Graced Life: The Writings of John Hughes

Graced Life

The Writings of John Hughes

Edited by

Matthew Bullimore

scm press

© Matthew Bullimore 2016

Published in 2016 by SCM Press
Editorial office
3rd Floor, Invicta House,
108–114 Golden Lane,
London EC1Y 0TG, UK

SCM Press is an imprint of Hymns Ancient & Modern Ltd
(a registered charity)
13A Hellesdon Park Road, Norwich,
Norfolk NR6 5DR, UK

www.scmpress.co.uk

British Library Cataloguing in Publication data

A catalogue record for this book is available
from the British Library

978 0 334 05447 4

Typeset by Regent Typesetting
Printed and bound by
CPI Group (UK) Ltd

Contents

For John's Godchildren
Alice, Freddie, Rosie and Thomas

Acknowledgements

John and I had many friends in common and since his death I have had myriad conversations about John's life and work. I am grateful to them all for sharing their wisdom and reminding me of all the good stories. The 'redoubtables' – Andrew Davison, Russell Dewhurst, Robert Mackley, Anna Matthews and John Munns – have matched their patron St Barnabas in encouragement and consolation and continue to inspire and to teach me in the fullness of Christian friendship.

Encouragement to pursue the project of collecting John's essays was given by Peter Candler, John Milbank, Adrian Pabst, Chad Pecknold, Catherine Pickstock and Graham Ward.

Necessary help along the way, which was gratefully received, was offered by all those at Hymns Ancient and Modern, including Rebecca Goldsmith, Stephen Platten, David Shervington, Christine Smith and Natalie Watson.

Those who read the introduction made it a much better piece. I am very grateful to John Bullimore, Francis O'Gorman, Robert Mackley, Althea Pipe, Peter Townley and James Walters for their thoughtful comments.

Pamela Allsopp, Delma Barnard and Glen and Sheila Monaghan graciously keep the parishes of St Peter, Felkirk and St John the Baptist, Royston in good order when I am engaged with other tasks. Caroline Harrison goes above and beyond the call of duty in assisting in the cure of souls and I thank her for many illuminating insights about grace.

I offer my heartfelt thanks to John's parents, Janet and Hywel Hughes, for their kindness, for helping me with stories about John's early years and for, quite simply, giving us John.

The family of a priest share him with so many other people and projects. Nothing would be possible without their patience, support and love, and so I thank God for Clare, Thomas, Anna and Katherine.

Matthew Bullimore

'Does it matter? Grace is everywhere ...'

   The priest in Georges Bernanos, *The Diary of a Country Priest*

As kingfishers catch fire, dragonflies dráw fláme;
As tumbled over rim in roundy wells
Stones ring; like each tucked string tells, each hung bell's
Bow swung finds tongue to fling out broad its name;
Each mortal thing does one thing and the same:
Deals out that being indoors each one dwells;
Selves — goes itself; *myself* it speaks and spells,
Crying *Whát I do is me: for that I came.*

Í say móre: the just man justices;
Kéeps gráce: thát keeps all his goings graces;
Acts in God's eye what in God's eye he is —
Chríst — for Christ plays in ten thousand places,
Lovely in limbs, and lovely in eyes not his
To the Father through the features of men's faces.

                                        Gerard Manley Hopkins

For the life of faith, lived liturgically, everything is superfluity, grace, and yet, when we have done everything, offered all our work, we must still say that 'we are unprofitable servants', precisely because all true work, inasmuch as it participates in God's work, is not ours but is given to us. Likewise, while we can have no control over the issue of our labour in this life, cannot secure it against being thwarted; nevertheless, we trust, in the hope of the Resurrection, that no good work will ultimately be lost.

                                        John Hughes, *The End of Work*

Introduction:
'Let's Exchange Charity'

This would have been a longer collection if it were not for John Hughes' immense capacity for friendship. John sought out the company of others and found as much time as he could to nurture friends old and new. Like many scholar priests, John also had to fit his academic pursuits around the other parts of his pastoral ministry. He was a conscientious and faithful priest and a well-regarded pastor, as attested to by all those who enjoyed the fruits of his priestly ministry during his curacy at St David and St Michael, Exeter, and then at Jesus College, Cambridge, where he served as Chaplain and then Dean. John made use of his academic gifts teaching in the Divinity Faculty at the University of Cambridge where he was much-loved as an able and stimulating tutor and lecturer. Despite these demands on his time, however, his publishing record was not unimpressive, as these essays demonstrate. The present collection bears witness to John's extraordinary theological imagination and the sheer range of his interests. John was also beginning to apply for some more senior academic posts to hold alongside his work as Dean and would no doubt have soon been successful. Nonetheless, the truth is that John was just as committed to enjoying the company of others as he was to reading or writing. Being so sociable was part of what made him such a good priest. When John died in a car crash aged thirty-five on St Peter's Day 2014 it was a tragedy for his family and the multitude of his friends but also for the academy and the Church. John would have been a leading academic priest and had so much to teach us. We will miss the joy he found in the world, his resilient faith in the Church of England and his irrepressible, if idealistic, hope for it. But most of all, of course, we will miss his friendship.

These chapters include all of his published material and two seminar papers.[1] They naturally bear upon John's primary interests but do so from a variety of perspectives. Among them there is a novel reading of

Shakespeare's *King Lear*, a survey of approaches to human labour in Europe's modern period, a treatise on apologetics and also a tentative proposal for the future direction of Anglican social thought. What binds these diverse topics together? At the heart of John's Christian faith and his intellectual project was an Augustinian emphasis on charity; on the exchange of the gift of love. John understood the essence of the divine life – as revealed to us most fully in the life, death and resurrection of Jesus – as love given and received. The reciprocity of love is thus the heart of the life of the Church. It is the true meaning and purpose of the Christian life, which for John was fundamentally social: the work of redemption is seen in and through community.

In his writings, John always held together the highest theological sophistication with the deepest concern for human being, hence his emphases on work, labour, art, social life and ethics. Of course, to write about the gift of charity is one thing. To be a good friend, son or priest was to enter more fully into relationships that participated in the divine life of exchanged charity. John entered into those relationships without reserve. His theological writing and his manner of life were of one piece. The concerns of his academic interests and projects were reflected in the pattern of his priesthood and his life and vice versa. They made sense of one another. And as far as John was concerned, what was the point of writing about charity if you were not enjoying it yourself and sharing it with others?[2]

I met John in 1997 in his first year as an undergraduate at a meeting of the Student Christian Movement. John was obviously prodigious. With his clarity of mind he always seemed able to cut through debates to see what was really at issue. John revelled in entering into intense discussion over a drink but never did so belligerently.[3] It would not be true to say that John suffered fools gladly, but suffer us he did, and was keen to guide us back to wisdom – as he saw it. I am peeved to say that in retrospect he often seemed to be right. In the seventeen years that I knew John, none of this ever changed. John became ever more incisive and his style matured but his ideas always gained their keen edge from discussion – and sometimes heated disputation – with a wide variety of friends. We remained in close contact throughout our graduate studies at different universities and came together again as ordinands at West-cott House in Cambridge where we both did doctoral research under the supervision of Catherine Pickstock. After ordination, John and I were in the same clerical cell group for mutual encouragement. My own theological learning and vocational life owe an enormous amount to John's continual charismatic presence, and it would be a fearful thing to imagine the Church or the academy without him if it were not for the extraordinary legacy he has left behind. At his Requiem Mass at Ely Cathedral on 10 July 2014, 120 clergy preceded the coffin in procession in the presence of a congregation of a thousand. It was a visible testimony to the love and affection in which he was held. John had shared himself lovingly in friendship and in service; a gift to those who knew him. Charity shared is not lost, however, for it draws us deeper into the shared charity that is the eternal heart of God.

Radical Orthodoxy

While we were undergraduates in the late 1990s, we were taught by those whose theological projects were then soon to be known collectively as 'radical orthodoxy'. Although John was a year below me, it was soon clear from our discussions who would be the teacher and who the pupil. John and I were both products of A level Religious Studies syllabi and first year undergraduate papers that taught us to pay heed to the so-called masters of suspicion such as Marx, Freud, Darwin, Durkheim and Nietzsche. We were aware of influential and powerful intellectual criticisms of religious faith. There were several routes that students so formed could follow. One was to decide to make the faith amenable to its critics as far as possible (which is probably fruitless for critics enjoy being critics). This route has the advantage of taking seriously philosophical critique but can denude the theological tradition of its own voice. It means that the tradition is always determined by outside positions. Another path is to retreat into a position of revelatory positivism in which all truth is averred to come from Scripture or the teaching of the Church so rendering all critique otiose. This path can take several forms: a conservative evangelical Protestantism; a caricatured version of neo-orthodoxy; an uncritical conservative Catholicism. While this path takes seriously theological sources of truth it is often characterized as being sectarian or even tribalist for refusing to engage with other disciplines and communities (a position often wrongly attributed to radical orthodoxy). At Cambridge there was also the possibility of following a 'death of God' theology that acknowledges the fecundity of religious language while denying it has any transcendent reference. John would, I think, have followed Evelyn Underhill in saying that the most interesting thing about religion, however, is God.

What made radical orthodoxy attractive to students like us was the fact that it offered a *via media* between these positions. I had to learn such a sensibility as something new to me, but I think that it more obviously chimed with John's best intuitions. John had a mind well-attuned to philosophical ideas and their practical consequences. He knew the richness of the theological tradition surprisingly well for someone of his age. He nimbly picked his way through the various complex debates underway in the academy and was one of the first to see the significance of this new theological style. It resonated with an élan that was already his own.

On the one hand radical orthodoxy accepts many of the criticisms of the faith, but sees them as valid responses to weaknesses in the development of the tradition. Yet, rather than merely remedially adapting the tradition and accommodating it to contemporary critique, it reaches back to the roots of the tradition to find resources that might also offer a convincing counter-narrative to the stories told by its modern and postmodern critics. The critics, then, are praiseworthy insofar as, first, they enable the recovery of stronger, earlier traditions that can be taken up into a newer presentation of the faith and, second, as they sharpen our critical faculties as we look at and listen to the world in which we live.

An oft-used strategy of radical orthodoxy is to narrate a genealogy of ideas that points out some of the wrong turns in theology. Furthermore, this strategy uncovers secular reason as itself being the product of those deviations and so susceptible of challenge by a rearticulated faith. A contentious example that is often associated with radical orthodoxy (although it is a much more established orthodoxy among continental thinkers (see Pickstock 2005)) is to argue that one of the key origins of modern secularism is found in the changing ways that the relationship between God and Being was articulated by theologians in the thirteenth century.

Previously, one of the transcendental attributes of God was Being. It described the essence of God, his fully active existence, who was therefore the source of the being of all things that exist. Creatures are given a share in God's Being – they are given and sustained in existence by God. Unlike their creator, however, creatures exist contingently. They are created. Later, God begins to be described as if he *has* Being. Being is something that is shared by God and creatures alike although God exists on an infinitely grander scale. This means, however, that the proper distinction between creator and creature is lost. We can begin to talk about God and creatures as if they were somehow on the same plane (though infinitely far apart). Being, as shared by God and creatures, becomes a category that supersedes them both as they are made subject to a prior term. Previously, theology as discourse about God necessarily involved discourse about his creative action and all creation. Theology was concerned with everything that was granted a share in God's Being. Afterwards, however, a science of Being itself – metaphysical philosophy – inevitably takes on that overarching role. Theology is thus relegated to talk about God and spiritual matters without reference to all else that shares in his Being. Various other scientific disciplines now begin to be used to describe the material universe without reference to its creator. Theology as a discipline is thus no longer necessarily concerned with the world and so the integral relation between the spiritual and the material, between spirit and body, revelation and reason is destroyed. It is then only a series of small steps to bracketing God out of the picture altogether. The upshot is the rise of secularism and immanent philosophies. What we lose is our trust in the world as something that reflects its origin as the gift of a transcendent, loving, good and personal God.

When we were training for ordination at Westcott House we wrote together a short introductory article about radical orthodoxy. It ended up being sent to *Telos*, the American political journal with which Catherine Pickstock had close connections (Chapter 7). We had immense fun writing it in my small top-floor room. It bears all the marks of being penned by two eager young students, full of caffeine, seeking to respond to some of the critics of the theologians who were having great influence upon them. John was always a little embarrassed by its gung-ho style but it gives a glimpse of what continued to excite us about the radical orthodoxy project.

Like the Catholic *ressourcement* movement, radical orthodoxy takes seriously the patristic and medieval roots of the faith as offering resources to tell a different story about the world in which we live. It had begun to look at Scripture in ways that were appropriately historical and literary while also seeing it as a collection of theological texts to be read and constantly reinterpreted by the Church so the word could be 'made strange' in each new generation. The orthodoxy that it finds in these radical sources always involves an imaginative re-presentation of Christian living. It is also radical in the sense that it is unafraid of engaging robustly, but not always unsympathetically, with critical theorists to sharpen the critique it offers of contemporary cultural, political and economic ideas and their attendant practices.[4]

One of the elements in the article, which was very much John's, was the insight that radical orthodoxy seeks to move us beyond dialectics. He saw that one of radical orthodoxy's moves is to take an apparent oppositional dualism (say, grace and nature or reason and revelation) and then show how they are *integrally* related. So, for example, in considering the apparent opposition between human reason and divine revelation, it might reject both the binary positions of, first, rational proofs for theism and, second, blind fideism. Instead, it might show how faith is reasonable (not nonsense) and how reason is a form of *trusting* in the meaningfulness of the world (see Chapter 6). John was not afraid of paradox and, like Eric Mascall, one of his academic forebears as a high-Anglican Thomist, and Henri de Lubac, one of the foremost theological influences upon him, he even saw paradox as crucial to Christian theology.

Heterodoxy is usually found in the overemphasis on one pole of an apparent dualism. By contrast, orthodoxy attempts to negotiate the paradoxical mystery, holding the poles together. For example, to say that Jesus was only human or only divine – or naively to say that he was somehow a bit of both, as if humanity and divinity were ontologically co-equal – is to miss the radicality of the creedal faith that he was fully man and fully divine. Using the language of paradox seemed to John to be a more faithful and honest way of describing the mysteries we encounter. Should we attempt to fix those mysteries in the limited categories of human language we usually opt for easier solutions, to say either this *or* that must logically be the case. We no longer hold together apparent contradictions and allow them to speak fruitfully and creatively. As John realized, this affects the way we understand the Christian life. In the example just used, the paradox of Christological orthodoxy, in which Christ's human nature is deified in its personal union with his divine nature, helps us to understand how the Church, as a people incorporated into Christ's humanity, are being transformed to participate in a divine pattern of life. Essentially, to revere paradox is to affirm that theological truth transforms and surpasses our reasoning. John taught us that theological imagination needs to be illuminated by the glorious mysteries of God, whose ways with the world nevertheless exceed our full comprehension.

In many of the following essays, then, we find John identifying the dualisms that structure an intellectual debate and then showing how, understood theologically, we can discern an integral relationship between them. John often shows how an appeal to transcendence prevents us from falling into a shuttle between opposing options. John learned much from Max Weber and Karl Marx about how ideas come with histories. What might appear to be eternal verities might actually be historically determined ideas that have become naturalized as the way a culture understands what structures the world.

In his monograph, *The End of Work*, for example, John shows how Marx revealed the scientific laws of the political economists to be actually only the ideas of a particular moment now solidified as a philosophical superstructure (see Chapter 4). Marx argued that such superstructures serve to mystify actually existing power relations, making them appear fixed rather than contingent. However, John then also criticizes Marx's attempt at a purely historical science that deemed all ideas as fully determined by a material base of historical power struggles. John argues that Marx's suspicion of all cultural and intellectual endeavour left him with an uncritical confidence in economic reality with no standard of truth, beauty or goodness by which to judge forms of human labour, production or consumption. When there is no way to judge their value, human activities serve no higher purpose and so: 'because there is nothing beyond for which things are ultimately employed, no greater end to which all usage strives, use or mere utility becomes an end in itself' (Hughes 2007, p. 93). This gave Marx no overarching means to account for the complex relations between things or their relation to that which might exceed them. Marx's insight that all ideas have histories made him too suspicious of them. Purging himself of all idealism he was left without any standards by which to evaluate the moral worth, purpose or meaning of material practices. If Marx was correct that idealism without historicism was naive and ultimately tyrannical, he did not make the correlative move of seeing pure historicism as necessarily relativist, pragmatic and as equally adept at obscuring hidden commitments and power relations. We are left with an immanent dialectics, a shuttle between naturalized and static ideals and a historicism without metaphysical warrant. John professed an incarnational theology that recognized that eternal truths were always historically and culturally mediated but not reducible to material practices. In the second essay on Sergei Bulgakov in this collection, for example, John articulates how a Christian 'praxeology' can make sense of the relationships between human sciences – 'economies of knowledge' – where each is seen as partial, yet nonetheless in their various ways pointing us towards a transcendent unifying truth. This is a truth that can only be revealed, however, in the practices of human living.[5]

John's work is clearly influenced by his radically orthodox teachers, to whom he would freely admit he owed an enormous debt of gratitude. Of course, such gratitude worked the other way too. Those teachers admit that to have a priest of John's irenic and lovable character practising his faith in a radically orthodox mood revealed the practicable – even prayerful – side of their intellectual virtuosity.

Finding Faith Together

John first encountered the Christian life by popping into the parish church on his way home from primary school in the village of Kenton in Devon. Sometimes he saw the flower guild at work and once he was given a tour up and over the rood screen by the churchwarden. He started attending church services with his mother after a family bereavement. He became a regular worshipper and, in time, became increasingly involved, for example by organizing a parish craft fair. Eventually as a teenager he asked if he could be confirmed. He told me he used to pore over the Book of Common Prayer that he found on his parents' bookshelf and was intrigued by the figure of Richard Hooker who sat proudly in the Cathedral Green in Exeter. This was the soil in which his catholic Anglicanism was nurtured and it is perhaps little wonder that John would admit to a romantic sensibility when it came to the Church of England.

Yet it was a romanticism that paid attention to the lived reality of people. It was a romantic Christian socialism: romantic in mind and heart but prudent and pastoral in practice.[6] Like anyone involved in a Christian community and later, in Christian ministry, John was not naive about the foibles that make themselves known and the difficulties that must be negotiated when people meet together. Yet he loved people and enjoyed them and knew that the love of God was known through the way Christians learned to bear with one another.

For John, catholic Christianity was a social phenomenon and not merely about individuals' piety. Salvation was experienced by incorporation into the body of Christ. It was at once an experience that must be personal, social, historical and spiritual. It was about the whole of human life in God. He would have agreed with Mascall that 'incorporation into Christ is incorporation into the Church, since the Church is in its essence simply the human nature of Christ made appropriable by men [sic], that all the thought, prayer and activity of Christians, in so far as it is brought within the sphere of redemption, is the act of Christ himself in and through the Church which is his Body' (Mascall 1946, p. v). There are no private Christians.

Intellectually John was also at heart a romantic. He liked to trace ideas across the ages and believed in the possibility of resolution and harmony. At Jesus College, he was influenced by the then Dean, the anthropologist Timothy Jenkins, who would show frustration as John made grand, sweeping statements about metaphysical verities. John was grateful that Tim taught him the need for the painstaking work of attending to complex historical and cultural details and practices. This is not to say that John's philosophical acumen was divorced from lived reality. As a Christian socialist, John had a deep interest in ethics; in the moral character of lives lived in the cosmos that his philosophical theology strove to understand. His Master of Studies degree was undertaken at Merton College, Oxford, under Oliver O'Donovan whose work in theological ethics had attracted John (see Chapter 12).

For John, theological ethics was not to be seen as a subset of a more universal discipline of ethics. Nor would John have wanted to treat ethics as confined to ethical dilemmas. Ethics was about attending to the practices of the community that was formed by the peace offered by Christ in his resurrection. It is a community of believers who share his human nature and who are together being transformed into his likeness, sharing his character of loving service. John's real interest was in the social aspects of ethics – on the shape of this community and the effects it had in a world that was still being redeemed. Ethics is primarily about the shape of a common life that is the fruit of a relationship. It describes a people's transformative relationship with God, integrating heart and action, self and community.

He had plans to write a book on interpretations of Jesus' Sermon on the Mount. He saw it as a manifesto for the Christian life. The sermon teaches that to be blessed is to be like the one who is teaching. How could it be understood otherwise when Christ's person, work and teaching are inseparable? It traces the way of the cross that each disciple must follow; a path that is a sharing together in Christlikeness in a world that is often un-Christlike. John delighted in the sermon's apparent paradoxes: its moralistic judgementalism ('be perfect as your Father in heaven is perfect', Matt. 5.48) and its tolerant amoralism ('judge not and you will be not judged', Matt. 7.1). Here he taught that the key to understanding the tension is forgiveness (see Chapter 1). Only the acceptance of forgiveness can render us perfect. We cannot will our own perfection. If we mask our failings by judging others it is nothing but hypocrisy and self-deception. It is in opening ourselves penitentially to divine love that we are transformed. In being made like Jesus we are enabled to forgive others. We then learn to see ourselves as God sees us and we learn to see God in others. The sermon is thus not a list of tasks for the Christian but concerns the gift of loving grace that perfects us: 'For it is love that demands nothing less than everything from us, and yet gives us that everything and forgives everything, stands always with arms open to receive us back, ever offering a new start.'[7]

Integral Christian Humanism

Central to John's project was an affection for the thinking of Henri Cardinal de Lubac, to whom he was introduced by reading the work of John Milbank and Catherine Pickstock. Formative for John was de Lubac's integral Christian humanism (see Chapter 8). De Lubac's account of the integral relationship between nature and grace – or between nature and the supernatural – illustrates the theological foundations of John's own integralist Christian humanism and, for that reason, is worth describing at length.[8]

In the twentieth century, the *ressourcement* movement in Catholic theology – pejoratively called the *nouvelle théologie* – sought to move beyond what it saw as the dry and sterile categories of neo-scholastic thought. One of its chief proponents, Hans Urs von Balthasar, explored the use of aesthetics and drama as appropriate means to interpret the tradition and allow the gospel to speak afresh. Henri de Lubac's work was a key part of this 'retrieval of the sources'. His controversial work *Surnatural* was aimed at breaking down an entrenched dichotomy of 'pure nature' and 'supernatural grace' and returning to a more authentic theological account of their integral relationship. He defended the idea that the integral relationship between them could be seen in our natural desire for the supernatural. What does this mean and why might it matter?

De Lubac's detailed historical research brought him to the conclusion that too often in early modern debates grace and nature bore only an extrinsic relationship to one another. A Renaissance naturalism lauded the accomplishments of nature and human culture and left little room for the mediations of grace or revelation. In reaction, Augustinians such as Michael Baius (1513–89) and Cornelius Jansen (1585–1638), like their

Protestant counterparts, stressed the utter depravity of fallen human nature and thus the exigency for grace. Baius saw in our prelapsarian innocence no need for grace, which was only a remedial measure after the fall that would bring us back to our primordial innocency. Jansen did see grace as having a role in Eden in making up for a lack in human nature so that we were nonetheless naturally constituted to obtain our supernatural end in God. Yet, the capacity of human nature was totally lost after Adam's refusal of grace in the fall and so an irresistible grace must be offered to enable us to follow God's commandments.

The positions of Baius and Jansen were both ecclesiastically condemned. De Lubac concurred. Grace for Jansen and Baius seemed only to operate as a corrective to sin and not as bringing human nature to a deeper participation in the life of God. In fact, human nature had no part to play in the postlapsarian dispensation. It seemed to him a denial of the glory of created human nature, however fallen. In Baius, grace was added to a depraved human nature to restore it to a graceless existence. In Jansen, before the fall, grace was seen as a constitutive part of human being and hardly a gracious gift at all, whereas, after the fall, it was all that there was, the capacities of human nature having been corrupted and destroyed. Thus it was styled as an invasive force and one now necessarily demanded of God. In neither case was there a relationship between created human nature and the gift of grace that raised and deified human nature. Here was no Christian humanism.

On the other hand, interpreters of St Thomas Aquinas (such as Thomas Cajetan (1469–1534) and Francisco Suárez (1548–1617)) sought to preserve the gratuity of grace by postulating a realm of pure nature. They were at pains to argue against the Augustinians' denial that human nature had any role after the fall. To safeguard the place of human nature they argued speculatively that God could have created us in a state of pure nature and that we could have achieved the purely natural ends we desired by virtue of our own natural capacities. Aristotle held that 'nature does nothing in vain', and so they argued that the ends our natures desired were owed to us as a matter of justice. It would be unjust for God to deny us the ability to achieve our natural ends. Grace was needed only for obtaining the supernatural end of the beatific vision, the vision of God. Their aim was to show that human nature was not utterly depraved and corrupt. This was not a denial of the fall but born of a desire not to evacuate created nature of the integrity with which it was created. It was an attempt to show that human endeavour (in politics, economics and social organization, for example) had autonomy and was intelligible by its own lights. This account of a pure nature then allowed them also to argue that grace was, indeed, gratuitous; a supernatural gift that was not obligatory but given to elevate human nature to its supernatural end. Blessedness was not something owed to human nature but a free divine gift. As such, it could potentially be denied to human creatures without injustice.

In this scheme de Lubac saw an essential contrast between nature and grace in which they were still only extrinsically related. Natural achievements seemed to need no divine assistance and human nature could operate according to its own teleology and under its own power. Grace was seen as something that arrived from without, over and above a natural realm that was coherent and relatively complete on its own terms. Grace, then, was only an addition that brought us to our eschatological end and remained unrelated to our natural existence.

De Lubac could not see how natural ends could be intelligible without reference to the supernatural end of human beings. He could not see the point of the theological game of positing a speculative 'pure nature' for that was not how God had created the world.[9] He saw in the idea of pure nature a world that was evacuated of grace. It appeared that all human work – and the ends to which it was oriented – was somehow indifferent to our supernatural end in God. It was almost as if we could get on with life for the most part without attention to God but needed that extra lift to achieve our supernatural end. This made grace sound like some *thing* added on to human nature rather than as a description of God's continual action upon us and his loving work of perfecting our nature.

For de Lubac our human nature could not be seen as explicable only with reference to merely natural, immanent ends and when somehow potentially closed off from its supernatural end. The experiment of 'pure nature' could not deliver what it promised. Rather than giving nature an integrity of which it was deprived by theologians of natural depravity, it separated off human life from its true *telos*. Nor could de Lubac see the theological validity of the idea that nature before the fall had no need of grace. If grace was not to be seen as something simply added on as a postlapsarian rescue package then it must always have been at work within human beings, enabling human nature to be most truly what it was called to be – in full communion with God. This was true even before the fall, but not in its postlapsarian remedial capacity. For de Lubac, all that we are and all that we do is open to the transforming work of grace.

With a truer Augustinian account of grace, de Lubac argued instead that St Thomas Aquinas had taught that humans have a natural desire for the supernatural. Human nature is created as *called* to a supernatural end that it can neither anticipate nor achieve by its own power. As the author of the letter to the Ephesians writes: God 'chose us in Christ before the foundation of the world to be holy and blameless before him in love. He destined us for adoption as his children through Jesus Christ, according to the good pleasure of his will, to the praise of his glorious grace that he freely bestowed on us in the Beloved' (1.3–6). We are created, then, with a desire for God to fulfil his promise and make good on his call upon our lives. As de Lubac writes: 'God's call is constitutive. My finality, which is expressed by this desire [to see God], is inscribed upon my very being as it has been put into this universe by God' (de Lubac 1998, p. 55). This is the created gift that is the natural desire for the supernatural. It is how we are made. As St Augustine put it at the beginning of *The Confessions* (I, 1, 1): 'you have made us and drawn us to yourself, and our heart is unquiet until it rests in you' (Augustine 1997, p. 39). It is not just that we have some potential or passive capacity to receive from God – as if to fill a void – but that there is some deep affinity between our nature and its supernatural destiny. It is an end that is unachievable for human nature alone but granted to us as a supernatural gift. De Lubac thus preserved the gratuitousness of grace by describing a nature that was created to desire an end that could only arrive as a gift.

The call to this supernatural end is thus seen to precede our creation. We are first given our existence as a gracious gift *because* we are called to the gift of the beatific vision. Nevertheless, the gift of beatitude – although it is what we are made for – is never fully anticipated nor commanded by us because it is a gift that surpasses our imaginings and gives more than we could ever demand. The collect for the sixth Sunday after Trinity draws the paradox well:

Merciful God,
you have prepared for those who love you
such good things as pass our understanding:
pour into our hearts such love toward you
that we, loving you in all things and above all things,
may obtain your promises,
which exceed all that we can desire;
through Jesus Christ your Son our Lord.[10]

Here love is a further gift added to us who already desire God and, by thankfully receiving that love, we are able to obtain the promises that in their bounty exceed our desires and expectations.

Aquinas' famous maxim holds that 'grace perfects nature and does not destroy it' (*Summa Theologiae*, Ia, q. 1, a. 8, ad 2). The work of grace is God's work, bringing the world to perfection. De Lubac argued that, for Thomas, nature is not thereby annihilated but neither should grace be seen as extrinsic to nature, as if it arrived from outside as something added on. Nature is already itself an effect of grace by virtue of the fact that it is created out of nothing and ever sustained in existence by the action of God. Our human nature is already a gift that is so ordered that it may receive the further gift of glory. The supernatural operation of grace is God working within us to bring us to a promised perfection to which we have always been called.

De Lubac insisted upon the adjectival form 'supernatural' to describe this *operation* of grace, the action of God, in created nature to prevent it being seen as something like a second storey that was extrinsically added on to nature from without and bereft of an integral connection. Grace is not a thing or a substance. To speak of the supernatural is to speak of how God *relates* to his creation by elevating it to reach the end that he has foreordained for it, but that it cannot reach by its own power.

For de Lubac, the relationship between nature and grace was thus to be seen as intrinsic; an integral relationship. Another maxim of Aquinas holds that 'grace presupposes nature' (*Summa Theologiae*, Ia, q. 2, a. 2, ad 1). Grace is not somehow alien, exterior or even unnatural, for if grace presupposes nature then they are made for one another. As Augustine writes, 'You were more intimately present to me than my innermost being, and higher than the highest peak of my spirit' (III, 6, 11. Augustine 1997, p. 83). Grace transcends nature and paradoxically makes nature more itself, but is nonetheless integrally related to it at the most intimate level. As John Milbank puts it, grace raises oneself as oneself to the beyond oneself (Milbank 2005, p. 39). Grace would be an abstraction without its relationship to the nature that it perfected. What would pure grace even look like? Grace *is* God's ever new expansion and development of a nature that is created precisely to be open to that work – it is the supernaturalizing of the natural. In a fallen world that grace is also necessarily redemptive but continues also to be supernaturalizing. It is a work of new creation and not just remedy. If grace is linked to pardon, mercy and forgiveness then it is what the supernatural looks like in a creation marred by sin.

De Lubac's thesis was roundly condemned by many of his con-temporaries and he was removed from his teaching positions.[11] The fear was that it naturalized the supernatural. Did it not mean that grace was no longer a free, unmerited gift but a matter of exigency, as if God was constrained to fulfil the natural human desire for the vision of God? Given the Aristotelian principle that nature does nothing in vain, was God not constrained for the sake of justice to grant the supernatural end of our natural desire? Did it not somehow anticipate the super-natural gift and so remove its status as a gift? Moreover, was it not a restatement of the Jansenist position that all was grace and that nature had no integrity? Another criticism was that it gave a pseudo-religious gloss to every aspect of human living so that it became almost a form of accommodation to all cultural mores.

De Lubac always contended that these criticisms did not hold good now that our heavenly call in Jesus Christ had been revealed. What we have been revealed to be, as created embodied spirits, could be nothing other than a desire for God; it is what it means to be a human creature. The desire is not something elicited from without or added to us as if we could be without that desire. There simply is no such thing as a natural human prior to having a desire for the supernatural. This we know because of the revelation of God's purposes in Jesus: 'creation as it exists, with the unique final end which it has ... [is] effected by God precisely with the object of giving himself to it ... creation [is] finally illuminated for us by the good news announced to mankind one night at Bethlehem' (de Lubac 1998, p. 131). The hypostatic union of divinity and humanity in the person of Jesus revises our theological anthro-pology. The true end of all that is human is for us to be embraced by the supernaturalizing work of divinity and so, in being united to divinity, to be brought in and with Jesus to the beatific vision of the Father. All that we do and are is in service of that end of adoption and filiation, of becoming children of God (John 1.12, 16). God is not constrained to grant the gift as if it were an economic debt: 'The supernatural is not owed to nature; it is nature which, if it is to obey God's plan, owes itself to the supernatural if that supernatural is offered to it' (de Lubac 1998, p. 94). God made us to respond to his call and to receive his gifts. The heavenly call precedes the created desire.

In this light, de Lubac felt that words such as grace, nature and supernatural were rather abstract and that what was required was something more personal. It makes more sense to speak theologically in terms of love – which can only be about gift and not demand, about relationship and not independence. Moreover, the operations of grace are best revealed and exemplified in the drama of the incarnation, passion and resurrection of Jesus.[12] Christ offers a renewal of our nature so that with him and in the Spirit we can see the Father as he himself does; we can share in the life of exchanged charity that is the divine life. This theology of recapitulation demonstrates that the purpose of creation is not that creatures should merely fulfil some natural ends but that they are ordered to glory, that they should find themselves in the image and likeness of God, new creatures renewed as the corporate body of Christ, drawn into the heart of God's own life of reciprocal love.[13] De Lubac refused to separate the orders of creation, redemption and salvation as if they could be understood in isolation. Creation is the means by which the will of God for creatures to be deified is accomplished, and redemption is the way in which that end is fulfilled despite the consequences of human disobedience. After Jesus, we can only speak of one human end. All living is for the sake of living well, a participation in eternal life.

To be a human creature is therefore to be grateful, to be eucharistic through and through. We are gifts, everything that we are and that we are called to be is given to us, and so we are naturally expectant and receptive. Having already received, we discover our final end as a promise. We have no self-sufficient stance from which we could demand anything. Yet, for de Lubac, this was not to deny nature any purchase. For him, nature was evacuated by presuming it had any immanent self-sufficient standing. This would be a form of materialism. A doctrine of pure nature was a doctrine of graceless nature. It was a nature indifferent to its supernatural end and so a nature destined eventually for secularity. A human nature that could be understood without reference to its transcendent end was also destined to separate almost every aspect of human living from the mediations of Christian living. Essentially it secularized society and privatized the Church. Worldly and bodily concerns were seen to be unspiritual. Grace only intervened to trump these natural and worldly activities and appeared as an alien imposition unrelated to and barely resonant with human living. In fact, de Lubac wondered how something apparently so alien to human concerns would even be recognizable.

For de Lubac, human nature does not receive its integrity by what it can offer in contrast or in competition with grace but has integrity by virtue of being created gift. The secular, the worldly, is upheld and sustained precisely because it is a gift to us that is being perfected. Henri de Lubac was a member of the Society of Jesus and one can detect the incarnational emphasis of his Ignatian spirituality. God is not to be found by looking outside the world or as at one afar off, but is found within and all around. Everyday life is where God is to be sought and not only in the supposedly religious, sacred or spiritual aspects of life. There is not a contrastive relationship between nature and grace because even though they are of different orders – natural and supernatural – they are made for one another. Another way of putting it is that God does not will to accomplish his will for us, without us.

John's work is defined by the same theological intuitions as fired de Lubac. His integral Christian humanism saw all human endeavour as shot through with the work of grace. In a created world, there is nothing that is not of theological importance, and there is nothing that cannot be redeemed. For John, there was no pure nature or neutral secular realm somehow separated off from God's involvement with his creation. All things could be seen, by the light of faith and interpreted through the Church, as graced and caught up in the redeeming love of God. The essays here in one way or another demonstrate his concern to read the world gracefully and his refusal of the 'extrinsicism' that would drive a disastrous wedge between the orders of nature and the supernatural. This is the thrust of the essay on the integralism John discerns in his native Anglican tradition (Chapter 8). He expands this concern in his essay on Anglican social thought (Chapter 12).[14] His companion piece on Benedict XVI's social encyclical *Caritas in Veritate* praises its integralism in the sphere of social ethics, arguing that the pope saw faith as transformative of our economic life (Chapter 10). He praises Benedict for speaking about 'development' in a theological idiom – using the language of love and speaking of the economy in terms of gift. Charity is not something added on to a common and universal concern for justice, but is the completion and inner meaning of justice. How we see justice is conditioned by our charity and not merely a prolegomenon to it. John argues that church reports with a theological coda to a sociological analysis are not sufficient. He saw Benedict as standing in the line of integralists like de Lubac and Jacques Maritain (who coined the term 'integral humanism'). John's critical essay on Maritain included here argues that this concern for integralism could be seen to be at work in both Maritain's liberal and conservative phases (Chapter 9).[15]

Association

This collection begins with John's astonishing essay on forgiveness which was the published form of his final year undergraduate dissertation. It begins where Christian theology must begin – not with creation but with new creation. John's was an Easter faith. The divine labour of new creation, of which the resurrection of Jesus is the supreme sign, was for him the central doctrine around which all others coalesced. The purpose of creation for the Christian can only be understood through what Christ accomplishes in his recapitulation of creation. What Christ gives in his resurrection is his peace. It is the offer of a social existence that is characterized by the exchange of charity which, in a fallen world, first looks like forgiveness (see Milbank and Pickstock 2015).

For the Christian tradition, then, human association is theologically primary. Peace, which is the gift of the risen Jesus, is only experienced in particular forms of communal life. This is why John paid so much attention to the spheres of lived human life and, in particular, human labour (Chapters 3 and 4). Beyond liberalism's oscillation between attention to the state and the individual, John was interested in those arenas in which substantial cultures and relationships are found. He saw civil society as that forum in which people could 'develop skills in collective organization in institutions that are relatively egalitarian with high levels of participation in governance in the pursuit of common social goods'.[16] It was here that cultures of true virtue could be discerned to be at work to transform labour and the working of capital – in professions, vocational work and social occupations like child-rearing and care of the elderly. He had a vision of an ethical socialism in which society could be seen as 'good' rather than as merely 'big' or 'open'. In Augustinian vein, John argued that it was in the living world of civil society that Christian practice could be culturally transformative by pointing social, political and ethical practices to an end that was not merely immanent and showing them that they are ordered towards the substantive peace that is the gift of God.

Like de Lubac, John was thus deeply concerned with the secular, if we mean by that the time that we call the everyday. It is the way we inhabit that time, our lived practices, that make it what it is. In secular time, we find churches establishing foodbanks, promoting credit unions, brokering relationships with the public and private sectors, working with children's centres, celebrating festivals, worshipping, supporting the living wage, forming Christian disciples, advising on governmental policy and seeking to civilize the economy. John thought that one of the often ignored triumphs of this renewal of social theology is the potential it evinces for a theology of the laity. The Christian practice of the people of God – individually, locally and corporately – has beneficial effects in a pluralistic environment. It promotes a Christian enculturation of society.

Culture was an important theme for John. Integralism was allied to historicism: the work of grace takes time, within history and forms communities of virtue with their own cultural particularities. Truth is revealed in the contingent. For example, like Richard Hooker, John could not see the Anglican settlement as somehow the inevitable outworking of the gospel record, but it was at its best a contingent, yet apt, result of the proclamation of the faith in England over time. In his essay on the possibility of Christian culture, John explores the idea of a Christian society (Chapter 11). Liberalism, despite many of its laudable gains, is essentially negative. It often presumes upon a secular neutrality that guards and defends freedoms, but John argues, by way of S. T. Coleridge and T. S. Eliot, that its indifference to particular cultures, traditions, heritage and communities of virtue is itself to take a position. John looks for an integralist mode of seeing how Christian culture works within society. He refuses a Christian quietist retreat into sectarianism as a move that would leave the secular as merely the secular. This would be to reinforce the concept of a pure nature in which God is removed from society and the Church is dehumanized. Here the Church would act only to pronounce who is saved and would no longer be working as leaven in society. John recognized that a Christian culture was not the same as a Christian theocratic state. Yet, neither did he think it was enough to remain at the level of sociological analysis in which the Church is to be seen as just another actor within the pluralistic environment of civil society. The essay is an initial probing of how Christian cultures and practices can gracefully shape a wider pluralistic social environment by instilling a desire to exceed themselves and be perfected.

John's great nemesis, which many of these essays engage in battle, was the culture of utility: 'a rational, calculating, quantifying spirit, which seem[s] determinedly destructive of traditional modes of thought and life, with materialistic, anti-theological prejudices, levelling qualitative differences to one commensurable, measurable scale, bracketing out moral and theological concerns in order to occupy a purportedly "neutral", empirically describable realm' (Hughes 2007, p. 217). This is a description of *mere* utility sundered from any transcendent end. Utility is here associated with instrumental rationality in which things only receive value insofar as they are useful for whatever task is being undertaken and without any reference to its inherent goodness. The spirit of utility lauds only the functionality of objects and, more disastrously, the functionality of people too, reducing us to manipulable machines given value only by our usefulness. Evidence of the spirit of utility is seen in the ubiquity of the language of the market that now pervades all aspects of life from education to health care. Now the provision of choice is seen as an end in itself rather than making good and wise choices. We judge the efficiency of professions by what we can measure without attending to the heart of what they offer. Politics succumbs to demagoguery and sophistry or, at best, becomes an exercise in managing scarce resources rather than the practice of forming a good society. Of course, things can be used for particular ends and used well, but without the means to judge the worth of those ends, utility becomes demonic, opposed to questions of goodness, beauty or truth. It becomes a self-grounding absolute end in itself. For John it was then that utility was revealed in all its bestial self-interest in which things are only ever useful as they are useful for me and for the satisfaction of my desires. It was the opposite of all that John held dear: gratuity, gift, charity, the absolute worth of all things and all people under God (see Mackley 2015).

John could always detect a whiff of utilitarianism and was keenly sensitive to its presence in church reports or ecclesiastical pronouncements. The Church, like creation, is not useful. It adds nothing to God who is overflowing superfluity and gratuity. Again, he would have agreed with Mascall (1953, p. 8) that 'the life of the Church, the organic act which constitutes its unity, is the life of the Holy Trinity imparted to men [*sic*] in Christ'. The end of all human relationships, all human living, all worship, all witness and mission was to bring people and the world to participate joyfully in the triune life of God. The Church is that part of the world where this end is made visible. The Church quite simply is the true end of human living and not a means to some other end. John always retained his faith in the Church. He believed that this people enacting the common good were undeniably powerful and transformative. This was because the Church is the name for that community living a gracious life of reciprocal love – a divine life. Participation in the Church's life was also the lens through which he believed we could learn to see grace at work in the world.

Attention to John's vision will continue to remind the Church that it is most truly itself not when it sets itself over and against culture or as subservient to it but when it sees its life as gracefully transformative of the world. He would remind us that Church needs to be humanist, concerned with aspects of human living. It needs to receive the world as a gift to be treasured and nurtured. He would remind us that all language of efficiency and use must be employed carefully and always in service of nurturing good relationships, for that is what God offers us as a participation in his life – nothing less than a common life of exchanged charity.

Plan of the Book

Part 1 concerns the work of creation. It starts with new creation and the work of salvation wrought by Jesus. The first essay is that on forgiveness. In the next essay John examines Sergei Bulgakov's criticisms of Thomas Aquinas' account of creation. Partly critical, for once, of Aquinas, John upholds Bulgakov's thesis while defending Aquinas from excessive criticism. John's concern is to defend the integral relationship between God's will and wisdom in order to show that creation can be rendered good and intelligible.

The next three essays offer an introduction to John's work on human and divine labour, which is worked out more fully in his monograph. Once again, he returns to Bulgakov and outlines the integralism of his sophiology. In a shorter essay, John traces a theological account of human labour in which forms of work that are better are the ones seen to participate in divine labour. This account is alternatively described in his essay on labour in modern European thought.

Part 2 contains those essays that deal with the Church in the world.[17] It begins with two essays on theological method, one on apologetics and one on radical orthodoxy. John's attention to social thought and practice is to the fore in his two essays on Anglican social thought and in his paper on Christian culture. He explores integral humanism in an essay on Maritain's intellectual development and a paper on Anglicanism.

Remembering John

One of John's favourite and oft-quoted lines came from David Jones'
poem *Anathemata*:

> The utile infiltration nowhere held
> creeps vestibule
> is already at the closed lattices, is coming through each door.
>
> (Jones 1972, p. 50)

The priest ('the cult-man') who guards the signs is the last bastion
against the creeping utilitarianism all around. We had always expected
John to be there in the Church and the academy leading a stand against
a now rampant instrumentalizing that deifies utility and shuns the true
ends of human living. He has left us to guard the signs and hold the line.
There are times when all seems lost and the powers arrayed against the
good news seem too strong. We are not bereft of grace, of course, and
he was a gift to us. So it is at those times of our fatigue and doubt that
I imagine John in his role as the cult-man. I remember his rhetorically
elaborate righteous indignation at some new folly. Sometimes I see him
with his head in a book, held up close to his reading eye, as he sits on
a lawn surrounded by friends. Sometimes he delightedly reads out a
purple passage and sometimes I see him lowering the book and frown-
ing as he swills an idea around his mind as if evaluating a fine wine. He
is always in company, sometimes dancing or barking with laughter, or
suggesting just one more glass of something to finish off the night. And
then I see him at the altar given to the beauty of holiness. For John,
there was only one way to stave off the encroaching tide of a demonic
utilitarianism and that was by living a life of friendship, of festival, of
worshipful thanks, of exchanged charity. I think he would be pleased if
I gave the last word to St Thomas:

> Sacris solemniis juncta sint gaudia,
> Et ex praecordiis sonent praeconia.
> Recedant vetera, nova sint Omnia
> Corda, voces et opera.
>
> *Let joys be joined to solemn feasts.*
> *Let praises from the depths resound.*
> *Let old things pass, make all things new.*
> *Let heart and voice and works abound.*
>
> (Anderson and Moser 2000, pp. 92–3)

Matthew Bullimore

References

Robert Anderson and Johann Moser (eds), 2000, *The Aquinas Prayer Book: The Prayers and Hymns of St Thomas Aquinas*, Manchester, NH: Sophia Institute Press.

St Thomas Aquinas, 1964–80, *Summa Theologiae*, London: Eyre and Spottiswoode.

St Augustine, 1997, *The Confessions*, London, Sydney and Auckland: Hodder & Stoughton.

Georges Bernanos, 2002 (1937), *The Diary of a Country Priest*, ET, Cambridge, MA: Da Capo Press.

Sergei Bulgakov, 1993 (1937), *Sophia: The Wisdom of God*, ET, Hudson, NY: Lindisfarne Press.

Matthew Bullimore, 2011, 'Radical Orthodoxy and the Anglican Social Tradition', *Crucible: The Christian Journal of Social Ethics*, July–September, pp. 23–32.

William T. Cavanaugh, 2011, 'The Sinfulness and Visibility of the Church: A Christological Exploration', in *Migrations of the Holy: God, State, and the Political Meaning of the Church*, Grand Rapids, MI and Cambridge, UK: Eerdmans, pp. 141–69.

Henri de Lubac, 1984 (1980), *A Brief Catechesis on Nature and Grace*, ET, San Francisco, CA: Ignatius Press.

Henri de Lubac, 1988 (1947), *Catholicism: Christ and the Common Destiny of Man*, ET, San Francisco, CA: Ignatius Press.

Henri de Lubac, 1996, *Theology in History*, ET, San Francisco, CA: Ignatius Press.

Henri de Lubac, 1998 (1965), *The Mystery of the Supernatural*, ET, New York: The Crossroad Publishing.

Henri de Lubac, 2000 (1965), *Augustinianism and Modern Theology*, ET, New York: The Crossroad Publishing Company.

Peter Groves, 2012, *Grace: The Cruciform Love of God*, Norwich: Canterbury Press.

David Grummett, 2007, *De Lubac: A Guide for the Perplexed*, London and New York: Continuum.

David Grummett, 2015, 'De Lubac, Grace, and the Pure Nature Debate', *Modern Theology*, Vol. 31, No. 1, January, pp. 123–46.

John Hughes, 2012, 'The Possibility of Christian Culture', unpublished seminar paper, delivered at the Society for the Study of Theology annual conference, University of York, 26–28 March.

John Hughes, 2013, 'Anglicanism as Integral Humanism: A de Lubacian Reading of the Church of England', unpublished paper, delivered to the Anglican Studies Research Seminar, Department of Theology and Religion, Durham University, 5 February.

Ruth Jackson, 2015, 'Of Life and Work', in Hugh Burling and Silvianne Bürki (eds), *Noesis: Theology, Philosophy, Poetics*, Cambridge: The Graduate Society for the Study of Philosophical Theology and Systematics, Faculty of Divinity, University of Cambridge, pp. 14–21.

David Jones, 1972 (1952), *The Anathemata: fragments of an attempted writing*, London and Boston: Faber & Faber.

Fergus Kerr, 2002, *After Aquinas: Versions of Thomism*, Oxford: Blackwell.

Fergus Kerr, 2007, *Twentieth-Century Catholic Theologians*, Oxford: Blackwell.

Robert Mackley, 2015, 'Communio Bonorum', in Hugh Burling and Silvianne Bürki (eds), *Noesis: Theology, Philosophy, Poetics*, Cambridge: The Graduate Society for the Study of Philosophical Theology and Systematics, Faculty of Divinity, University of Cambridge, pp. 11–13.

Michael Martin, 2015, *The Submerged Reality: Sophiology and the Turn to a Poetic Metaphysics*, Kettering, OH: Angelico Press.

Eric Mascall, 1946, *Christ, the Christian and the Church: A Study of the Incarnation and its Consequences*, London: Longmans, Green & Co.

Eric L. Mascall, 1953, *Corpus Christi: Essays on the Church and the Eucharist*, London: Longmans, Green & Co.

Eric L. Mascall, 1956, *Via Media: An Essay in Theological Synthesis*, London: Longmans.

E. L. Mascall, 1959, *The Importance of Being Human: Some Aspects of the Christian Doctrine of Man*, London: Oxford University Press.

E. L. Mascall, 1976, *Nature and Supernature: St Michael's Lectures, 1973*, London: Darton, Longman & Todd.

John Milbank, Catherine Pickstock and Graham Ward (eds), 1999, *Radical Orthodoxy: A New Theology*, London and New York: Routledge.

John Milbank, 2005, *The Suspended Middle: Henri de Lubac and the Debate Concerning the Supernatural*, Grand Rapids, MI and Cambridge, UK: Eerdmans.

John Milbank, 2009, 'Sophiology and Theurgy: The New Theological Horizon', in Adrian Pabst and Christoph Schneider (eds), *Encounter Between Eastern Orthodoxy and Radical Orthodoxy: Transfiguring the World Through the Word*, Farnham and Burlington, VT: Ashgate, pp. 45–85.

John Milbank and Simon Oliver, 2009, *The Radical Orthodoxy Reader*, London and New York: Routledge.

John Milbank and Catherine Pickstock, 2015, 'The Work of Forgiveness', in Hugh Burling and Silvianne Bürki (eds), *Noesis: Theology, Philosophy, Poetics*, Cambridge: The Graduate Society for the Study of Philosophical Theology and Systematics, Faculty of Divinity, University of Cambridge, pp. 37–41.

Adrian Pabst and Christoph Schneider (eds), 2009, *Encounter Between Eastern Orthodoxy and Radical Orthodoxy: Transfiguring the World Through the Word*, Farnham and Burlington, VT: Ashgate.

Catherine Pickstock, 2005, 'Duns Scotus: His historical and contemporary significance', *Modern Theology*, Vol. 21, Issue 4, October, pp. 543–74.

Aaron Riches, 2008, 'After Chalcedon: The Onenness of Christ and the Dyothelite Mediation of His Theandric Unity', *Modern Theology*, Vol. 24, No. 2, April, pp. 199–224.

James K. A. Smith, 2004, *Introducing Radical Orthodoxy: Mapping a Post-Secular Theology*, Grand Rapids, MI: Baker Academic.

Andrew Dean Swafford, 2014, *Nature and Grace: A New Approach to Thomistic Ressourcement*, Eugene, OR: Pickwick Publications.

Rudolf Voderholzer, 2008, *Meet Henri de Lubac: His Life and Work*, ET, San Francisco, CA: Ignatius Press.

Hans Urs von Balthasar, 1991 (1976), *The Theology of Henri de Lubac*, ET, San Francisco, CA: Ignatius Press.

Frances Young, 2013, *God's Presence: A Contemporary Recapitulation of Early Christianity*, Cambridge: Cambridge University Press.

Published Works by John Hughes

2001, 'The Politics of Forgiveness: A Theological Exploration of *King Lear*', *Modern Theology*, Vol. 17, No. 3, July, pp. 261–87.

2002a, 'Bulgakov's move from a Marxist to a Sophic Science', *Sobernost*, Vol. 24:2, pp. 29–47.

2002b, 'What is Radical Orthodoxy?', *with Matthew Bullimore*, in *Telos*, No. 123, Spring, pp. 183–9.

2004, 'Unspeakable Utopia: Art and the Return to the Theological in Adorno and Horkheimer', *Cross Currents*, Vol. 53, No. 4, Winter, pp. 475–92.

2007, *The End of Work: Theological Critiques of Capitalism*, Oxford: Blackwell.

2010, 'Jacques Maritain: Pre-Conciliar conservative or Thomist liberal democrat?', *Theology*, Vol. CXIII, No. 871, Jan/Feb, pp. 12–22.

2011a, 'Integralism and Gift Exchange in the Anglican Social Tradition, or Avoiding Niebuhr in Ecclesiastical Drag', in Adrian Pabst (ed.), *The Crisis of Global Capitalism: Pope Benedict XVI's Social Encyclical and the Future of Political Economy*, Eugene, OR: Cascade Books, pp. 219–33.

2011b, 'Proofs and Arguments', in Andrew Davison (ed.), *Imaginative Apologetics: Theology, Philosophy and the Catholic Tradition*, London: SCM, pp. 3–11.

2011c, 'Work, prayer and leisure in the Christian Tradition', *Crucible: The Christian Journal of Social Ethics*, Jan–Mar, pp. 7–15.

2013a, 'Creatio Ex Nihilo and the Divine Ideas in Aquinas: How Fair is Bulgakov's Critique?', *Modern Theology*, Vol. 29, Issue 2, April, pp. 124–37.

2013b, (ed.), *The Unknown God: Sermons Responding to the New Atheists*, Eugene, OR: Cascade Books.

2013c, 'Work and Labour', in Nicholas Adams, George Pattison and Graham Ward (eds), *Oxford Handbook of Theology and Modern European Thought*, Oxford: Oxford University Press, pp. 149–68.

2014, 'After Temple? The Recent Renewal of Anglican Social Thought', in Malcolm Brown (ed.), *Anglican Social Theology: Renewing the Vision Today*. London: SPCK, pp. 74–132.

Secondary Sources on John Hughes

2014, obituary in *The Times*, 22 July, p. 46.

Hugh Burling and Silvianne Bürki (eds), 2015, *Noesis: Theology, Philosophy, Poetics*, Cambridge: The Graduate Society for the Study of Philosophical Theology and Systematics, Faculty of Divinity, University of Cambridge.

Andrew Davison, 2014, obituary in *The One Hundred and Tenth Annual Report* of Jesus College, Cambridge, pp. 83–4 (as in *The Church Times*, 11 July 2014, p. 45).

John Rutter, 2015, 'The Quest' in his collection *The Gift of Life: Six Canticles of Creation and Seven Sacred Pieces*, commissioned in memory of John Hughes.

Janet Soskice, 2014, obituary in *The One Hundred and Tenth Annual Report* of Jesus College, Cambridge, pp. 79–81.

Reviews of *The End of Work*

Malcolm Brown, 2009, *Reviews in Religion and Theology*, Vol. 16, Issue 3, July, pp. 432–5.
Kelly Johnson, 2009, *Modern Theology*, Vol. 25, No. 3, July, pp. 521–3.
David Martin, 2011, *The Times Literary Supplement*, 22 August, www.the-tls.co.uk/tls/public/article706998.ece.
Eva Poole, 2008, *Faith in Business Quarterly Journal*, Vol. 12:1, pp. 27–8.
Marcus Pound, 2010, *Studies in Christian Ethics*, Vol. 23, No. 1, February, pp. 106–9.
Keith Ward, 2008, *Times Higher Education*, 21 February, www.timeshighereducation.com/books/the-end-of-work-theological-critiques-of-capitalism/400706.article.
Myles Wernz, 2008, *Religious Studies Review*, Vol. 34, Issue 4, December, p. 272.

Notes

1 One published essay (Hughes 2004) became a chapter in his monograph, *The End of Work: Theological Critiques of Capitalism* (Hughes 2007), and therefore has not been included.

2 In the copy of the issue of *Modern Theology* that John gave to me, which includes his essay on forgiveness (Hughes 2001), the handwritten inscription reads, 'Let's exchange charity', from *King Lear* V:III:165.

3 That being said, I was once sitting near John at a formal dinner when we were ordinands. John found himself sitting next to an undergraduate's father who turned out to be a tabloid journalist keen to share his views on his abhorrence of religion. It was not a happy ending. For the journalist.

4 On radical orthodoxy see Chapter 7 and for John's acknowledgement of his debt to its proponents see Chapter 12. For introductions to radical orthodoxy see: Milbank, Pickstock and Ward 1999; Milbank and Oliver 2009; Smith 2004; Bullimore 2011.

5 Chapter 5. In our first year of doctoral research when I was struggling to put pen to paper, John dusted off this review essay because it 'interested' him and was never part of his plan for inclusion in his dissertation.

6 For an account of John's Christian socialism see Jackson 2015.

7 Unpublished sermon delivered at St David, Exeter and St Michael, Exeter on the Fourth Sunday of Advent, 2007.

8 For pertinent works of Henri de Lubac see: de Lubac 1984, 1988, 1996, 1998 and 2000. The grace–nature debates are well described by Eric Mascall in: Mascall 1946, 1956, 1959 and 1976. Fergus Kerr (2002, p. 145) suggests that Mascall (1956) provides the best account in English of Thomas Aquinas' theology of nature and grace. For other explanatory literature see: Grumett 2007, 2015; Milbank 2005; Swafford 2014; Groves 2012; Kerr 2002, 2007; von Balthasar 1991; Voderholzer 2008.

9 In Chapter 2 John similarly argues against postulating alternative creations. God does not create our world by willing one of many possible divine ideas. This would suggest an arbitrariness to God's creative action because it separates God's faculty of willing from his divine wisdom. In God, wisdom, will and power are integrally related. God freely wills only what is good and accords with his wisdom. In creation we see the fruit of God's good and wise will. This is why we can be assured that the

world is ordered, loved and graced. The act of creation is God making his own nature and character imitable by creatures even in their finitude. It is not the arbitrary choice to make actual one of many possibilities.

10 This is the collect as found in the Church of England's *Common Worship: Service and Prayers for the Church of England*, London: Church House Publishing, 2000. It is the collect of the day from the Sarum rite by way of The Book of Common Prayer.

11 Whether or not de Lubac is the target of Pius XII's encyclical *Humani Generis* is a disputed question. See, e.g., Swafford 2014, pp. 55–63 and Milbank 2005, pp. x, 8–10, 33–47. The encyclical states: 'Others destroy the gratuity of the supernatural order, since God, they say, cannot create intellectual beings without ordering and calling them to the beatific vision.' (Quoted in Milbank 2005, p. ix.)

12 Aaron Riches' rather forbidding sounding article on the oneness of Christ and the Dyothelite mediation of his theandric unity (2008) demonstrates the necessity of describing the work of supernaturalizing grace through the lens of the biblical narrative of Christ's life and, in this case, the story of Christ's agony in the garden of Gethsemane. William Cavanaugh, like Riches, uses the thought of St Maximus to argue similarly in his essay on the visibility of the Church (2011).

13 For a recent articulation of a theology of recapitulation, see Young 2013.

14 No doubt John would have traced connections between the ecclesiological sensibility of the Church of England and the Anglican Churches across the world but in these essays 'Anglican' describes the Church of England. Characteristically, John was less interested in the rules governing the worldwide Anglican Communion and more inclined to build relationships. John spent time with the Delhi brotherhood during his ordination training, taught in a seminary in Kenya as a curate and, as a priest, preached Holy Weeks at Christ Church, St Laurence, Sydney and St Clement, Philadelphia.

15 John was beginning to explore his integral Christian humanism using the Russian sophiological tradition, which was of course freer of neo-scholastic habits of thought and more content to speak in a poetic and mystical mode. It was not embarrassed, for example, to speak of creation as being for the sake of deification. Like de Lubac's natural desire for the supernatural, it sought to find ways of speaking of the paradoxes of divine–human mediation. See: Bulgakov 1993; Martin 2015; Milbank 2009. John reviewed the volume (Pabst and Schneider 2009), in which Milbank's essay is included, in *International Journal for the Study of the Christian Church*, Vol. 11, Issues 2–3, May 2011, pp. 24–35.

16 'The Good Society: Can Labour Develop a Radical Agenda on Civil Society' (unpublished paper) delivered to the Blue Labour conference at Nottingham University, 6 July 2012.

17 The two seminar papers are printed as delivered.

PART I

New Creation, Creation and Labour

The Politics of Forgiveness:
A Theological Exploration of
King Lear (2001)

Introduction

This essay will present a theological reflection upon forgiveness as a social and political practice, but one distinctively based upon theological premises. In order to illustrate this account of forgiveness, I shall trace its emergence as a third possibility from the space opened by the conflict between two alternative unforgiving, 'non-theological' ideologies within Shakespeare's *King Lear*. Forgiveness will be shown to differ from, and be incomprehensible to both the conservative and radical models of sociability presented in the play, because of the transcendent horizon upon which forgiveness depends.

Why *Lear*? It may seem an unusual choice, yet this play in particular lends itself to a discussion of the often overlooked *political* significance of forgiveness.[1] *Lear* emerges from a historical climate of increasing tension between two ideologies – the old, static and conservative feudal order and the new renaissance bourgeois individualism – and has been read as arguing for *both* these positions.

Traditionally the play had been seen as a conservative and moralistic illustration of the Jacobean social wisdom that anarchy results from challenging the received political order and distributing power to the young, women or bastards. Such a reading gains some plausibility from the dating which would place the play's composition around the time King James was seeking parliamentary approval for the Act of Union, when a play about the 'evils of disunion' for the island of Britain might be most opportune.[2]

This view came to be challenged more recently by those who saw *King Lear* as opposed to traditional morality and social order.[3] To these revisionists, *Lear* becomes a revolutionary, almost proto-Marxist, political critique of the injustices of Jacobean society, aligned not with establishment interests, but with subversive Anabaptist radicals and the egalitarianism of anarchist groups such as the Levellers and Diggers.[4] A more extreme form of this radical reading has linked the play with the new renaissance scepticism of Montaigne and Bacon and its Machiavellian politics of naked power.[5] The play then becomes a 'subversive critique of ideology' *per se* (Dollimore 1984, p. 4), a 'demystification of Christian charity' (Kronenfeld 1998, p. 170), a rejection of the very possibility of any justice, authority and virtue.

Against both of the above accounts, it will be argued here that *neither* of these two ideologies actually emerges victorious within the play, and that their apparent opposition hides a more fundamental dialectical similarity, in their dependence upon a foreclosed, materialist account of the world which, as such, is haunted by the fear of death and thus is unable to envisage hope and unable to accommodate forgiveness. Thus we will see that, against Jonathon Dollimore and others, *King Lear* contains not only a radical critique of conservative values, but also a critique of the emerging radicalisms of nonconformist individualism and neopagan anarchism based upon the survival of the fittest, which have frequently been regarded by recent criticism as the triumphant voice within the play. Furthermore, we will argue that *Lear*, however bleak, is not finally an utterly sceptical, nihilist play, completely without ethics or virtue. Against Dollimore's argument that *Lear* embodies a 'demystification of Christian charity', I will suggest that it is rather *power* that is demystified, and charity which, by being decommodified, becomes almost remystified, re-enchanted.

It should be clear that this discussion does not entail arguing for any particular reconstruction of Shakespeare's own theological views, or even providing a systematic account of the 'moral' of *Lear* into which everything must be integrated. I am unconvinced that Shakespeare employed such a simplistic attitude to writing, and besides am primarily interested in the question of how he might assist a consideration of forgiveness. Hence there will be no treatment of the often debated portrayal of the gods in *Lear*, or of the 'problem' of the ending.[6] Rather, we are simply suggesting that some of the aporias in the play's ideological dialectic and its implicit treatment of certain key themes can be read as pointing towards a vision of forgiveness that is illuminating to current debates within Christian theology. In this light the setting in pre-Christian times, in a Britain that is still pagan, is no longer merely

4

incidental (as J. C. Maxwell has argued, in Muir 1984, p. xv). In a world without the hope of resurrection (which, it will be argued, is vital for forgiveness) any prescience of forgiveness can only remain a shadowy and hidden affair. This 'pagan' tragedy can thus be read in the manner of the Church's typological readings of the Old Testament – as pointing towards another dispensation. The emergence of forgiveness is certainly not something clearly articulated in *Lear*; it is the two non-forgiving ideologies that dominate our attention. Yet we shall argue, as Eagleton hints, that 'both [these] modes of being are a kind of nothing, and "something" only emerges in the play elusively, glimpsed fitfully in the dialectic between them' (Eagleton 1986, p. 80). Forgiveness, it will be argued, is intimated in the mutual self-deconstruction of the alternative possibilities, and in the occasional moments of epiphany where certain characters point towards the possibility of what might be.

The essay will thus divide into two halves: the first will consist of an analysis of *Lear* indicating the twofold portrayal of the destructive logic of violence at work within the text; the second, more substantial yet also more tentative, part will attempt to go beyond *Lear* to consider something of the 'logic' of Christian forgiveness, gestured towards within the play, although far from explicit, which suggests a possible way to resist the entrapment of the aporias in the former logic.

1 The Destructive Logic of the Economy of Vengeance and Violence

Out went the candle and we were left darkling.[7]

What are the politics of the two ideologies unable to accommodate forgiveness? This question can be approached through their representative characters.[8] The distinction between two quite different meanings of 'Nature' within the play has been noted before by various critics (see, for example, Danby 1949). These two accounts of what it is to be 'natural', with their consequent perspectives on the themes of Power and Justice, provide a useful way to outline the distinctions between the two competing ideologies.

The conservative perspective is represented within the play by the foolish parents – Lear and Gloucester. For these two old men, Nature signifies the received social order, understood in a static, essentialist fashion (the unchanging *ius divinum*) (Dollimore 1984, p. 95). Thus any questioning of the symbols of status which legitimate social order is regarded as dangerous, because of its potential to lead to the total breakdown of society into anarchy ('in cities, mutinies; in countries, discord; in palaces treason; and the bond crack'd twixt son and father', I:II:103–6). The apparent benevolence and order of Nature on this account is seen when Lear prays to her as a 'dear goddess' (I:IV:273) while Gloucester, thinking that Edmund has been faithful to him, calls him his 'loyal and *natural* boy' (II:I:83; cf. II:IV:176). On the inverse side of this binary construal of nature, those who do not perform the obligations appropriate to their role within society and even try to subvert the received social order are repeatedly termed 'unnatural' (for example, I:I:218; I:II:73). The political implications of such an account of Nature are clear: the Natural/ Unnatural opposition is used unconsciously by Lear and Gloucester to underwrite their own political status, and to prevent any attempts to challenge this distribution of power.

Lear and Gloucester may seem to be in favour of the social realm, advocates of justice and peaceful order and opposed to individualism and anarchy. While this is partly true, their account of the social realm is problematic. As conservatives, they construe it as something given, fixed and unchangeable, rather than something that continues to arrive and thus is more fluid, constantly open to being reconstituted afresh (the task of forgiveness). They are blind to the radical contingency of any actual society and to its artificiality and injustices, precisely because of their belief in the divine right of kings and nobility – that is, the ontologizing of the current distribution of power. In thinking things cannot be otherwise, they mistake culture for nature and words for reality, as can be seen when they are tricked by vain appearances and flattering words. In the first act, Lear mistakes the empty rhetorical performances of Goneril and Regan for genuine affection ('power to flattery bows', I:I:147), while failing to recognize the more truly real, albeit modest, love of Cordelia. Likewise Gloucester is easily duped by Edmund into suspecting his other son Edgar of plotting against him. Their inability to see leaves them naive when they should be suspicious, and suspicious when they should be more unsuspecting.

Their conservative attitude to moral order and accountability is as static and rigid as we might expect. Because of their conviction that the current social order is naturally ordained and unchanging, they possess a harsh and punitive view of moral responsibility and justice reminiscent of the *lex talionis* – 'an eye for an eye and a tooth for a tooth'. Lear is quick to judge moralistically, spending much of the early scenes condemning people and crying for 'vengeance' (II:IV:92; cf. III:VI:15 and IV:6:185). He believes it ridiculous to think that he could seek forgiveness, because his pride precludes the humbling this entails: 'Ask her forgiveness? Do you but mark how this becomes the house' (II:IV:149). Likewise neither he nor Gloucester show sympathy to the poor and weak: 'O! I have ta'en too little care of this', Lear admits later (III:IV:32).

The second ideological perspective is embodied by the young and healthy rather than the old and weak. It is championed by the mutinous children – Edmund, Goneril and Regan. Their alternative view of Nature is illustrated by Edmund's prayer to '*Nature* ... my goddess' (I:II:1, my italics). Here he appeals to biological naturalism ('my dimensions are as well compact, my mind as generous') against the 'plague of custom' (that is, the social convention that regards him as inferior because illegitimate). This relativizing recognition that 'law and morality have their origins in custom rather than with an eternal order of things' (Dollimore 1984, p. 16) not only challenges the ideological basis of the current moral and political order, but through the disclosure of the artificiality of the processes of legitimation, questions the very possibility of any ethics and justice as anything more than ideological disguises for naked power.[9] Nature is now regarded not as static but as dynamic, not benign but rather violent, iconoclastic and antisocial. Whereas Lear and Gloucester can be seen, in terms of the Jacobean political situation, as representing the views of the old aristocratic feudal interests, their rebellious children perhaps embody the values of the rising mercantile bourgeoisie[10] – the triumph, through competitive conflict, of the strongest at the expense of the weak, the constant desire to exceed one's position and increase one's power ('I grow, I prosper; Now, gods, stand up for bastards!', I:II:22). The 'natural man' is now the bare beast who is stripped of all social disguises, and who imposes his will upon others by force; as can be seen from the repeated association of Edmund, Goneril and Regan with wild animal imagery (tigers, bears, rats, serpents, and so on) and in more explicitly negative tones with the terms 'monster' and 'monstrous' (for example, I:I:215). This account of Nature leads to exactly the opposite view of justice and responsibility from the foolish parents. Rejecting convention, the only law that Edmund, Goneril and Regan recognize is that of the jungle; hence the world is seen in completely amoral and egoistic terms: 'All with me's meet that I can fashion fit' (I:II:181).

It is hardly necessary to indicate that for each view, the other's model of virtue is their supreme vice. Nothing is more wicked to the conservative view than to have 'son against father' (I:II:107); while nothing is more miserable to the radical perspective than to have the old and weak still clinging to a power that is theirs on account of convention rather than strength. We might note that from the stance of a prudent Jacobean politician, both sides would seem to embody genuine wisdom (a weak monarch may be as disastrous for the kingdom as the more 'immoral' traitor).

Who is to be victorious?

Who is to be victorious in this battle of the two Natures? Is it to be Lear and Gloucester who think that it is 'natural' for children to care for their parents and for the socially inferior to look up to their superiors, and 'unnatural' to challenge this arrangement? Or Edmund, Goneril and Regan who think it is 'natural' that the strong should rule, and the weak (frail old kings and dukes) should go to the wall?

Upon the heath, the radical view seems initially to triumph. A wild and violent Nature (represented by the howling storm) proceeds to 'crack nature's mould' (III:II:8) – to destroy the 'natural', essentialist, moral and social order that Lear believed in, reducing him to a bestial nature without the trappings of society and status – a 'poor, bare forked animal' (III:IV:106–7). Brute force seems to have conquered social convention; the embodiment of conservative order and justice is deconstructed to reveal what renaissance neopaganism claimed man to be – an agent or victim of naked power. In the light of this, all attempts at justice and morality seem like weak disguises hiding the exercise of violent force. It is Lear himself who gives voice to the demystification of the moral and political ideological structure that he represented.

> 'They told me I was everything. 'Tis a lie: I am not ague proof ... change places, and, handy-dandy, which is the justice, which is the thief ... The great image of Authority: a dog's obeyed in office ... through tattered clothes small vices do appear; robes and fur gowns hide all. Plate sin with gold, and the strong lance of justice hurtless breaks; arm it in rags, a pigmy's straw does pierce it.' (IV:VI:105, 151, 156, 162–5)

Yet is this the final word? Are we to conclude that justice, virtue and charity are impossible and any attempts are always deceptions? That human relations are no more than the violent dominance of one over another? That man is no more than beast? Many have concluded so; but I shall argue that the play is more subtle than this and points us beyond the truth of the radical critique of society towards something else.

Against those who argue that Edmund, Goneril and Regan represent the play's triumphant conclusion, we should begin by indicating the various negative images of wild beasts, corruption, venereal disease and death associated with them. The play clearly does not uncritically embrace such views as positive, suggesting at various points that they might be 'barbarous', 'degenerate' (for example, IV:II:43), even demonic. Beyond this, the gruesome fate that eventually overcomes all three characters – as, beset by suspicion and an unquenched desire for still more power, they gradually turn against one another until all lie dead – suggests an awareness that the ideology they embody is not merely undesirable, but ultimately untenable. The radical, pagan option, which appeared triumphant, is thus seen to be self-refuting in that it is ultimately self-destructive.[11] To live by violent force and the triumph of strength not only creates the civil anarchy so feared by the parents, but even destroys those who advocate and live by its rule so that, 'Humanity must perforce prey on itself like monsters of the deep' (IV:II:49).

The Common Materialist Agenda: The Primacy of Power and Violence

Nothing will come of nothing. (I:I:89)

In the movement of using one ideology to deconstruct another and then exposing the self-destructive nature of that ideology, we can glimpse a more fundamental similarity beneath the apparent opposition of these two worldviews. The theologian is perhaps particularly well placed to notice this (when the literary critic seems not to have done so!) as it lies in their metaphysic or fundamental ontology. By this is meant how they narrate the way things ultimately are, the picture of the world that is posited as the backdrop to all their activity. First we may note a common disregard for the poor and weak uniting the parents and children. Both groups appeal to Nature to legitimate their own power at the expense of others. Both also construe the structure of society as fixed and unchanging and are thus incapable of imagining a different pattern of sociability. This applies not only to Lear and Gloucester, but

also to Edmund, Goneril and Regan who may conceive of a revolutionary change of who holds power, but do not contemplate any alteration
to the basic structures of power (hence their radicalism is merely an
inadequate one that inverts rather than transforms society). Ironically,
then, it seems that the apparently 'benign' Nature of the conservatives
is actually as violent as that of the radicals in its corrupt justice and
disregard for the weak, while the apparently 'dynamic' Nature of the
radicals remains in reality as static as the conservative account in its
inability actually to change the structures of power. The two groups are
ultimately united by a common obsession with 'power, property and
inheritance' (Dollimore 1984, p. 198), which underpins the violence
and hostility to change of both.

These common factors all point towards the realization that the
ontology or underlying picture of the world for both ideologies is a
foreclosed materialist one. The clue to this materialism is given in
Lear's repeated assertion that 'nothing can come of nothing'.[12] We are
reminded of this throughout the play as the references to 'nought' and
'nothing' become more frequent with the increase of the tragedy, suggesting a sense of the onset of anarchy pictured as the primal Nihil, the
nothing that preceded creation. For a materialist outlook, it is of course
the case that nothing can come from nothing, and that therefore what
exists must always have done so (the doctrine of the eternity of matter),
yet this is not so for Christianity, for which it is crucial that God creates
ex nihilo. For the materialist, there can be 'nothing new under the sun'[13]
as there is no transcendent from which a *novum* might arrive; like any
foreclosed system, the universe must be beset by what the Preacher calls
'vanity', doomed to collapse upon itself, spiralling towards an endless
death: 'This great world shall so wear out to naught.'[14] Hence the world
is conceived as a place of finite scarcity rather than eternal bounty (the
'doctrine of the limited good'),[15] which in turn produces a competitive,
violent construal of selfhood in terms of possession; thus all things,
including even happiness, become *commodified* as, being limited, one
can only possess them at the expense of someone else.[16] Everything is
therefore haunted by a desire for possession and control, and a suspicion of rejection and fear of loss, and ultimately death – as one cannot
trust that one's acts of generosity will not remain finally unreturned
and so tragically futile. For such a view of the world, forgiveness (and
indeed love) must remain impossibilities.

Exactly this process of the commodification of charity, founded upon
materialism, is central to *Lear* where, in a scene rich in the language of

finance and capital, Lear attempts to extort love from his daughters in exchange for land.[17] The scene opens with 'a bout of severe linguistic inflation' (Eagleton 1986, p. 76) as Lear treats 'love' as a sort of finance capital or abstract quantifiable commodity ('Which of you shall we say doth love us most?', I:I:50), and it is by joining this game that Goneril and Regan are able to respond with a 'speculative venture' – a rhetoric which in claiming to be hyperbolically 'beyond what can be valued rich or rare' (I:I:56) is in fact worthless. It is this materialist commodification (begun by Lear) and the consequent competitive territorial greed (of Edmund, Goneril and Regan) that is the ultimate cause of all the violence and tragedy within *Lear*.

The common agenda of power and property uniting conservative and radical is noted by Dollimore, who sees it as a failure of Edmund's radicalism to escape the dominant conservative ideology that it opposes (Dollimore 1984, pp. 198–201). We might agree here, but not with the implication that if Edmund were just a little more 'radical', more sceptical and iconoclastic, he could do this. In fact, ironically for one who is so willing to dismiss Christianity as essentialist, it is the persisting essentialism of Edmund's view of Nature (now neopagan rather than conservative), which Dollimore himself uncritically endorses, that is the real problem. By this we mean that to say that: 'Power and property ... are somehow prior to the laws of human kindness rather than vice versa (likewise with power in relation to justice)' (Dollimore 1984, p. 197) is itself a form of essentialism, claiming that things must necessarily always be so, and cannot be otherwise.

This attribution of ultimacy to power rather than charity, now more widespread than ever through the work of the 'neo-Nietzscheans', is however merely one way of narrating the world (what John Milbank calls an 'ontology of violence').[18] Furthermore, we have seen that it is precisely this foreclosed materialist ontology, which Dollimore neglects to question, that actually unites the two ideologies and prevents them from envisaging any forgiveness or social transformation. Dollimore's essentialism lies in his acceptance of Edmund's neopagan account of Nature as necessarily true, failing to recognize that it is not a positivist 'scientific' truth, but rather simply another form of the materialist ontology, which one may or may not inhabit. Such a bestial image of humanity is not so much an exposure of our true nature, but an instantiation of our cultural potential for subhuman behaviour.[19]

Only Nihilism?

The two unforgiving ideologies are indeed inevitably locked into a destructive battle to the death in which neither can be truly victorious. Both are enslaved to the logic of fear, suspicion, vengeance, violence and death. Is there any way out of this dialectic? Many commentators in recent years, recognizing the horrific ugliness and immorality of the neopagan account of bestial human nature, nevertheless believe it to be irrefutable in its 'awful truth' (Dollimore 1984, p. 197). For them *Lear* has no politics or ethics whatsoever. It is rather a painfully accurate description of the utter nihilism of the human condition, a world where people do prey upon one another and from which there is no escape.

Yet it is simply not the case that Lear is left howling upon the heath. This is not the play's conclusion. The storm functions not so much as a destructive force alone, but rather more like the purifying furnace of purgatory[20] which dissolves society in order to rebuild it again. The imagery of clothing and nakedness throughout the play, with its undertones of the relationship between Nature and Culture, can illustrate the same point. As Judy Kronenfeld has argued, the imagery of Lear's nudity is neither purely positive, nor the play's conclusion (1998, ch. 4, especially p. 91). Stripping may signify exposing the truth, but it also has connotations of humiliation and dehumanization (as the monster/ bestial imagery indicates); while clothing can represent protection, civilization and 'seemly apparel' as much as it can mean false pomp and deceptive disguise. We might suggest that this imagery functions within the play not according to a simple 'clothing = bad, stripping = good' dichotomy, but rather operates after the pattern of Christian baptismal imagery of being stripped of one's old garments before donning new ones. On this account, the destruction of the old Lear upon the heath is merely the necessary prelude to the birth of the new. Thus the radical voice appears not as the final word within the play, but simply a stage or tool in the deconstruction of one particular model of society (not the possibility of society in general). Society is dismantled in order to be reconstructed. Lear must be reclothed (Lerner 1963, p. 158).

When searching for pointers to what form this reclothing might take, we should note that the dialectic of vengeance does not account for all the characters within the play. There remains a third group comprising Cordelia, Edgar and Kent. Could it be these characters are the embodiment of something else, signs of the possibility of virtue and indications of the 'clothes' that Lear should assume on leaving the heath? It is often claimed that all the characters are engaged in an endless series of parodies, disguises and performances ('Edgar I nothing am', II:III:21) from which it is impossible to extract any coherent account of human identity, let alone virtue. In response to this, it is certainly the case that at any one moment in the play it is problematic to isolate the virtuous characters from the wicked: Cordelia's refusal to play the game of flattery might be construed as stubborn, priggish and miserly; Edmund's claim that his illegitimacy is not his own fault seems fair; Goneril and Regan's refusal to accommodate their father's riotous retinue could be seen as prudent; Edgar's acting the bedlam beggar might be seen as torturing his father, and so on. However, this way of reading the play makes the crucial mistake of ignoring *temporality*, which is the dimension in which virtue and the possibility of imagining a different ontology emerge ('Time shall unfold what plighted cunning hides', I:I:279). It is in fact clear to an audience, through the duration of the play, that Cordelia, Kent and Edgar are truly virtuous in their consistent faithfulness and loyalty towards others, which is unshaken even in the most extreme situation of chaos and rejection. Likewise the truly vicious nature of Edmund, Goneril and Regan is not something that remains open to doubt for one who has followed the play's passage through time. A consistent portrayal of Virtue is manifested within the play through its performance in time.[21]

We will now proceed to consider forgiveness as the key to this alternative social practice, which alone can escape enslavement to violence.

2 The Practice of Redemption: Forgiveness

L'arc-en-ciel entre Dieu et les hommes, c'est le pardon.[22]

Our analysis of *Lear* has shown how the play contains a residual hope for something else that can break out of the cycle of vengeance and violence. What form must this alternative ideology and practice take? If the problem is an order characterized by the endless exchange of violence, then the solution must be something that breaks this circle and transforms this violence into peace. Already we can see here that the solution must resemble the Christian understanding of redemption; namely, the process of reconstituting a divided and broken Babel world into the harmony and peace of the Kingdom of God. We have seen how these forms of violence involve a competitive mistrust of others

(Lear, Gloucester, Edmund, Goneril and Regan), which leads people to be quick to judge others, while being resistant to being judged themselves (as when Lear protests he is 'more sinned against than sinning', III:II:60). Believing in the rightness of one's own cause and the iniquity of any who stand in its way, such people are easily prone to a sense of being wronged, and easily incited to seek vengeance. Thus any solution must enable the renewal of trust of others, the recognition of wrongs committed and the pardoning of offences received; the suspension of judgement and the forgoing of vengeful retaliation.

Such a transformation requires a radical change of hearts, a repicturing of the world. Within the play we witness such a transformation of Lear and Gloucester (and perhaps briefly Edmund as well)[23] as they painfully unlearn the ways of dominance and judgement, regret their errors, and learn compassion and charity. This transformation is not, as is often suggested, learned simply through their humbling and humiliation, which alone could have been simply destructive (both Lear and Gloucester go through a stage where they have unlearned judgement without learning charity). The transformation does not proceed *ex nihilo*, from an effort of will in response to an experience of suffering; rather it is a gift painfully given by the agents of redemption – Edgar, Kent and Cordelia – who act like midwives in bringing to birth the new Lear and Gloucester. These characters manifest faithful love towards the two old men despite their errors, even when this entails painfully enduring the consequences of their folly. This constant, transformative loving-faithfulness is what we understand by the social and political practice of forgiveness. Such a reading is encouraged by the redemptive language associated with these figures, as when Edgar is described as having 'sav'd [Gloucester] from despair' (V:III:190), and, more evidently, with Cordelia, who cries 'holy water from her heavenly eyes' (IV:III:30) and 'redeems nature from the general curse' (IV:VI:203). She is a 'soul in bliss' whose kiss will 'repair those violent harms' and, in language again reminiscent of baptism, take Lear 'out o'th'grave' (IV:VII:28, 45–6). She opposes the dissemblance and violence not with another form of force, but with honesty and love. Forgiveness is precisely this radically non-violent opposition to violence.

To present forgiveness as a solution to the social and political deadlock of the conservatives and radicals in *Lear*, offers an attempt to indicate how forgiveness can and should be understood as a social and political option. Such a conclusion, however, runs counter to the arguments of many, both theologians and secular moral or political theorists, who have insisted that forgiveness can serve at most as an interiorized psychological event, but can have no possible place within the social and political realm. This view was maintained by early pagan critics of Christianity and then endorsed by some of the apologists in response. The Reformers' exegesis of the prohibition of judgement as not applying to people acting ex officio continued this exclusion of forgiveness from the political sphere (Bonhoeffer 1959, pp. 128–9); while the interiorizing and therapeutic rhetoric of forgiveness often used by the Church today merely perpetuates it further.[24]

Political theorists and philosophers can be even more confident in their dismissal. To forgive a political offence is seen as implicitly endorsing it and enabling its continuation; forgiveness is thus opposed to the rule of law upon which political society is founded.[25] This argument assumes that violence can only be countered with violence (albeit in legitimated forms such as the police) and that forgiveness, in renouncing this, must be cowardly and life-denying, becoming complicit with violence and ultimately being crushed by it – as is so powerfully indicated by the limp body of Cordelia in the final scene.

To counter these arguments and show how our political understanding of forgiveness is not only possible but necessary, we must indicate how it operates not in an ideal vacuum, but amid its very antithesis – the persisting order of vengeance and violence. We will seek to do this by correcting certain (interiorized, purist, extrinsicist, sadomasochistic) views of forgiveness that we believe to be inadequate, learning in particular from recent discussions of historical shifts in the understanding of Christian charity. This comparison is based upon the claim that forgiveness *is* Christian charity, albeit in the mode of interaction with a fallen and sinful world – that is, in the mode of redemption. Recently there have been a number of attempts to rehabilitate a view of charity as a concrete and social practice over time, which resembles our presentation of the forgiveness offered by Cordelia, Kent and Edgar. We shall now consider how the discussion of the place of self-interest and reciprocity within Christian charity might be helpful to our concept of forgiveness.

The Role of Self-Interest and Reciprocity

Let's exchange charity. (V:III:165)

Edgar's words 'Let's exchange charity' may seem awkward to our ears. We are not inclined to see charity, which if our definition is accepted includes forgiveness, in terms of an 'exchange' – a reciprocal, two-way relationship – preferring to figure it as an altruistic, unilateral and unreturnable gift.

Many theologians follow this by opposing the reciprocity of the economy of vengeance (its tit for tat exchange) to the unilateral, unmerited and unreturnable divine gift of forgiveness.[26] The former is then pictured as a circular relationship, while the latter is very much a linear one-way relation. Similarly, the former is aligned with the self-interest of worldly *eros*, while the latter is linked with the disinterested altruism of Christian *agape* (see Nygren 1953, pt 1, ch. 3 and *passim*). On this account, our sinful human ways are dominated by considerations of 'what we will gain from this', merits and rewards; God's ways, by contrast, are utterly selfless, other-centred, unmerited.

Drawing upon Linda Woodhead and John Milbank's critiques of some forms of sadomasochistic altruism within Christian ethics, we shall suggest that this account of charity and forgiveness as ideally disinterested and non-reciprocal is deeply flawed and inadequate, and should be replaced with the more Augustinian eudaemonist perspective upon charity that has been championed by John Burnaby and Oliver O'Donovan.

The problems with unilateral, disinterested altruism as the ideal model for human relations and for a political account of forgiveness can be illustrated by considering unrequited love. It is intuitively obvious that this is usually an unhealthy state, a painful and unbalanced relationship. (This is not to claim that equivalence and sameness are necessary for an ideal relationship; indeed, healthy parent–child relationships are obviously asymmetrical, yet remain reciprocal.) It seems necessary to recognize the point made by feminist commentators that: 'the hope and desire for a response of love from the one who is loved – indeed for communion with the loved one – is not only a natural but a legitimate aspect of love and that there is nothing sub-Christian about it ... at its best love is a reciprocal relationship rather than a one-way self-offering' (Woodhead in Elwes 1992, p. 67).

The alternative – unilateral altruism – is ultimately more sinister than we might believe. If virtue is about the absolute concern for the other and the total exclusion of erotic self-interest,[27] then it would seem that suffering is dangerously close to becoming a virtue per se[28] and replacing the happiness of the Beatific vision as the goal of the Christian life. Such an account renders Christian virtue a form of sadomasochism: secretly celebrating the suffering of another as the occasion for its own holiness (Milbank 1997, p. 24), and ultimately seeking its own annihilation, in a suicidal will to death (Milbank 1997, p. 16). Furthermore, if this utterly unreciprocated altruism is the supreme model of Christian virtue, then one should not only hope for the rejection of one's offerings of love and forgiveness (which would thus become more holy), but as has been suggested,[29] the most virtuous Christian would be an atheist one, whose intention is thus purified from 'contamination' by the hope of a reward in heaven – 'Christianity's true destiny is to be demythologised and secularised' (Milbank 1997, pp. 16–17; cf. Derrida 1995, p. 112). Ultimately, one should also then admit that such an altruism is finally impossible; we must await its eternally postponed arrival (Milbank 1995, pp. 130–1). The 'gift' of love and forgiveness cannot be given,[30] precisely because such an absolute purity of intention and detachment from our own interests and hope for return is in practice impossible, as even the minimal return of someone's grateful thanks contaminates the 'pure' intention.[31]

Yet we can insist that such a picture of Christian virtue is in fact a distortion. Christian charity is neither to be equated with neo-Kantian ethics of rational duty, from which self-interest must be excluded, nor with a 'Stoical' securing of interior purity against dependence upon external influences. There are many reminders of the need for mutuality and erotic self-interest throughout the Christian tradition.[32] Indeed we can claim that this has been the dominant 'ontological' or 'eudaemonist' view of Christian charity held by Augustine and Aquinas, which came to be gradually undermined by various 'subjectivist' theologians.[33] Analysing the commandment to 'Love your neighbour as yourself', Woodhead (in Elwes 1992, p. 77), points to its stress on mutuality: 'For neighbourhood is a reciprocal notion. As Augustine said, "nobody can be a neighbour except to a neighbour".' Within the New Testament the legitimate desire for happiness and hope for immediate or eschatological return are not excluded from the practice of virtue. Thus even the injunctions to do things without expectation of worldly praise are followed by the promises: 'your Father who sees in secret will reward you' (Matt. 6.4; cf. Luke 14.14). As von Balthasar puts it: 'L'amour pur does not exclude the thought of being rewarded.

Love rejoices over the "reward" and the prospect of being united forever with the beloved' (1995, p. 88). The shift towards the dominance of an interiorized and unilateral account of Christian charity, such as we have argued against here, has been traced within a particular period of Western history. Theologians of the twelfth and thirteenth centuries were among the earliest proponents of such views, while later, in the fifteenth and sixteenth centuries, John Bossy detects a shift in the everyday sense of the word 'charity': 'the decay of the notion that reciprocity and some kind of personal relation (on the beggar's part praying for the soul of his benefactor) were necessary characteristics of an act of charity' (Bossy 1985, p. 146), until the Augustinian view of charity as a 'state of enlarged sociability' is all but replaced by the more familiar sense of charity as acts of 'civility and activism' directed towards an 'abstract and rather passive neighbour'(Bossy 1985, p. 143). A similar development in views of forgiveness can be seen through this period. It is seen, first, in confessional practices, which became increasingly interiorized and lost their social dimension with the replacement of public by auricular confession in the tenth and eleventh centuries, and the eventual fading out of the practice altogether among Protestant traditions (Jones 1995, p. 38; cf. Bonhoeffer 1959, pp. 260f.). Where confession persisted, penitential manuals testify to a growing preoccupation with personal (usually sexual) sins, rather than social ones.[34] Second, these same developments can be found in changing accounts of divine forgiveness in the doctrine of the atonement during this period: the Anselmian account of the cross as an 'equitable and objective exchange' (God in Christ offers his humanity to the Father on behalf of all humanity), the restoration of friendship through a social transaction, according to the model of kinship relations, came to be replaced by the Lutheran picture of a more unilateral, isolated, unmerited and unreturnable act from God to the believer (God offers his divinity, in Christ, to us) which we simply passively receive (Bossy 1985, pp. 93–4).

If, then, we seek to resist these various developments, we must follow Milbank's rejection of the construal of the ideal gift as unilateral, linear and unreciprocated, an interpretation that has become even more predominant in modernity, in favour of an endless reciprocal gift-exchange.[35] It then becomes more clear, first, how we can and should speak of 'exchanging' charity and also how, in a world where 'all have sinned', the 'gift' of forgiveness can never be purely one-sided if it is to be fruitful. The practice of reconciliation, the restoration of peace, must always be a reciprocal task.

The Problem of Commodification

The hostility to reciprocity does however require some consideration, as it can point us to a different problem with forgiveness. Why have self-interest and reciprocity been regarded as so suspect? If self-interest and reciprocity are regarded as somehow less holy and ideal, this is even more so (especially for Protestants) when it comes to the relationship between God and humanity. To Protestant ears, talk of any exchange between heaven and earth, of self-interest in our salvation, may sound dangerously close to suggesting we can 'merit' our salvation, making God into some sort of business partner. Why should this be so? I want to suggest that there is an authentic concern underlying this protest – a mistaken response to a misidentified, yet very real, danger that affects all relationships – the danger of *commodification*, perhaps the most serious threat to the possibility of both love and forgiveness. We can illustrate this by examining the originating event of the Reformation (for it is no accident that Protestants should be so particularly hostile to self-interest and reciprocity in their ethics as much as their theories of the atonement!) – the protest at the sale of indulgences, the greatest theological controversy about forgiveness. Using the analogy of human love and friendships we can suggest how these developments can be resisted by identifying the genuine problem of commodification, which threatens charity and forgiveness, human and divine, alike.

If we consider an ordinary relationship we can see that it is not properly self-interest and reciprocity which are problematic in themselves, but the commodification which can distort these qualities: a couple who are in love are not being unhealthy in desiring that the other person will return their love, nor in taking delight in their love. However, we would be justified in describing as diseased a relationship which was infected by suspicion and fear of loss rather than trust, and which consequently treated the other person's love as a scarce commodity to be bought, possessed and controlled. The symptoms of such a commodification of love would be a sense of proprietorial ownership and rigid obligation ('You are my wife, therefore you owe me ...'), an anxious calculation and expectation of equivalence ('If I bring home a box of chocolates then I might get this out of her ...') rather than spontaneity and inexact generosity, an alienation of the gift of love from the personal giver, and a quantification of this love as something that can be measured. This is of course precisely the same process that makes indulgences abhorrent: the penitential system degenerates into a form of early capitalist economy, where forgiveness, in terms of quantifiable days off purgatory, can be calculatingly and anxiously purchased as a commodity independent of actual relationships, and then possessed as a secure right or guarantee against fear. Interestingly this process of turning forgiveness into a form of spiritual capital ('the Treasury of the Church'), which developed from 1300 onwards, seems to have been particularly encouraged by the Franciscans who had so adamantly renounced material property (Bossy 1985, p. 55).

If this was the real problem with indulgences, maybe we can begin to speak once again of reciprocity as ideal not only in human relations, but even in divine ones (albeit asymmetrically). Such a reflection would avoid rendering humanity purely passive[36] in accounts of redemption, and would enable us instead to recover more reciprocal terms for the relations between heaven and earth such as 'covenant'[37] and 'friendship' (Jones 1995, pp.xii–xiii). Indeed it is important to note that the doctrine of the Trinity suggests a God whose relations are reciprocal *in se*.[38]

How does this exchange between heaven and earth work for forgiveness? While it does not seem meaningful to speak of us 'forgiving' God (Jones 1995, p. 52), it is not the case that we should simply accept divine forgiveness and then do nothing. Rather, this should overflow towards others and thus return to God, so that within the always-already prior activity of divine grace and forgiveness, we can and should 'offer up' to God our acts of forgiveness in the hope that they will continue to be non-identically returned in his merciful forgiveness towards us. This is supremely manifested in the Lord's Prayer where a promise of forgiveness is trustingly offered in the hope of being returned: 'Forgive us our trespasses, as we forgive those who trespass against us.' The same movement of the endless exchange of offerings between heaven and earth might be said to be found in the Eucharist, where the Gift *cannot* be alienated from the Giver nor unreturned for, in truly Trinitarian fashion, it is God who offers Godself back to God (for example, 'Thou on earth both priest and victim in the eucharistic feast').[39] We will return to consider exactly how human forgiveness is linked with this movement of divine forgiveness later.

Our examination of the dangers of commodification makes it necessary to insist that forgiveness, like love and salvation, is not a commodity that can be bought or possessed, not something that can be abstracted from real people and relations, expected as a right, secure from anxiety or fear of loss, nor a gift that should be quantified or given calculatingly. As France reminds us: 'Love's not love when it is mingled with regards that stand aloof from th'entire point' (I:I:236). Rather, like the love of a healthy friendship, forgiveness should proceed spontaneously and generously from trust and hope.

The Theological Horizon

It should not be surprising to see that it is commodification of love and forgiveness that threatens their reciprocity and thus their very possibility. We have already argued that commodification is integral to the materialist ontology that causes the violence of the two opposing ideologies in *Lear*. Thus it is obvious that a different view of the world will be necessary to sustain the trust and hope of forgiveness, one which can oppose this violence and the suspicion and fear upon which it is based. A different ontology is required to sustain reciprocity without commodification.

More positively we can indicate that the very logic of reciprocity itself requires the recognition of a *transcendent* horizon as the condition for its possibility. Such a recognition is simply the reverse of the earlier observation that a completely altruistic, disinterested love must exclude the possibility of heavenly reward; if love *must* be reciprocal, then it *requires* the hope of heaven.[40] Why is this so? If forgiveness is an endless circle where each forgiving person is implicated in the experience of being forgiven, we are left with a problem of infinite regress: who starts this circle off or completes it? A circle, by definition, has no beginning or end. Thus, in a manner similar to Aquinas' argument from motion, we can say that forgiveness requires the existence of a perfect being who does not require forgiveness and cannot be other than forgiving as the condition for its very possibility.[41] In more concrete terms, the political process of forgiveness, while needing to be reciprocal to be successful, also demands that someone make the risky and costly step of taking the initiative to break the circle of recrimination and violence in order to get the circle to begin at all.[42] Without such an initiative, the two sides will remain in a state of deadlock, waiting for the other to make the first move. Yet if, for fallen humanity, forgiveness is not an effort of the rational will that proceeds *ex nihilo*, but must be received as gift, erotically drawn forth by the prior experience of love, then it would seem such an initiative is impossible for us. However for Christians this is not the case, as our acts of love and forgiveness are made possible by the experience of the always-already love of God for us in

Christ, which forms the motivation for such acts and the grounds for hoping they will not ultimately be unrequited, even when there can be no such grounds forthcoming from other people.[43] The prior initiative and posterior response of God is the framework that makes possible such a way of living – the love behind us and before us that draws forth our love. Such a view of our 'horizontal' forgiving as inhering within the 'vertical' economy of forgiveness between heaven and earth is evident in the New Testament where the difficult call to love one's enemies is justified specifically on the basis of divine precedent ('He makes his sun rise on the evil and the good', Matt. 5.45), while Paul urges his readers to forgive one another 'as God in Christ has forgiven you'.[44] Likewise potentially unrequited acts of forgiveness are encouraged on the basis that God will 'underwrite' them ('If you forgive men their trespasses your heavenly Father also will forgive you', Matt. 6.14), gathering up our unrequited gifts of charity and returning them to us either now, or eschatologically, at the resurrection ('give and it will be given to you; good measure, pressed down, shaken together, running over, will be put into your lap', Luke 6.38). Forgiveness thus requires a combination of trust that one is forgiven and hope that one will receive forgiveness back. Without the trust that it is in giving that one receives (from a transcendent source) and the hope that one's dispossession will not ultimately leave one with any the less and so will not involve self-diminution, forgiveness (and indeed love) must remain impossible, and human relations must remain dominated by the violence inherent in conceiving of people as competitive territories. Forgiveness then is impossible upon the basis of the foreclosed materialist ontology, which we explored earlier, but is dependent upon a distinctively theological horizon of trust in grace and hope for resurrection as the condition of its very possibility. Indeed, any act of forgiveness implicitly posits such a horizon.[45]

If our forgiving is an imitation of and participation in the circular divine economy of forgiveness then it seems that, when this practice is to encounter and transform the world, we may well be called upon to imitate the divine initiative ('while we were still far off you met us in your Son', *The Alternative Service Book 1980*, p. 144) in order to break the *nihil ex nihilo* of violence and revenge – to make the first move. This is what it means to love those who have not shown love, to love even enemies. Such a move may indeed be both risky and costly, as it entails an abandonment of security, placing oneself in a position painfully vulnerable to rejection. Thus forgiveness may even entail the supremely difficult vocation to martyrdom. Cordelia, Kent and Edgar all sustain their devotion when it is unreturned, or even returned with hostility ('We are not the first who, with best meaning, have incurred the worst', V:III:3–4), and are able to do this because their behaviour is founded on something deeper than the contingencies of the king's affections. Their love must precede the transformation of Lear and Gloucester in order to make it possible. For Christianity the divine initiative of incarnation was itself met with rejection and finally crucifixion, although it was not defeated by this, and we can only trust that ours likewise will be finally vindicated.

How is such a potential for martyrdom to be distinguished from the life-denying morality with which forgiveness has been identified? Forgiveness has been seen as beset by a pathological self-denial that is almost a will to death. It is the value not of heroes, but of victims; a degenerate otherworldly 'ascetic' piety that has suppressed the natural order of vengeance and retaliation, enabling the weak to hold power while society becomes ever more sickly. This view is found supremely among Nietzsche's writings, where forgiveness is an excellent example of Christianity's usual practice: 'weakness is being lied into something meritorious ... the inoffensiveness of the weak man, even the cowardice of which he has so much ... here acquire flattering names ... his inability for revenge is called unwillingness to revenge, perhaps even forgiveness'. Forgiveness then is nothing more than the 'vengeful cunning of impotence'.[46] Such a 'Nietzschean' critique is voiced within *Lear*, when Goneril condemns her husband's virtue, with its obvious resonances of turning the other cheek, as cowardice: 'Milk-liver'd man! That bear'st a cheek for blows, a head for wrongs' (IV:II:50–1; cf. Matt. 5.39 and Muir 1972, p. 147). Yet this exposes the critique as itself based upon the very violent ontology which we have already argued can and must be resisted.

It is certainly possible to reject its caricature of forgiveness: Christianity is not an extension of suicidal stoicism[47] (despite superficial similarities) in that it involves completely abandoning oneself in faith to grace; quite the opposite of an attempt to secure happiness against the vulnerability of rejection by utterly interiorizing virtue into the 'pure intention' which is immune from outside influence.[48] Likewise we should note that with Edgar, Kent and Cordelia it is *love* (unto death) that is redemptive, not death itself.[49]

This subtle yet crucial difference separating Christian virtue from a selfish and nihilistic death wish is manifest in the trick that Edgar plays upon his father in order to enable him to overcome such 'stoicism'.

While it may seem bizarre to dupe his father into believing he has been miraculously spared death having jumped from a cliff, this is actually successful in enabling Gloucester to overcome his life-denying suicidal death wish: in receiving his life back as an unexpected gift ('Thy life's a miracle', IV:VI:55) he is enabled to return to life ('henceforth I'll bear affliction till it do cry out itself "Enough, enough"', IV:VI:76). It is perhaps supremely here, in this bizarre scene, which has so annoyed many critics with its implausibility upon the stage, that we can see a response to the most penetrating criticism of forgiveness as a nihilistic and self-denying death wish. It is not difficult to observe how Gloucester's suicidal denial of life is quite different from the voluntary self-abasement for service (*kenosis*) of his son: the former is premised upon despair and seeks only a selfish self-annihilation, which can only add to the suffering of others, while the latter is based upon hope and endures present suffering because it seeks eventual self-fulfilment in mutual happiness.

The Relationship of Forgiveness to Law and Justice

'Judge not, lest ye be judged'; what a beautiful refrain.[50]

From what has gone before, we can now make some observations regarding the relationship of forgiveness to the rule of law, which is so often cited as the incompatibility that requires the exclusion of forgiveness from the political sphere. This inherent tension between forgiveness and law has produced a considerable body of discussion, from political philosophers such as Spinoza, Kant and Hegel[51] to contemporary popular wisdom,[52] but can briefly be summarized: Justice requires judgement to be passed upon certain actions and people; likewise, it seems justice entails some form of retaliation (albeit a restrained, impersonal and passionless sort) which is legitimated by the processes of law. Forgiveness, however, involves the suspension of judgement and the forgoing of retaliation ('Judge not, that you be not judged' and 'if any one strikes you on the right cheek, turn to him the other also', Matt. 7.1 and 5.39) and thus seems to threaten the very foundation of the rule of law, or as Ambrose claimed against the emperor Theodosius: 'It is necessary for judgement to yield to religion' (O'Donovan 1996, p. 200). What are we to make of this dilemma?

It seems necessary to admit that forgiveness is beyond law. To those who claim that it is offensive to demand forgiveness as an imperative, we should partly agree on the basis of our analogue of charity: the very idea of love being a duty or legal obligation that can be commanded is inherently odd, as it evidently proceeds not so much from an effort of the will on the basis of reason, as from being erotically drawn forth from without, by the attraction of the object of love.[53] It has been standard for Christian theologians to attempt to make sense of the paradoxical *commandment* to 'love your neighbour' in these terms, arguing that our love for God is solicited by the erotic draw of the supreme Good who is himself perfect beauty and the fulfilment of all our desire. Love for neighbour is not self-grounding, but proceeds from this prior attraction of God, involving a (metaphysical) perception of the same beauty of Christ (the *imago dei*) in all people.[54] Thus we should insist that forgiveness, like charity, is supernatural and excessive (beyond the behaviour of tax collectors and gentiles, see Matt. 5.46–47). It is neither something that could be commanded of someone else, like a law, nor an effort of rational will (both of which would presume a 'Cartesian' model of the self as a completely autonomous and self-possessed will),[55] but a charism or gift that must be received from outside oneself.

Yet while it may be beyond law, forgiveness, like love, is not antithetical to justice, but is its consummation (cf. Matt. 5.17). Situated between and against the radical and conservative accounts of justice and responsibility that we considered earlier, forgiveness possesses its own political import: it resembles the radical perspective by subverting our capacity to judge others, yet does so *without* the nihilistic and antisocial rejection of all justice and morality, by turning this judgement back upon ourselves and demanding our own transformation ('Why do you see the speck that is in your brother's eye, but do not notice the log that is in your own eye?' Matt. 7.3 f.). This role of forgiveness as a form of judgement and call to repentance can be seen within *Lear*. On the heath the king is forced to abandon the harsh, static and punitive judgementalism of the conservative ideology, as he recognizes the sheer contingency and artificiality of any social arrangement of power, which means the judge may be no more virtuous than the felon. At first this recognition pushes him towards the amoral laissez-faire stance of Edmund, Goneril and Regan: 'None does offend, none, I say, none ... Let copulation thrive' (IV:VI:166, 114). Yet at other moments, and perhaps finally, both he and Gloucester come to recognize their own failings ('I am a very foolish fond old man', IV:VII:60; 'I stumbled when I saw', IV:I:19) and their need for repentance ('I'll kneel down and ask of thee forgiveness', V:III:11) and for the continual radical reordering of society based upon true justice and the exchange of charity ('Take physic Pomp; expose thyself to what wretches feel, That thou mayest shake the superflux to them and show the Heavens more just', III:IV:30; 'So distribution should undo excess and each man have enough', IV:I:69). Properly, the recognition that the judge may be as guilty as the thief can be understood not as universal innocence, but as universal need for forgiveness and transformation ('all have sinned', Rom. 3.23). Thus, against all the caricatures that we have encountered, forgiveness is not properly a form of licence to reoffend (as in Protestant satires of the confessional), a laissez-faire abandonment of all morality (despite its inevitable potential to degenerate into this); rather, forgiveness is the intervention of a higher judgement, which overrules all inferior judges. When Christ disbands the stoning of the woman taken in adultery, this is transformative love passing judgement on both the accused and the accusers.[56] As Bonhoeffer recognized, it is not a question of 'whether we judge', but '*how* we are to judge' (Jones 1995, pp. 14–15, 145). The particularity of forgiveness, like love again, is more truly just in its attention to the specificity of a situation, than an arbitrary formalist justice based upon equivalence which thus ignores individual difference (hence Christian justice is better expressed by the principle 'from each according to his abilities; to each according to his needs' than Liberalism's 'all men are born equal').[57] For God, judgement neither precedes, nor is separable from his loving forgiveness, but is identical with it. We can go further and say that, for God, there is no judgement other than his forgiveness.[58] When we pass judgement, as we are tragically bound to continue to do within a fallen world, it should seek to model this simultaneity of judgement and love, as is particularly illustrated within *Lear* by Kent: it is *because* he has 'lov'd [Lear] as my father' and is not afraid to lose his life for the king's wellbeing, that he will not succumb to flattering the king, and insists on speaking the judgement of 'plainness', telling Lear to 'see better' and that 'thou dost evil' (I:I:140, 147, 157, 164).

The practice of worldly justice which is essential to the rule of law, is thus exposed as a poor shadow of divine justice, manifest in the cross, where judgement is identical with mercy and reconciliation (O'Donovan 1996, p. 256) – more of the containment of violence by another more controlled form of violence, than its subversion, absorption and cessation by peace. And yet, in a fallen world, prior to the eschatological separation of the wheat from the chaff, law will remain a tragic necessity. Since, as Augustine says, 'We should not before the appointed time desire to live only with those who are holy and righteous' (O'Donovan 1996, p. 202), it seems that, against all purist and extrinsicist accounts of forgiveness, Christians should not seek withdrawal from the political sphere and so cannot avoid the messiness of the interaction of law and forgiveness. Such an interaction will radically relativize the judgements of law, by recalling their provisionality and the subordination of both accusers and accused to the higher divine law, for it is only God who, being perfect, can ultimately pass judgement. Forgiveness thus stands in judgement of all our judging.

Holy Foolishness

Our explorations have suggested that forgiveness is, in one sense, 'irrational' as its critics have maintained.[59] Such a recognition is not unprecedented within the Christian tradition, going back to Paul's description of the gospel as 'the foolishness of God which is wiser than the wisdom of men' (1 Cor. 1.25). It was common even to regard Christ as a 'Fool', and holy foolishness as a mark of a saint (Foucault 1995, pp. 78–82). In this light, the role of the Fool within *Lear* becomes particularly illustrative of the 'holy foolishness' of forgiveness. His foolishness is often more genuinely wise and truthful than the flattering wisdom of the court ('Jesters do oft prove prophets'),[60] and it is possible to see his faithful accompaniment of Lear and determination to force him to face the truth as containing overtones of a Christlike redemptive figure.[61] The Fool also reminds us mockingly of the 'foolishness' of the other virtuous characters, as when he says to Kent: 'If thou follow him thou must needs wear my coxcomb' (I:IV:102). It is evidently not 'wise', in the sense of politically prudent or conducive to one's self interest, to '[take] one's part that's out of favour' (I:IV:97) or to seek to remain faithful to those who have become hostile, as Kent and Edgar discover when both are mistreated for their loyalty by the very men they are seeking to serve. Yet it is clear that without the 'foolishness' of this loyalty the transformation of their abusers would be impossible.

Forgiveness is irrational because it does not promise the immediate success that a utilitarian calculus might require, nor can it be deduced from some universifiable principle of pure reason (like the categorical imperative). We have argued that it cannot be founded upon a purportedly 'neutral', rational analysis of the human situation, but only upon a specific self-grounding theological metaphysic. Forgiveness is a practice that is implicitly committed to a certain view of the world –

the very act of forgiving is itself an imaginative positing of a particular ontology that alone makes such an act possible and 'rational'. Such an ontology thus cannot be irresistible; it will remain open for people either to practise forgiveness or not. If perceptions are implicit in the practices one embodies, as has been argued, then those who do not engage in forgiveness must inevitably see the world differently, and to them forgiveness will be absurd and an abomination, as Albany recognizes: 'Wisdom and goodness to the vile seem vile' (IV:II:38–9). Thus it would seem that ultimately the only way to render forgiveness plausible to its opponents will be to engage them in the venture of its practice, more specifically through an apprenticeship within a community of the forgiven and forgiving, and through the recollection of past exemplars (Jones 1995, p.xii).

Conclusion

I have attempted to indicate how an analysis of *Lear* can suggest how the Christian practice of forgiveness, properly understood, might relate to the political order. In contrasting it with two opposed, yet identically secular and materialist political ideologies represented within *Lear*, it has been seen that forgiveness must differ from them in terms of its underlying ontology. In arguing that the logic of forgiveness requires this distinctively theological horizon of grace and resurrection, it must follow that forgiveness as such is incoherent and impossible outside this. However it has also been seen that this same theological horizon of trust and hope provides forgiveness with an advantage that the other ideologies lack.

What difference does it make exactly? This theological 'ontology' enables forgiveness to be understood, like love, as legitimately involving a proper self-interest and reciprocity (against the parodies of forgiveness which have justly been viewed as cowardly and suicidal), while at the same time avoiding the process of commodification – which we have claimed is the genuine problem that has made self-interest and reciprocity seem unhealthy. Our analysis of the competing ideologies within *Lear* led us to suggest that it is in fact this materialist picture of the world, implicit in the process of commodification with its fetishized possessiveness and concomitant fear and insecurity, that continually threatens to overwhelm human relations, which is the real cause of the economy of violence within the play, and which simultaneously prevents the possibility of envisaging any escape from this. Forgiveness alone, while recognizing this ever present threat, is capable of resisting paralysing enslavement to it and breaking the downward spiral of the endless repetition of retributive violence and destruction, by positing a different, theological ontology – one constituted by trust and hope. While the restraint of violence by force will remain a tragically inevitable aspect of postlapsarian relations until 'heaven and earth have passed away', it is nevertheless the case that if this was all, its logic would seem to lead necessarily to the utter breakdown of all sociability. Therefore, while it cannot escape the messiness of coexisting and interacting with the old order, it is forgiveness alone that makes possible the 'social miracle' (Bossy 1985, p. 57) – the endless reconstitution of social relations through the costly practice of reconciliation. Forgiveness, far from being apolitical or antisocial, is nothing less than the ongoing business of society being reborn afresh, as a *novum* received from outside itself.[62]

References

1980, *The Alternative Service Book 1980*, Cambridge: Cambridge University Press

1986, *The New English Hymnal*, Norwich: Canterbury Press

Aeschylus, 1956, *The Oresteian Trilogy*, Harmondsworth: Penguin

St Augustine, 1997, *On Christian Teaching*, Oxford: Oxford University Press

Francis Bacon, 1985, *The Essays*, Harmondsworth: Penguin

Dietrich Bonhoeffer, 1959, *The Cost of Discipleship*, London: SCM Press

John Bossy, 1985, *Christianity in the West: 1400–1700*, Oxford: Oxford University Press

Andrew Bradley, 1905, *Shakespearean Tragedy*, London: Macmillan

John Burnaby, 1938, *Amor Dei*, London: Hodder & Stoughton

John Danby, 1949, *Shakespeare's Doctrine of Nature*, London: Faber & Faber

Jacques Derrida, 1995, *The Gift of Death*, ET, Chicago, IL: University of Chicago Press

Jonathon Dollimore, 1984, *Radical Tragedy*, New York: Harvester Wheatsheaf

Terry Eagleton, 1986, *William Shakespeare*, Oxford: Blackwell

Teresa Elwes (ed.), 1992, *Women's Voices: Essays in Contemporary Feminist Theology*, London: Marshall Pickering

Paul Fiddes, 2000, *The Promised End*, Oxford: Blackwell

Michel Foucault, 1995, *Madness and Civilisation*, ET, London: Tavistock Routledge

Gregory Jones, 1995, *Embodying Forgiveness: A Theological Analysis*, Grand Rapids, MI: Eerdmans

Julian of Norwich, 1987, *Revelations of Divine Love*, London: Hodder & Stoughton

Judy Kronenfeld, 1998, *King Lear and the Naked Truth*, Durham, NC: Duke University Press

Nicholas Lash, 1996, *The Beginning and the End of 'Religion'*, Cambridge: Cambridge University Press

Laurence Lerner (ed.), 1963, *Shakespeare's Tragedies*, Harmondsworth: Penguin

Hugh Ross Mackintosh, 1927, *The Christian Experience of Forgiveness*, London: Nisbet

John Milbank, 1990, *Theology and Social Theory: Beyond Secular Reason*, Oxford: Blackwell

John Milbank, 1995, 'Can a Gift be Given? Prolegomena to a Future Trinitarian Metaphysic', *Modern Theology*, Vol. 11, Issue 1, January, pp. 119–61

John Milbank, 1997, 'The Midwinter Sacrifice: a Sequel to "Can Morality Be Christian?"', *Studies in Christian Ethics*, Vol. 10, No. 2, August, pp. 13–38

Michel de Montaigne, 1958, *Essays*, ET, Harmondsworth: Penguin

Kenneth Muir (ed.), 1972, *King Lear*, London: Methuen

Kenneth Muir (ed.), 1984, *King Lear: Critical Essays*, London: Garland

Anders Nygren, 1953, *Agape and Eros*, ET, London: SPCK

Oliver O'Donovan, 1980, *The Problem of Self-Love in St Augustine*, New Haven, CT and London: Yale University Press

Oliver O'Donovan, 1994, *Resurrection and Moral Order*, Leicester: Apollos

Oliver O'Donovan, 1996, *The Desire of the Nations: Rediscovering the Roots of Political Theology*, Cambridge: Cambridge University Press

Michel Perrin (ed.), 1987, *Le Pardon*, Paris: Beauchesne

Donald Shriver, 1995, *An Ethic for Enemies: Forgiveness in Politics*, Oxford: Oxford University Press

Dorothee Soelle, 1974, *Political Theology*, Philadelphia, PA: Fortress Press

Hans Urs von Balthasar, 1995, *The Grain of Wheat: Aphorisms*, ET, San Francisco, CA: Ignatius Press

Rowan Williams, 2000, *On Christian Theology*, Oxford: Blackwell

Notes

1 The need for such an account is recognized by Jean Deleumeau (in Perrin 1987, p. 7), and L. Gregory Jones claims his entire book, *Embodying Forgiveness* (1995) seeks to offer something of this.

2 J. W. Draper, e.g., argues this view (cited in Muir 1972, p. xxii).

3 Arnold Kettle, Walter Cohen, John Danby, Annabel Patterson and Jonathon Dollimore all represent this contemporary consensus.

4 See, for example, Charles Hobday, Walter Cohen, John Danby. For a good summary of their views, see Kronenfeld 1998, pp. 170, 200.

5 This view is particularly represented by Jonathon Dollimore.

6 This is because even if these aspects are seen as offensive to a Christian reading and lead people to see this play as an anti-Christian text (and I remain unconvinced that this is the case anyway, see Fiddes 2000, pp. 71–2, 75), this would still not prevent someone so totally immersed in Christian culture from continuing to think in thoroughly Christian categories, as Kronenfeld (1998, p. 229) notes: 'The Christian promise to the repentant is not fulfilled on earth, nor in a play ending there. Nevertheless – for those whose everyday experience was coded in its terms – that does not necessarily diminish its meaningfulness …' Incidentally, Fiddes' stimulating book

appeared after the original writing of this essay, preventing a more detailed consideration of his theological analysis of *Lear*. However I would broadly agree with most of his views, although he is not so concerned with the social and ethical dimensions of the play as I am. I would also want to question the boldness with which he asserts that Lear is 'not redeemed' (p. 64), and to go further than he does in stressing the unnaturalness of death against Heidegger, Tillich and Rahner (pp. 68–9).

7 I:IV:218. All quotations from *King Lear* are given as *Act:Scene:Line* and are taken from Muir 1972.

8 We should note that the division of the characters into the same three groupings that are used here can be found at least as early as Bradley 1905, p. 225.

9 For a detailed account of the subversive potential of these ideas and their currency among such conservative figures as Machiavelli, Montaigne and Bacon, see Dollimore 1984, chs 1 and 10.

10 While Kronenfeld argues against any such attempts to align characters with specific political 'classes', I suspect she is overreacting here to the more crudely anachronistic readings of some recent political criticism. I would, however, agree with her ultimate conclusion that the play does not finally represent the interests of any one partisan grouping within society, but rather calls all to account on the basis of the common Christian culture to which they were all at least in theory committed.

11 'Nemesis does operate in *Lear*; evil does undo itself' (Kronenfeld 1998, p. 229).

12 I:I:89 and I:IV:130. Apparently this was proverbial as *ex nihilo nihil fit*, see Muir 1972, p. 9, n. 89.

13 Eccles 1.9; cf. Bacon 1985, p. 228.

14 IV:VI:133; cf. the discussion of the theme of cosmic decay and elemental chaos in Elizabethan and Jacobean literature in Dollimore 1984, pp. 92–103.

15 Ascribed to Dante in Bossy 1985, p. 36.

16 Cf. 'On Envy' (in Bacon 1985, p. 83) and 'That one man's profit is another's loss' (in Montaigne 1958, p. 48) for an indication of the currency of these ideas.

17 Thus indicating, against Dollimore, that he is in fact as much of a materialist as the rebellious children.

18 Milbank 1990, ch. 10. For a good summary of this argument see Lash 1996, ch. 12.

19 This critique of Dollimore depends upon a certain perspective on the relationship between nature and culture which, as Eagleton (1986, pp. 77–81), has shown, is implied both in *Lear* and throughout the Shakespearean corpus. This perspective can be summarized thus: Culture is 'natural' for human beings and so not to be rejected (against Edmund, Goneril and Regan); yet Nature is always a cultural production and so open to transformation (against Lear and Gloucester); the theologian might add that this parallels the recognition that salvation is at once the natural end of human striving, and yet somehow also 'supernatural'. Sadly, while applauding Shakespeare's recognition of this problematic, which becomes ever more intense in capitalist societies, Eagleton rejects his vision of how it might be overcome, regarding this as romantic and reactionary.

20 A suggestion of R. W. Chambers in Muir 1984, p. xv.

21 'Cumulative dramatic clues, then, gradually establish whether characters are good or bad in terms of an overarching Christian cultural framework' (Kronenfeld 1998, p. 245).

22 Jean Delumeau, in Perrin 1987, p. 6.

23 Edmund's deathbed regret of his mistakes and reconciliation with his brother (V:III) appear genuine, if rather implausibly sudden and unanticipated. There is no evidence of any similar final redemption for Goneril and Regan.

24 For an account of this popular psychologizing of forgiveness and a critique, see Jones 1995, pp. 35–46. A theologian of the calibre of Hugh Ross Mackintosh is not immune from such dangers, as can be seen from his tendency to neglect the 'horizontal' dimension of forgiveness in favour of the 'vertical', and to see forgiveness as addressed more towards psychological guilt than external social relations (see Mackintosh 1927).

25 Bernard Rousset, 'La possibilité philosophique du pardon' in Perrin 1987, p. 190; cf. Levinas's objection to Christian forgiveness (Jones 1995, p. 104).

26 E.g., Mackintosh 1927, pp. 63, 94, ch. 6 and passim, where this hostility towards reciprocity and self-interest (in terms of merits and rewards) is manifest in his treatment of forgiveness.

27 As Nygren (1953) seems to argue and even Levinas can suggest (see Milbank 1997, pp. 18–19).

28 Simone Weil as cited by Woodhead (in Elwes 1992, p. 70).

29 E.g., by Jan Patocka, Jacques Derrida (Milbank 1997, pp. 16–17) and George Bataille (see Milbank 1995, p. 132).

30 The argument of this entire section is indebted to Milbank 1995.

31 Interestingly it seems that such an immoral, incoherent and unchristian account of altruism is the object of Richard Dawkins' misdirected Selfish Gene polemics.

32 See the Augustinian critique of Nygren's denial of erotic self-interest and reciprocity in Burnaby 1938, especially chs I and X, and O'Donovan 1980.

33 Including St Bernard, Duns Scotus, Luther and Fénélon, see Burnaby 1938, ch. IX; cf. O'Donovan 1994, pp. 250–3.

34 Bossy 1985, pp. 35–7. The post-Vatican II renaming of confession as the sacrament of reconciliation is a welcome step towards rectifying this. Priestly absolution should encourage the socio-political practice of forgiveness, providing it is understood as an exemplary way that the ordained priest formally instantiates the duty of proclaiming God's reconciling forgiveness (the power of the keys) which is incumbent upon the priesthood of all believers in their daily lives (Matt. 18.18; John 20.23). Thus in answer to the question of the Pharisees (and their modern puritan heirs!), 'Who can forgive sins but God alone?' (Luke 5.21), the Church should reply, 'Yes, but in Christ, he wills to do this through every believer.'

35 Milbank 1995, p. 144. Indeed we can now see that the earlier characterization was mistaken. It is actually the apparent circularity of vengeance, which is truly linear and unilateral, because it ultimately spirals downwards to a zero point of mutual extinction; whereas it is the circular exchange of charity between God and his beloved which is, for Christian hope, never-ending.

36 Catherine Pickstock has suggested that the relations between heaven and earth are better understood in terms of the liturgical 'middle voice' rather than active or passive.

37 A suggestion of Helen Oppenheimer, cited by Woodhead in Elwes 1992, p. 68.

38 Oppenheimer cited by Woodhead in Elwes 1992, p. 68.

39 W. Chatterton Dix, 'Alleluia Sing to Jesus', No. 271 in The New English Hymnal; cf. also Milbank 1997, pp. 37–8 and Milbank 1995, p. 152.

40 See the discussion of love and its reward in O'Donovan 1994, pp. 250–3, which takes issue with Kenneth Kirk's Kantian opposition of virtue and reward.

41 Likewise, just as God's forgiveness cannot be a change of mind on his behalf, a royal pardon that would be arbitrary and unjust, but is part of his unchanging faithfulness (as was recognized by Julian of Norwich in her *Revelations of Divine Love* (1987, chs 45–9)), so our forgiveness should seek to model this eternal faithfulness in time by a constant disposition of love that entails the endless repetition of forgiveness, not just a one-off decision (thus the stubborn persistence of Kent, Edgar and Cordelia illustrates Christ's answer to Peter that one must forgive 'seventy times seven times', Matt. 18.22).

42 The need for divine initiative to overcome vengeance by uniting justice and mercy is suggested by Aeschylus in 'The Eumenides' (1956, pp. 170–5), where Athene intervenes, silencing the vengeful furies, founds the court of the Areopagus and acquits Orestes.

43 'A way out of the cycle of lovelessness', Woodhead in Elwes 1992, pp. 80–1; although note that such a trust and hope can itself only be mediated through other people and communities (e.g., the Church).

44 Ephesians 4.32. Throughout this account of forgiveness I am arguing for a 'participatory' account of the relations between earth and heaven, rather than the more 'dialectical' model of Mackintosh. Human forgiveness is not antithetical to divine forgiveness in Christ, but replicates it in time and participates in it through the Church's incorporation into Christ. A good critique of the depoliticizing of forgiveness in dialectical theologies is given by Soelle (1974, ch. 8), and I am broadly sympathetic to her alternative presentation, although she perhaps neglects the importance of the 'vertical' dimension of forgiveness, in her enthusiasm to reinstate the 'horizontal' dimension.

45 This linking of Christian ethics with the specifically theological and realist horizon of resurrection has been advocated recently by O'Donovan 1994, pp. 13f., and Williams 2000, pp. 265f.

46 'On the Genealogy of Morals', essay 1, cited in Jones 1995, pp. 244–5.

47 This distorted view of Christian ethics is similar to that of Schopenhauer, and arguing from this perspective Crampe-Casnabet concludes that forgiveness is impossible, '*La Pitié et le Pardon*' in Perrin 1987.

48 Such a 'stoicism' resembles the materialist doctrine of the limited good in its possessive and atomistic inability to see individual happiness as fulfilled in a social, *common* good.

49 Hence Cordelia's tragic death should not be regarded as sacrificial or salvific. This is perhaps also suggestive with regard to how one might have a theology of the atonement that avoids the celebration of death and violence.

50 Lyrics from REM's 'New Test Leper', from the album *New Adventures in Hi Fi* (1996).

51 See Rousset's '*La possibilité philosophique du pardon*' in Perrin 1987, which discusses the hostility these rationalist thinkers have towards forgiveness.

52 I am reminded of episodes of the British television chat show '*Kilroy*', where Christians arguing for forgiveness always come across as naive and soft!

53 This is not to succumb to rather naively romantic views of love as a purely passive affection that is enslaved to its own fickle coming and going. Of course, love is at once both a discernment of beauty and an active craft that must be practised even when the feelings may abate, and a habit to be learned.

54 See, e.g., Augustine's description of how it is not appropriate to love things for themselves (which would be idolatrous) but only in their participation in God, who alone is truly lovable, in *On Christian Teaching* (1997, Book I, p. 21).

55 I am grateful to Alice Wood for this observation.

56 This point is made by Augustine, cited in O'Donovan 1996, p. 20.

57 Consider the apparent injustice of the partiality shown towards the prodigal son and the workers in the vineyard who arrived last.

58 This point was also recognized by Julian of Norwich (1987, chs 45–9).

59 Rousset agrees that forgiveness is beyond philosophy, Perrin 1987, p. 196.

60 V:III:72; cf. the Beatitude-like paradox of Cordelia who is 'most rich, being poor; most choice, forsaken; and most loved, despised!', I:I:249–50.

61 E.g., it might not be too fanciful to see echoes of Christ's death at noon in the Fool's parting line: 'And I'll go to bed at noon', III:VI:83.

62 For practical illustrations of how some of the ideas suggested here might be applied, one can consider the courageous example of the Justice and Reconciliation commission in South Africa. Donald Shriver's book, *An Ethic for Enemies: Forgiveness in Politics* (1995), similarly indicates how forgiveness might operate politically in specific situations, although his account of the tradition (pp. 33–63) is somewhat dismissive.

2

Creatio Ex Nihilo and the Divine Ideas in Aquinas: How Fair is Bulgakov's Critique? (2013)

What is the place of the divine ideas in the doctrine of creation *ex nihilo*? Are they a Platonic hangover that properly belongs in a demiurgic model of creation such as the *Timaeus* and contaminates creation *ex nihilo* with a vestige of pantheistic necessary emanation? Or is it rather that, properly understood and reconceived in the light of the revealed truth of creation *ex nihilio*, the divine ideas actually guard *against* the notion of necessity in creation (as Aquinas claims), and also prevent this doctrine from falling into extreme voluntarism? The latter position has been suggested by a number of writers (for example, Roger Arnaldez) but requires further explanation.[1] It is commonly claimed that the doctrine of creation *ex nihilo* was developed out of the revealed experience of divine sovereignty and freedom – there is nothing over and against God restricting his creative intention. Creation, according to Jews, Christians, and Muslims, should be understood as a *free* intentional act, rather than according to a scheme of necessary emanation. Yet this leaves the question of how this divine freedom should best be imagined. Or to put it another way, if creation *ex nihilo* means that creation proceeds solely *ex Deo*, then is this from the 'nothingness' of arbitrary divine choice, or rather does it proceed somehow from the plenitude of form which is the divine wisdom and essence (yet without necessity)? If Arnaldez thinks that the divine ideas prevent Christian understandings of creation *ex nihilo* from descending into voluntarism, others have taken the opposite view: that it is the notion of divine ideas as an infinite timeless warehouse of essences from which God 'chooses' a world to create which leads to voluntarism. According to this view, the divine ideas are a Platonic world of ideal essences which detracts from the 'existentialist' priority of the actual which, it is claimed, is the great achievement of Aquinas and his Aristotelian revolution.[2] While I shall be mainly following Arnaldez in arguing that the divine ideas help to understand creation *ex nihilo* as neither necessary nor purely voluntarist in an arbitrary sense, we shall see that there are certain conceptions of the divine ideas that can suggest a priority of the possible and thus open the door to voluntarism.

Bulgakov's Reading of Aquinas on Creation

In this article I hope to explore these debates through the particular lens of Sergei Bulgakov's critique of Aquinas on creation *ex nihilo*. Bulgakov's own sophiological method is particularly concerned with this question of the relation between divine and creaturely being. In *The Bride of the Lamb*, written by 1939 as the third of his trilogy on Divine-Humanity, but only published posthumously in 1945, Bulgakov begins with a survey of classical, patristic, and medieval views on creation before offering his own 'Sophianic' account. Christian views of creation need, he says, to avoid two alternative positions: 'pantheistic or atheistic monism on the one hand and the dualistic conception of creation on the other'.[3] Because the world is created *ex nihilo* 'the world exists only in God and by God' (Bulgakov 2002, p. 7).[4] Sophia, or wisdom, thus names, for Bulgakov, both the existence of the world in God, the divine ideas or prototypes of all creatures eternally pre-existing in the mind of God (the 'divine Sophia'), and the existence of God in the world, the potential divine life and form in all creatures ('creaturely Sophia'). According to Bulgakov's account of the history of 'sophiology', the Christian tradition has not clearly formulated this question, but has remained under the unhelpful influence of pagan sophiologies that do not fully grasp the Trinitarian logic of creation.

What is Bulgakov's specific critique of Aquinas' account of creation? He begins with the familiar charge of twentieth century Orthodox theologians (and some Protestants) against Western scholastic theology, that it is contaminated by the excessive influence of Aristotle: 'As his point of departure Thomas Aquinas takes not the Christian dogma of the personal, trihypostatic God, but Aristotle's impersonal divinity' (p. 19). As evidence of this Bulgakov points to Aquinas' understanding of God as prime mover (*primus motor*) and efficient cause (*causa efficiens*) and particularly to Aquinas' position on the eternity of the world. Although Aquinas rejects this Aristotelian doctrine, he does so, according to Bulgakov, for purely *fideistic* reasons, admitting its theoretical possibility. For Bulgakov this is 'a compromise between Moses and Aristotle, a compromise that is unconvincing for Aquinas himself as a theologian and philosopher, and that exposes in this question his hidden or unconquered Aristotelianism' (pp. 20–1). The relationship between God and the world in Aquinas is understood according to these Aristotelian categories of motion and causation, according to Bulgakov, and is therefore defined 'statically, so to speak, not dynamically' (p. 21). Although Bulgakov admits that a more Trinitarian account of creation *ex nihilo* exists in Aquinas he argues that this account is mixed with Aristotelian metaphysics in a way that does 'not form an organic unity' (p. 22). The influence of Aristotle is particularly evident for Bulgakov in Aquinas' account of the relationship between God's knowledge and will in creation, which brings us to the tension between necessity and freedom. 'Aquinas uses both *intellectus* and *voluntas* without any reference to the personal God', claims Bulgakov (p. 22). For Aquinas, the knowledge of God is the cause of things (*scientia Dei est causa rerum*) *and* the will of God is the cause of things (*voluntas Dei est causa rerum*) (*Summa Theologiae*, Ia, qq. 14 and 19). Although it is necessary that God knows things other than himself and God's knowledge is eternal, yet creation is not (*Summa Theologiae*, Ia, q. 14, aa. 5 and 8). Aquinas therefore distinguishes two modes of God's knowledge: knowledge of that which will exist at any time ever (the knowledge of vision, *scientia visionis*) and knowledge of that which is possible but will never be (the knowledge of simple understanding, *scientia simplicis intelligentiae*). 'This is a highly obscure and arbitrary distinction', says Bulgakov, 'which admits in God an abstract, unreal thinking of bare possibilities, contrary to the fact that God's thoughts are also his deeds. This is pure anthropomorphism' (p. 22). While Bulgakov recognizes that the notion of will is an advance upon the Aristotelian view of God as impersonal thought thinking itself, he claims that Aquinas' position, that 'God's knowledge necessarily causes the existence of things while his will freely causes this existence', is inconsistent, an abstract account of the faculties of will and mind in God (p. 23).

Bulgakov sees the same problems even more acutely manifest in Aquinas' treatment of the divine ideas, where he says Platonism is 'brought into the very heart of Christian philosophy' (p. 24). 'The doctrine of ideas is', he says, '*not* brought into a connection with the doctrine of the Holy Trinity, does not belong to the trinitarian doctrine, but refers, so to speak, to the pre-trinitarian or extra-trinitarian (more

Aristotelian than Christian) doctrine of God as mind, *noesis*' (p. 24). For Aquinas, forms or ideas of things exist in the mind of God. God does not simply create by chance, or will alone, but according to his intellect, intentionally, like an artisan, so these divine ideas are the exemplary causes in the mind of God of all things. God knows other things through his own essence, which is the likeness of all things. Although the divine mind is absolutely simple and without composition, nevertheless the divine ideas are plural for Aquinas, following Augustine, because they are the various ways in which diverse creatures participate in the divine nature (*Summa Theologiae*, Ia, q. 15). But here again the same tension arises for Bulgakov as before, in that Aquinas distinguishes the ideas according to those which are realized and are therefore exemplars, by which God creates in the manner of an artisan, and those which are mere possibilities (*rationes*) never to be realized and therefore known speculatively (*per modum sepeculationis*) (*Summa Theologiae*, Ia, q. 15, a. 3). 'What a strange, contradictory, and unreal notion of abstract "speculation" in God', exclaims Bulgakov (p. 25). Bulgakov sees in Aquinas' account of creation a conflict between a 'doctrine of the Divine Sophia and the creaturely Sophia in their identity and difference' and residual Platonism and Aristotelianism. He is particularly concerned by the inclusion of 'thoughts of God that never become a reality', in opposition to Aquinas' own position that the divine knowledge is the cause of things (*scientia rerum est causa rerum*) (pp. 25–6). Bulgakov sees this as connected to another significant problem with Aquinas' doctrine of creation, that the world is not understood as 'unique in its design and perfect' but 'as imperfect, only one of many possible types of worlds' (p. 26). This is opposed to healthy cosmology, anthropology, and Christology for Bulgakov, and 'introduces an element of irrational accident and arbitrariness in the relation of the Creator to creation' (p. 26). We are left with 'a quantitative noncorrespondence of ideas and things ... The domain of ideas is larger than the domain of things; divine Sophia does not coincide with creaturely Sophia' (p. 26). But if the divine ideas were originally introduced as the exemplary prototypes of things, what would be the point of unrealized ones?, asks Bulgakov.

From all this we can sum up Bulgakov's critique of Aquinas on creation and the divine ideas which, it is worth noting, is not directed against Aquinas alone, but is part of a larger account of the 'unfinished' nature of sophiology in patristic as well as scholastic thought, in the East as well as the West. For Bulgakov, Aquinas' account of creation and the divine ideas is insufficiently Trinitarian and too much influenced by Platonic and Aristotelian philosophy. As a result it works with an overly anthropomorphic account of the faculties of divine intellect and will in creation, with intellect being identified with necessity, and will with arbitrariness. This distinction 'brings into divinity the element of accident and arbitrariness', pure occasionalism (p. 31). The divine ideas likewise are pictured as the speculative surplus of possible worlds in the divine essence from which God arbitrarily selects some to be exemplars for the creation of this world, which as such is neither unique nor perfect. The ideas on this account are not understood 'sophiologically', but merely extrinsically, instrumentally, in their relation both to God and the world. They are left 'ontologically suspended in the air ... situated somewhere between God and the world' (p. 33). But is this a fair reading of Aquinas?

Aquinas on Creation and the Divine Ideas

The claim that Aquinas' thought is too pagan and philosophical and insufficiently Christian is of course not a new one. First made by some of his more conservative contemporaries, anxious about his use of the 'dangerously secular' new Aristotelianism, these charges have been repeated by many since, especially among Protestants and Catholics of a more Augustinian temperament. In the mid-twentieth-century, just after Bulgakov was writing, this view reached something of a crescendo, perhaps in reaction to the textbook approach to Aquinas taken by the Leonine neo-Thomists and anti-modernists who used him as the basis for an independent 'natural theology' and rationalist apologetics. This criticism of Aquinas often focused on the structure of the *Summa* and the placing of the discussion *de Deo uno*, built upon the supposedly universal purely rational foundations of the *quinqae viae*, before coming to the revealed doctrine of God as Trinity only in question 27. It is frequently claimed that this move unwittingly establishes a Deist account of God at the foundation of Aquinas' thought. Not only Barth, Moltmann, Pannenberg, and Gunton, among Protestants, and Lossky among the Orthodox, take this view, but perhaps more surprisingly Rahner and von Balthasar express similar misgivings (Kerr 2002, pp. 181–3). Another critique of Aquinas' indebtedness to Aristotle, which may also have influenced Bulgakov, is made from a rather different philosophical position by Heidegger, who famously attacked the account of God as *causa sui* (Kerr 2002, pp. 85–8). But if these readings of Aquinas have been widespread, they have not been universal. Indeed, the defence of Aquinas has been vigorously made by many Thomists, particularly in the French tradition of Maritain, Gilson, and Chenu, which has often laid more stress on Aquinas as theologian rather than simply a philosopher. As various authors have pointed out more recently, the structure of the *Summa* need not be construed as giving priority to natural theology before revelation; rather the initial account of the divine unity can be understood instead in terms of the unfolding of salvation history and Israel's confession of faith in one God which preceded the revelation of God's triune nature.[5] While the five ways certainly all have classical precursors, they are set by Aquinas firmly in the context of the revelation of the divine name 'I AM THAT I AM' to Moses and the scriptural claim that 'the invisible things of him from the creation of the world are clearly seen' (Rom. 1.20), indicating that there is no bracketing of revelation here, but rather Aquinas' thought is inseparable from revelation from the beginning. More importantly for the questions raised by Bulgakov, it is not clear that the adoption of non-scriptural categories from pagan antiquity such as 'motion' and 'causation' necessarily involves the wholesale importation of their original metaphysical contexts. Indeed it seems ironic that Bulgakov should object to such adoption of non-Christian language when he himself faced similar accusations from other Orthodox theologians in relation to his use of German idealism in his sophiology. It is equally plausible to maintain that Aquinas freely moulds and develops Platonic and Aristotelian categories to do new and different tasks within his own Christian metaphysics. In particular it seems unfair of Bulgakov to accuse Aquinas of a purely impersonal and mechanical account of creation, when Aquinas goes to such considerable lengths to distinguish free, intentional creation from necessary emanation. Aquinas insists that God acts by will not by natural necessity (*Deum agere per voluntatem, non per necessitatem naturae, Summa Theologiae*, Ia, q. 19, a. 4, rep.), and puts as much stress on the more personal and intentional modes of causation (exemplary and final) as upon what we might think of as more naturalistic modes such as efficient causation and motion (indeed some see an ascent within the ordering of the five ways from lower models of creation towards higher more personal ones).[6] Likewise the charge that Aquinas reduces God to the first in a series, on the same ontological plane as his creation, seems to ignore the point noted by so many commentators, that Aquinas goes to great lengths precisely to stress the absolute uniqueness and therefore relative incomprehensibility of creation, the distinction between God who has being and all other things which receive their being from him, and the at most analogical rather than univocal nature of the five ways. For example, Aquinas stresses that although our spatio-temporal minds cannot help but picture it in these terms, creation cannot actually be a change or motion for there is nothing that precedes it to be acted upon ('creation is not a change', *creatio non est mutatio, Summa Theologiae*, Ia, q. 45, a. 2, ad 2). It is hard not to suspect therefore that Bulgakov's allergy to images of causation and motion for creation says more about his own (post-Kantian) position, and perhaps the distortions of Aquinas presented by textbook apologetics, than about Aquinas himself. As Fergus Kerr puts it: 'Thomas's God is not the perfect being of Greek metaphysics, the supreme entity at the top of a hierarchy of atomistically conceived substances ... Whatever else is to be said, Thomas is plainly out to save God from being turned into one more entity' (Kerr 2002, pp. 200, 204).

If it is unfair to accuse Aquinas of a purely philosophical, Aristotelian, mechanistic, and impersonal account of creation, is he nevertheless guilty of being insufficiently Trinitarian? Would Bulgakov's critique be more plausible if we restricted the claim to saying that Aquinas' account of creation is generically monotheistic and not truly Trinitarian and Christian? In particular is it more dominated by the anthropomorphic faculties of divine intellect and will rather than shaped by the Trinitarian life? While this might seem an initially plausible accusation, it does not obviously stand up so well to closer inspection. For in fact the treatment of divine knowledge and will (Ia, qq. 14, 15, and 19), although it precedes the articles on the Trinity, is very obviously neither Aristotelian (Aristotle's deity does not have any will to speak of), nor anthropomorphic in some univocal way. Rather these questions are already oriented towards the discussion of the Trinity, in that divine intellection and will are, following St Augustine, identified with the internal processions of the Son and the Spirit respectively (*Summa Theologiae*, Ia, q. 27, aa. 1–5; q. 45, a. 7). When Aquinas says that God's intellect and will are the cause of things he is making precisely the Trinitarian claim that the Father creates through the Son and the Spirit:

Deus est causa rerum per suum intellectum et voluntatem, sicut artifex rerum artificiatarum. Artifex autem per verbum in intellectu conceptum et per amorem suae voluntatis ad aliquid relatum operatur. Unde

*et Deus Pater operatus est creaturam per suum Verbum, quod est
Filius, et per suum Amorem, qui est Spiritus Sanctus.*[7]

Bizarrely Bulgakov quotes these very articles before concluding 'the
creator of the world is, strictly speaking, the impersonal Aristotelian
divinity' (p. 27). The implication seems to be that Bulgakov believes
the Trinitarian processions are being subordinated to an abstract prior
account of divine will and intellect, whereas it is surely more plausible
that the opposite is the case, that intellect and will are being understood
in a Trinitarian fashion. Creation, according to Aquinas, is absolutely rooted in the Trinitarian inner life of God: 'The comings forth
of the divine Persons are causes of creation', *processiones divinarum
Personarum sunt causa creationis* (*Summa Theologiae*, Ia, q. 45, a. 6,
ad 1).

Yet, if Aquinas' account of creation can be said to be not only personal
but also Trinitarian, nevertheless Bulgakov's charge that intellect is
identified with (eternal) necessity in God's own life and will with (external) freedom in creation is harder to dismiss and potentially troubling.
Will in God is not understood quite as anthropomorphically as Bulgakov suggests, as pure arbitrariness. God's will is free in the sense of
not being determined by any external cause (*nullo modo voluntas Dei
causam habet*)[8] and in being intellectual and intentional rather than a
matter of natural necessity, like the appetite of a plant or animal (*Deum
agere per voluntatem, non per necessitatem naturae*).[9] But this does not
mean that it is therefore empty and contentless, like many more modern
notions of the will. For God's will is not, according to Aquinas, a 'seeking what is not possessed' but a 'delighting in what is'.[10] As will is, for
Aquinas, a tending towards a good, so God's will is the possession of
his own goodness, which is his nature (*objectum divinae voluntatis est
bonitatas sua, quae est essentia; unde cum voluntas Dei sit eius essentia*).[11] Aquinas can compare God's will to the sun (*Summa Theologiae*,
Ia, q. 19, a. 4, ad 1, following Dionysius), and even speak of it as having a certain necessity in itself, in common with the divine knowledge:
*sicut divinum esse in se est necessarium, ita et divinum velle et divinum
scire.*[12] But then he goes on to make significant qualifications to this
claim: God's being, unlike that of creation, is 'not of a determinate
kind, but contains in itself the whole perfection of being' (*esse divinum
non sit determinatum, sed contineat in se totam perfectionem essendi*,
Summa Theologiae, Ia, q. 19, a. 4, rep.), so it seems as if whether any
particular idea is realized or not in reality is determined by God's will,

which is not necessary (*quia forma ut est in intellectu tamen non deter-minatur ad hoc quod sit vel non sit in effectu, nisi per voluntatem*).[13] Thus, according to Aquinas, God wills his own goodness absolutely necessarily, just as our will is necessarily ordered towards our own happiness (*bonitatem suam Deus ex necessitate vult, sicut et voluntas nostra ex necessitate vult beatitudinem*, Summa Theologiae, Ia, q. 19, a. 3, rep.), but everything other than himself that he wills through his happiness he does not will absolutely. This is because God could will his happiness through different means just as, Aquinas says, we could choose to take a journey by horse or on foot. Although God wills creation for his goodness, he does not need creation and it adds nothing to his perfection so he does not will it *absolutely* necessarily (*alia a se eum velle non sit necessarium absolute*).[14] Creation does however have a *hypothetical* necessity, because what God wills he wills from eternity and cannot be unwilled (*quod velit, non potest non velle, quia non potest voluntas eius mutari*).[15] We might think that Bulgakov would be sympathetic with the subtle argument that Aquinas is developing here: that creation adds nothing to God, is not needed by him, and is therefore personal and free, against all pantheistic schemes of neces-sary emanation (the Latin Averroeists are presumably the immediate concern). Yet, despite all the careful qualifications, and the repeated insistences that will and intellect are ultimately one in God, there is undoubtedly an alignment here of intellect with internal necessity and will with external freedom and contingency, which remains troubling. This means that creation is at times conceived surprisingly anthropo-morphically, not simply as free, but as an act of free *choice, liberum arbitrium* (*Summa Theologiae*, Ia, q. 19, a. 10).

Where does this leave the divine ideas? They seem to be in danger of being conceived anthropomorphically as an infinite set of possible worlds known by God, not really identical with the goodness of his nature, from which he arbitrarily chooses one to create. This is, as we saw earlier, the heart of Bulgakov's criticism of Aquinas' account of creation *ex nihilo*: 'The domain of ideas is larger than the domain of things; divine Sophia does not coincide with creaturely Sophia' (p. 26). The evidence for this claim can be seen in questions 14 and 15 of the *prima pars*, but their interpretation is not straightforward.[16] Aquinas follows Augustine and others in saying that 'God's knowledge is the cause of things', for 'God's knowledge stands to all created things as the artist's to his products' (*scientia Dei est causa rerum. Sic enim scientia Dei se habet ad omnes res creates, sicut scientia artificis se habet ad artificiata, Summa Theologiae*, Ia, q. 14, a. 8, rep.). Then, perhaps fearing that this could imply that creation follows necessarily from God's necessary knowledge, he adds that 'an intelligible form does not indicate a principle of activity merely as it is in the knower, unless it is accompanied by an inclination towards producing an effect; this is supplied by the will'. Therefore God's knowledge is the cause of things 'when it is conjoined with his will' (*secundum quod habet voluntatem conjunctam*) and this is termed 'knowledge of approbation', *scientia approbationis* (*Summa Theologiae*, Ia, q. 14, a. 8, rep.). This invocation of will is surely correct, yet need not in itself imply a choosing between things, unless the relationship between intellect, will and goodness is conceived extrinsically. Such a notion does however appear in the following article where Aquinas asks if God has knowledge of non-existent things. This question leads him to distinguish between God's knowledge of things that are or ever have been or will be existent and his knowledge of those things that will never exist, following on St Paul's expression in the letter to the Romans: 'Who calls the things that are not, as the things that are' (Rom. 4.17). Those things which will exist at any time are known by God's knowledge of vision, *scientia visionis*, while those things which never are, except potentially in the mind of God, are known by his knowledge of simple understanding, *scientia simplicis intelligentiae* (*Summa Theologiae*, Ia, q. 14, a. 9, rep.). Of these things that only ever exist potentially, God has a purely speculative knowledge as he does of his own nature; while all things that actually exist are known by God through practical as well as speculative knowledge (*Summa Theologiae*, Ia, q. 14, a. 16). This is the crucial distinction and the will is brought in to justify the difference between the two: 'it is not necessary that all that God knows should exist at some time, past, present or future, but only such things as he wills to exist or permits to exist' (*Summa Theologiae*, Ia, q. 14, a. 9, ad 3). When Aquinas comes to say more of the divine ideas, he preserves this same distinction. Ideas are forms existing apart from the things themselves and can serve two purposes: 'either to be the exemplar or pattern of the things whose form it is said to be', corresponding to practical knowledge, or 'the principle of knowing that thing', corresponding to speculative knowledge (*Summa Theologiae*, Ia, q. 15, a. 1, rep.). It seems as if there are two sorts of divine ideas: those that are realized and those that are not. The ideas used by practical knowledge are exemplars, while the ideas that are never realized and known only speculatively are purely principles, *rationes* (*Summa Theologiae*, Ia, q.

15, a. 3, rep.). Such an account does indeed seem to have the elements of anthropomorphism and arbitrariness of which Bulgakov accuses it. For *why* does God choose to realize these ideas and not others, to make this world and not different ones? This does appear to represent an opening for both later voluntarism and possibilism. And is not a wedge driven here between the necessary intellect and the arbitrary will in God, which by extension means also between the Son and the Spirit? But this is only because freedom and necessity are being understood all too humanly. Bulgakov's alternative account is surely more convincing here when he says that in God 'all is equally necessary and equally free' and that 'against the idea of different and manifold *possibilities* in God, actualized and unactualized, we must oppose the idea of the *uniqueness* of the ways of God, a uniqueness that excludes all other unactualized possibilities' (p. 31). In fairness we should note that there are moments when Aquinas seems to lean more in this direction. He does, for example, insist that 'God's knowledge has the same extension as his causality' (*intantum se extendit scientia Dei inquantum se extendit eius causalitas*, *Summa Theologiae*, Ia, q. 14, a. 11, rep.), and his entire account of the divine ideas emphasizes their intentional dynamic creative exemplarity, after Dionysius's *paradeigmata*, as against purely cognitive views of the ideas.[17] Similarly, Aquinas often speaks of the divine ideas more in terms of a single perfect plan, identical with God's own wisdom or essence, and not simply an unconnected collection of thoughts: *Idea in Deo nihil aliud est quam eius essentia*.[18] Likewise, as more recent anti-Platonist commentators are keen to point out, Aquinas frequently insists that the ideas are not a separate realm of forms existing 'between God and the world', nor even really distinct relations in God, but only the diverse ways that God knows his own nature as imitable by creatures, and that therefore the ideas are extended, beyond the neo-Platonists and Avicenna, to individuals and matter.[19] In this respect, David Burrell is surely correct when he wishes that Aquinas had taken the analogy of the artisan to its radical conclusion and rejected the residual Aristotelian priority of speculative over practical reason. For an artist does not 'choose' from a set of options whether to create this work of art or that one, 'like a jury in an architectural contest', as Burrell puts it (1993, p. 111). Rather those other possibilities which were never realized have at most a shadowy, virtual existence, merely 'penumbral' to this practical knowledge which creates (Burrell 1993, p. 110). It is not that the ideas are the problem which must be abandoned, but rather that they must be understood in this more integral, intentional, practical way or, as Bulgakov puts it, in a more Trinitarian and Sophiological way. And at times this is exactly what Aquinas seems to say, restricting the divine ideas in their truest sense to those which are exemplars, and describing the *rationes* of those things which never exist as merely virtual.[20] All these elements of Aquinas' account of the divine ideas certainly seem to reduce their instrumental and accidental character, of which Bulgakov is so afraid, but they do not altogether do away with the problems we have noted.

These problems, concerning the existence of a surplus of unrealized divine ideas, from which God arbitrarily chooses some to actualize, do in the end seem to leave a certain ambivalence towards the very goodness of creation, despite all Aquinas' supposed affirmation of the world. As Bulgakov claimed, the world is not understood as 'unique in its design and perfect' but 'as imperfect, only one of many possible types of worlds' (p. 26). This can be seen in Aquinas' discussion of divine power. Here, having repeated that 'God can do what he does not do' (*Deus potest facere quod non facit*, Summa Theologiae, Ia, q. 25, a. 5, sed contra) and 'can make things differently from how he has made them' (*Deus potest alia facere quam quae facit*, Summa Theologiae, Ia, q. 25, a. 5, rep.), he makes the strange and speculative claim 'God can make a better thing than anything he has made' (*qualibet re a se facta potest Deus facere aliam meliorem*, Summa Theologiae, Ia, q. 25, a. 6, rep.). Aquinas goes on to qualify this: God could not improve *this* universe without upsetting its harmony, but he could 'make other things, or add them to those he has made, and there would be another and better universe' (*et esset aliud universum melius*, Summa Theologiae, Ia, q. 25, a. 6, ad 3). The reasoning behind this position is, exactly as Bulgakov claimed, because the divine Sophia does not coincide with the creaturely Sophia: God's power is limited by his wisdom (*divina sapientia totum posse potentiae comprehendit*),[21] but this is not exhausted by the current course of events. Therefore 'divine wisdom is not limited to one fixed system in such a manner that no other course of things could flow from it' (*Summa Theologiae*, Ia, q. 25, a. 5, rep.). If, as Aquinas says, it is the divine will which chooses which aspects of divine wisdom are to be realized, then this will seems only accidentally or instrumentally related to divine wisdom, not intrinsically.

It is worth returning to the role that the divine ideas are meant to perform in Aquinas' account of creation *ex nihilo*. According to the *De Veritate*, the divine ideas are essential to a correct view of creation (*De Veritate*, q. 3, a. 1). For the ideas simultaneously rule out the view that everything is simply a matter of chance, as Aquinas claims the Epicureans believed, *and* the view that everything is simply determined by natural necessity, as he believed Empedocles and others to have thought. Plato is thus praised by Aquinas for avoiding these two options, while he also accepts Aristotle's criticisms of an independent realm of substantial forms by embracing the Augustinian position that the ideas exist in the mind of God. But Aquinas is even more explicit about the connection of the divine ideas with a Trinitarian view of creation: he cites Augustine's claim 'whoever denies the existence of the ideas is an infidel because he denies the existence of the Son' (*qui negat ideas esse, infidelis est, quia negat filium esse, De Veritate*, q. 3, a. 1) and also insists that a knowledge of the Trinity is needed in order to have a right view of the creation of all things.[22] Because we know that God made everything by his Word and his Love we avoid thinking of creation as necessary (*excluditur error ponentium Deum produxisse res ex necessitate naturae*) and that he made creatures from his own goodness, not because of any need or compulsion (*neque propter aliam causam extrinsecam, sed propter amorem suae bonitatis*).[23] For Aquinas, the divine ideas are clearly not some hangover from Platonic demiurgic or emanationist schemes of creation, but rather, understood according to the logic of the Trinity, are crucial to understanding creation as truly free and personal rather than proceeding from natural necessity, but also as in accordance with the intrinsic order of divine goodness and wisdom rather than simply formless, random, and arbitrary. And yet it seems that in one particular respect, as we have seen, there is an instability in this account which can introduce an element of arbitrary will into the picture.

In conclusion, I have argued that some of Bulgakov's criticisms of Aquinas on creation reflect the widespread prejudices of his time against Leonine Thomism and do not stand up to closer attention. It is not the case that Aquinas' account of creation is impersonal, mechanistic, or non-Trinitarian. Bulgakov's sophiological concerns do however draw attention to the way that the divine ideas were crucial in Christian understandings of creation *ex nihilo*. It seems that the image of the artisan and the divine ideas, understood according to a Trinitarian logic, enabled Christian theologians to articulate creation *ex nihilo* in terms that avoided both necessary emanation and arbitrary choice. God creates not without any reason or order, according to the arbitrariness of pure will, nor according to some external plan constraining his freedom, but according to the divine ideas which are his own self-knowledge, his intellection of himself and the ways in which creatures can participate in his being. He creates not simply by thinking these thoughts, in some passive or speculative necessary manner, but simultaneously by actively willing them as goods, or as participations in his own goodness. This creation by the ideas, in and through God's thought and will, enabling creatures to share in his own truth and goodness, is a form of practical reason, comparable to the way an artist brings his ideas to fruition. But the inevitable limitations of this analogy when applied to the unique case of the act of creation by the entirely simple, perfect and eternal One, leave a number of potential dangers of anthropomorphism. Principal among these is how we should understand the uniqueness of this creation in relation to divine knowledge and will. Is it really appropriate to imagine a surplus of unrealized divine ideas from which God chooses, apparently without reason, to make this particular creation? Here Aquinas' mode of expression, perhaps intended to avoid the necessitarianism of the Averroeists, may well have unwittingly opened a door to later more extreme forms of voluntarism and possibilism, against which he is normally presented as an heroic champion of the priority of actual existence.[24]

References

St Thomas Aquinas, 1967, *Summa Theologiae*, Vol. 8, London: Eyre and Spottiswoode

Roger Arnaldez, 1977, '*Intellectualism et voluntarisme dans la pensée Musulmane*', in *1274, année charnière: mutations et continuités*, Paris: Editions du Centre Nationale de la Recherche Scientifique

Vivian Boland, 1996, *Ideas in God according to Saint Thomas Aquinas: Sources and Synthesis*, Leiden: E. J. Brill

Sergei Bulgakov, 1993, *Sophia: The Wisdom of God*, ET, Hudson, NY: Lindisfarne Press

Sergius Bulgakov, 2002, *The Bride of the Lamb*, ET, Edinburgh: T. & T. Clark

David Burrell, 1993, *Freedom and Creation in Three Traditions*, Notre Dame, IN: University of Notre Dame Press

W. Norris Clarke, 2009, *The Creative Retrieval of St Thomas Aquinas*, New York: Fordham University Press

Gregory T. Doolan, 2008, *Aquinas on the Divine Ideas as Exemplar Causes*, Washington, DC: The Catholic University of America Press

Étienne Gilson, 1924, *The Philosophy of St Thomas Aquinas*, Cambridge: Heffer and Sons

R. J. Henle, 1956, *Saint Thomas and Platonism*, The Hague: Martinus Nijhoff

Fergus Kerr, 2002, *After Aquinas: Versions of Thomism*, Oxford: Blackwell

Josef Pieper, 1962, *Guide to Thomas Aquinas*, New York: Pantheon Books

James Ross, 1990, 'Aquinas's Exemplarism; Aquinas's Voluntarism', *American Catholic Philosophical Quarterly*, Vol. LXIV, No. 2, pp. 171–98

Robert Slesinski, 2007, 'Bulgakov's Sophiological Conception of Creation', www.geocities.ws/sbulgakovsociety/slesinski_creation.doc

Rudi te Velde, 1995, *Participation and Substantiality in Thomas Aquinas*, Leiden: E. J. Brill

A. N. Williams, 1997, 'Mystical Theology Redux: The Pattern of Aquinas's *Summa Theologiae*', *Modern Theology*, Vol. 13, No. 1, January, pp. 53–74

John F. Wippel, 1993, *Thomas Aquinas on the Divine Ideas*, Wetteren: Universa

Notes

1 Arnaldez 1977, p. 125: '*La première conséquence de ce volontarisme, c'est la negation des Idées exemplaires en Dieu ... De la négation des Idées résulte la négation des natures et des lois naturelles.*'

2 This seems to be the fear for Thomas Gilby (see Aquinas 1967, pp. xxv, 149) and also for David Burrell (1993, p. 63). R. J. Henle speaks of the 'awkwardness' of the divine ideas in Aquinas' thought (1956, p. 360), while W. Norris Clarke describes them as an aspect of neo-Platonism which 'stubbornly resists coherent assimilation' in Christian thought (2009, p. 88). These authors see the ideas as contrary to the Christian valuing of creation, history, and incarnation, and claim that Aquinas only incorporated this alien element into his metaphysics of act out of deference to St Augustine. Henri Bergson, who, via Étienne Gilson, may be behind much of this tradition, spoke of '*la maladie des archetypes*' (cited in Boland 1996, p. 327).

3 Bulgakov 2002, p. 3. For an introduction to Bulgakov's sophiology, see Bulgakov 1993.

4 All subsequent references to Bulgakov 2002 will be by page number within parentheses in the main body of the chapter.

5 Kerr 2002, pp. 183–4; Pieper 1962, p. 93; Williams 1997. Cf. also Robert Jenson, cited in Kerr 2002, p. 205: The five ways 'occur within a specifically biblical apprehension already in place' because 'the entire body of Thomas Aquinas' *Summa Theologiae*, encompassing alike the propositions supposed to be available by nature to all humans and those attributed to historically specific revelation alone, is shaped by a narrative of creational-incarnational procession from and return to God'.

6 See Robert Slesinski's interesting essay 'Bulgakov's Sophiological Conception of Creation' (2007), which helps to explain Bulgakov's hostility to the 'mechanistic' language of motion and causation.

7 *Summa Theologiae*, Ia, q. 45, a. 6, rep.: 'God is the cause of things through his mind and will, like an artist of works of art. An Artist works through an idea conceived in his mind and through love in his will bent on something. In like manner God the Father wrought the creature through his Word, the Son, and through his Love, the Holy Ghost.'

8 *Summa Theologiae*, Ia, q. 19, a. 5, rep.: 'God's willing is not in any way caused.'

9 *Summa Theologiae*, Ia, q. 19, a. 4, rep.: 'he works through will, and not ... through necessity of his nature'.

10 *Summa Theologiae*, Ia, q. 19, a. 1, ad 2.

11 *Summa Theologiae*, Ia, q. 19, a. 1, ad 3.: 'The objective of God's will, however, is his own goodness, and this is his nature.'

12 *Summa Theologiae*, Ia, q. 19, a. 3, ad 6.: 'As the divine existing is essentially necessary so also is the divine knowing and the divine willing.'

13 *Summa Theologiae*, Ia, q. 19, a. 4, ad 4.: 'Whether an idea conceived in the mind is or is not realized in fact depends on the will.'

14 *Summa Theologiae*, Ia, q. 19, a. 3, rep.: 'there is no absolute need for him to will [things other than himself]'.

15 *Summa Theologiae*, Ia, q. 19, a. 3, rep.: 'on the supposition that he does will a thing it cannot be unwilled, since his will is immutable'.

16 See also *De Veritate* 1:3; *Scriptum in IV Libros Sententiarum*, 1, 36, 2, 1; *De Spiritualibus Creaturis* 10, ad 8; *Lectura super Ioannem*, 2:77. The best overviews of this are Boland 1996; Wippel 1993; Doolan 2008. See also: Gilson 1924, pp. 111ff.; Velde 1995, pp. 102–16.

17 Wippel 1993, pp. 37–8. See also Boland 1996, ch. 3, where he stresses how Dionysius fuses the Platonist tradition of the ideas with more explicitly biblical, intentional notions such as 'pre-destinations'.

18 *Summa Theologiae*, Ia, q. 15, a. 1, ad 3.: 'an Idea in God is simply the divine essence'.

19 *Summa Theologiae*, Ia, q. 15, a. 2, rep.; cf. Henle 1956, p. 361.

20 Wippel notes how Aquinas' position on this seems to shift slightly from the commentary on the Sentences, where he is unclear as to whether purely possible things have ideas of their own, through the *De Veritate*, where they are known actually as *rationes* by *scientia simplicis intelligentiae*, but only virtually as exemplars, to the *Summa Theologiae*, where they are not known as exemplars at all, but only as *rationes* (1993, pp. 36–7, 46–8). See also Doolan 2008, pp. 22–3 and *passim* on this gradual restriction of the term exemplar, under the influence of Dionysius, to things which are actually made.

21 *Summa Theologiae*, Ia, q. 25, a. 5, rep.: 'divine wisdom covers the whole range of power'.

22 In the light of this claim by Aquinas, it is difficult to agree with those whose anti-Platonism makes them determined to see the divine ideas as unimportant and out of place in Aquinas' thinking, or with those who see his account of creation as deistic and non-Trinitarian.

23 *Summa Theologiae*, Ia, q. 32, a. 1, ad 3: 'we avoid the error of those who held that God's nature compelled him to create things [he created] not because he needed them nor because of any reason outside himself, but from love of his own goodness'.

24 These tensions can be seen in the debate generated by James Ross' article (1990), followed by the replies of Armand Maurer, Lawrence Dewan, and Ross in *American Catholic Philosophical Quarterly*, Vol. LXV, No. 2 (1991), pp. 213–43. Ross argues that Aquinas' Aristotelian metaphysics meant that he effectively rejected any residual 'photo-exemplarism' despite paying lip-service to Augustine's account of the divine ideas. This determination to resist any account of possibilism, of really distinct ideas of things before they exist (like a 'row of tin soldiers'), which Ross shares with Maurer and the Gilson tradition, leads him to assert a voluntaristic view of creation which they generally do not share. Dewan on the other hand seeks to defend the surface meaning of Aquinas' position on the divine ideas (particularly their inclusion, even if only virtually, of things which will never actually exist, especially in the *De Veritate*), although at times this leads him in the direction of the sort of possibilism about which Ross and in a different way Bulgakov are not unreasonably concerned.

3

Work, Prayer and Leisure in the Christian Tradition (2011)

Parameters of the question

Even though work itself has only entered into consciousness as a theological issue in its own right in the last century or so, yet we can still discern the shape of a number of key questions in relation to the treatment of 'work' in the Christian tradition. First there is the question of how broadly or narrowly work itself is defined. The scope ranges from the narrow definition of work as purely economic, this-worldly activity oriented towards subsistence ('labour' in Hannah Arendt's typology), through broader accounts of work in terms of production, creativity and art ('work' for Arendt), to the entirety of human activity (Arendt 1998).

The second question concerns the relation of work to its apparent antonym, rest or leisure. This opposition of leisure/rest to work usually corresponds to a hierarchy of values in which work is placed at the bottom, with the implication that, unlike rest, work entails an element of toil and suffering. However, we can note already that this applies more obviously to the narrow definition of work than the broader ones, where the contrast becomes more problematic. If true work is free, pleasurable, creative and oriented to more than just worldly subsistence then it begins to look much more like leisure.

Following on from this there is the question of the relation of work to prayer, liturgy and worship. Again, drawing particularly on the Sabbath tradition, the obvious move would be to link prayer and worship with rest and leisure in opposition to work. However, again this applies well for the narrow definition of work, while for the broader definition it might make more sense to see prayer and worship as the archetypal and supreme human activity, rather than its antithesis.

Finally, and perhaps crucially underlying these other questions, stands the debate about the relationship between human and divine works. Is work something peculiarly human, worldly, or even fallen, or can we speak in some analogous way of God's work as the perfect form and ideal of all human working? While the tradition has generally regarded it as inappropriate to speak of God 'toiling', it has been more willing, with certain important qualifications, to speak of God working and even 'creating' in ways analogous to human work and creation. This analogy between human and divine labour can then form the basis for Christian discernment or judgement of work, what makes for good or godly work or not.[1] In this paper I will attempt to give a critical survey of how these interlocking questions have been negotiated in the Christian tradition (this is a slight reworking and development of some of the material from the introduction and first chapter of my book, *The End of Work* (Hughes 2007)).

Old Testament

Within the Scriptures we can of course find a diversity of apparently differing views of work lying side by side, which cannot easily be reconciled. Although it is a gross simplification, we might still generalize by saying that the Old Testament has a broadly positive view of labour but usually regards it as this-worldly, while the New Testament is less interested in work in the sense of 'secular employment', but has more to say about spiritual 'works'.

In the traditions which make up the creation narratives in the first two chapters of Genesis we can see some of the tensions which will be important sources for future discussion in the tradition: In the priestly narrative, humanity is commanded by God to 'subdue' (*kbsh*) the earth and to have 'dominion' (*rd*) over all living creatures (Gen. 1.28), just as for the Yahwist we are entrusted with the task of 'tilling and keeping' the garden (Gen. 2.15, *shmr* and *'bd*). Prelapsarian Eden was not, it seems, supposed to be a place of idleness. However, after the primordial disobedience we are told that our labouring for food will be characterized from now on by the curse of 'toil' (*'tsbwn*) and the 'sweat' of our face.[2] Work, in the creation narratives as we have received them, seems in some sense to be inseparable from the nature of humanity in its aboriginal Edenic goodness; yet this seems not to be necessarily the same as much of the reality of work as we experience it, which is characterized by toil and struggle.

The Israelites continued to explore this twofold character of work in the narrative of the exodus, where the slavery of the people in Egypt comes to symbolize the oppressive and alienating side of work (for example, Ex. 1.11–14, *sbl* and *'bdh*), and in the vision of the Promised Land as so abundant as to require minimal effort in cultivation ('flowing with milk and honey', Deut. 30.20, and so on), which becomes a symbol of emancipated labour ('For the land that you are about to enter to occupy is not like the land of Egypt, from which you have come, where you sow your seed and irrigate by foot like a vegetable garden. But the land that you are crossing over to occupy is a land ... watered by rain from the sky', Deut. 11.10–11). The contrast between Egypt and the Promised Land is not exactly one between work and rest; rather it concerns the difference between work as slavery, working for an oppressive other, and work as free and fulfilling, and perhaps therefore more 'rest-like' or leisurely, when everyone shall sit 'under their own vines and under their own fig trees' (Micah 4.4; 1 Kings 4.25). The transition from slavery to freedom is also linked to the possibility of worship: 'Let my people go, so that they may worship me' (Ex. 8.1).

Unlike the modern Romantics however, the Israelites did not link their positive account of free work with a positive interpretation of artistic craft, which remained somewhat suspect as a decadent luxury, or even as blasphemous presumption. In the prophetic literature, for example, the polemic against the fabrication of idols is extended into a suspicion of artifice more generally: 'All who make idols are nothing ... the artisans too are merely human ... they shall all be put to shame' (Isa. 44.9–11). By contrast, some of the histories and priestly literature do offer an account of cultic crafts and liturgical work as 'Spirit-inspired', as in the artisans Bezalel and Oholiab (Ex. 35.30–35).[3]

In the Wisdom writers there is a strong pragmatic moral condemnation of idleness ('Consider the ant you sluggard', Prov. 6.6f.; 'do not let your hands be idle', Eccles. 11.6) alongside a more philosophical and perhaps world-weary critique of the ultimate vanity of all human work ('What do people gain from all the toil at which they toil under the sun? ... I saw all the deeds that are done under the sun; and see all is vanity and a chasing after wind', Eccles. 1.3, 14). Both these perspectives regard work as primarily this-worldly, regardless of whether it is positively or negatively valued. Similarly, when leisure is commended in the Wisdom tradition it seems once again to be for entirely worldly reasons: 'Go, eat your bread with enjoyment and drink your wine with a merry heart' (Eccles. 9.7). However there are hints of a closer link between divine and human work in the figure of Wisdom herself, who is initially represented as the means through which God exercises his creative power ('the Lord by wisdom founded the earth', Prov. 3.19; cf. 8.22f. and Wisd. 7.22), and then comes also to be understood, particularly in the more Hellenistic apocryphal Wisdom literature, as the divine gift which inspires creativity in human actions: 'who has learned your counsel unless you have given wisdom from on high?' (Wisd. 9.17).

This interest in God's work is not something completely novel, but has roots in much earlier strands of Old Testament tradition, such as many of the psalms, which speak of God's creative and redemptive 'works' (for example, Ps. 8.3; 9.1; 19.1; 26.7; 40.5; 66.5; 78.7; 86.8; 92.4; 104.24; 111.7; 145.4, and so on, where the most common words used are $p'l$ and $m'sh$). The analogy of human artisanship for divine creation can also be found in the prophetic literature in the image of the divine potter (Jer. 18.3–6; Is. 64.8 ($ml'kh$); Job 10.8–9; Gen. 2.7 ($ytsr$)).[4]

These hints of some relation between divine and human working bring us to what is perhaps the supreme focus of Old Testament reflection on work, rest and worship: the institution of the Sabbath. In the Sabbath the resting from ordinary labour was placed at the heart of the covenantal relationship with God in the Decalogue and linked with national and cosmic foundation narratives: it recalls both the deliverance from slave labour in Egypt ('Remember that you were a slave in the land of Egypt ... therefore the Lord your God commanded you to keep the Sabbath day', Deut. 5.15) and, even more significantly, the divine rest from creation on the seventh day ('For in six days the Lord made heaven and earth ... but rested the seventh day; therefore the Lord blessed the Sabbath day and consecrated it', Ex. 20.11; cf. Gen. 2.1–3).[5] In the notion of the Sabbath as consecrated to God, we find a divinely ordered priority of rest over work and a linking of rest with the worship of God. The Sabbath, unlike the quotidian working days, is cultically set apart from 'secular' time just as the Temple or the priesthood are set apart from ordinary places and people. The Sabbath might be said to provide here a teleology for work, perhaps in the double sense of a goal towards which work aims, and a limit which keeps it in its bounds. The cosmic setting of the Sabbath in the priestly tradition situates this teleology in the context of a clear analogy between human and divine work and rest, which will open up questions later in the tradition.

New Testament

In the New Testament Christ himself uses many images of labourers in his parables, such as the labourers in the vineyard (Matt. 20.1–16) and especially the parables of the talents and the separation of the sheep and the goats (Matt. 25.14–46) might be said to provide the basis of a theology of 'good works'. However, Christ's teaching, particularly in the Sermon on the Mount, appears to have a pronounced hostility towards trading and the accruing of riches (for example, 'you cannot serve God and mammon', Matt. 6.24; cf. Matt. 19.24; 21.12–13) and much more to say about rest and the liberation from toil and labouring than any positive 'theology of work': for example, 'Consider the lilies of the field, how they grow; they neither toil nor spin' (Matt. 6.28), and 'Come to me all you that are weary and carrying heavy burdens and I will give you rest' (Matt. 11.28).[6] St Paul, on the other hand, is more concerned about the dangers of idleness and has strict warnings for those who will not work to support themselves: 'Anyone unwilling to work should not eat' (2 Thess. 3.10).

For a broader account of work, beyond the purely subsistent and economic, and its relation to our salvation, we can look particularly to St John and St Paul. St Paul uses the Rabbinic language of works to speak of acts fulfilling the Law, and famously rejects the idea that such works are the basis of our justification: 'we hold that a person is justified by faith apart from works prescribed by the law' (Rom. 3.28; cf. 11.6; Gal. 2.16). However, Paul also speaks of spiritual works in a much more positive light. He often refers to his ministry as an apostle in terms of a work, sometimes even describing the churches he has established or built up as his own work: 'Are you not my work in the Lord?' (1 Cor. 9.1), or again: 'According to the grace of God given to me, like a skilled master builder I laid a foundation ... the work of each builder will become visible for the Day will disclose it, because it will be revealed with fire and the fire will test what sort of work each has done' (1 Cor. 3.10, 13). In both of these cases, Paul is careful not to claim the work as his own in opposition to God; rather his work is 'in the Lord', or 'according to the grace of God given to me', yet it is still his work, and hence he carries responsibility for it. This is particularly clear in the second passage where these works take on an eschatological significance, being judged on the final day, with the good works enduring into the new creation. The collaborative language of working with God is developed in more explicitly participatory terms by Paul: 'there are varieties of works [*energematon*], but it is the same God who works them all in everyone' (1 Cor. 12.6).[7]

In John's Gospel we find a more spiritual concern with the 'works of God', which seems to pick up the language of the psalms: When the people ask Christ, 'What must we do to perform the works of God?' he replies, 'This is the work of God, that you believe in him whom he has sent' (John 6.28–29). This particular case is interesting in that it both presumes an analogy, or better a participatory relationship between human and divine works, and also because the reply resists any narrowly worldly interpretation of such works and even subverts such notions by identifying this work with something apparently more passive, belief. At other points John speaks of the miraculous signs and healings as 'God's works' (for example, John 5.16; 9.3) and confirms the participatory language of our sharing in the works of God: 'the Father who dwells in me does his works ... the one who believes in me will also do the works that I do and, in fact, will do greater works than these' (John 14.10, 12).

This broad Johannine account of human participation in divine works, rooted in the Trinitarian relations between the Father and the Son and their indwelling through the Spirit, also provides a new perspective on the Sabbath. A superficial reading of Christ's teaching on the Sabbath, particularly in the Synoptics, could be seen as either simply a restoration of the original humanitarian purpose of the Sabbath against formalist legalism ('the Sabbath was made for humankind, not humankind for the Sabbath', Mark 2.27), or even a practical abolition of the Sabbath, comparable to contemporary liberalization. However John and Matthew hint at an alternative more theological interpretation which links back to the original meanings of the Sabbath. John has Jesus give the explanation that, 'My Father is still working [on the Sabbath] and I also am working' (John 5.17). The implication here seems to be that the divine work did not just finish on the sixth day but is in some sense continuing and that therefore such work, participating in the divine work as opposed to the drudgery of postlapsarian toil, is appropriate to the Sabbath. The examples that Christ provides of the legitimacy of circumcision and priestly activity in the Temple on the Sabbath can be interpreted as suggesting that the divine work that he is working has the same 'liturgical' quality (John 7.22; Matt. 12.5). In Matthew's version the phrases 'something greater than the Temple is here' and 'the Son of Man is Lord of the Sabbath' can be read in a more epochal fashion, so that Christ's attitude to the Sabbath should be understood in terms of the arrival of the Kingdom which is itself the Sabbath of Sabbaths, going beyond the postlapsarian provision of the Sabbath as exceptional foretaste. For Christ and his followers every day has become the Sabbath. If this is so, then it seems that under the New Covenant, for the priestly people who work the works of God, the divisions between work, rest, and worship might not be so clear, but rather these three may be moving towards some ideal convergence: work that is leisurely (in the sense of free and joyful) and worshipful.[8]

Patristic and Medieval Views

The early Fathers of the Church, building upon these New Testament emphases, gave relatively little attention to work in the narrow sense of employment or physical labour, other than to condemn idleness and certain specific occupations. Such a stance may also reflect the largely urban setting of early Christianity, or perhaps the sense of imminent eschatology, which gave little importance to the continuation of worldly affairs. However the Fathers did continue to develop the New Testament language of good works or spiritual works.

It was the rise of asceticism in the fourth and fifth centuries which enabled a much more positive evaluation of physical, subsistence labour to develop within the Christian tradition and for this to be linked more explicitly with prayer, as seen in the Rule of St Benedict for example.[9] During the same period Greek notions of the philosophical life as founded upon *otium*, leisure, began to enter into Christian thinking, finding their fullest expression in the scholastic account of the supremacy of the *vita contemplativa* over the *vita activa*.[10] This might seem no different from the biblical priority of the Sabbath over work and to be compatible with the ascetical view, and yet increasingly it came to be mapped onto a more pagan aristocratic social division of labour, moving away from the earlier ascetic positive valuation of manual work towards the creation of non-labouring monastic classes whose existence was justified by their contribution to the work of prayer. On the other hand, the Renaissance marked a new Christian appreciation of human artistic creativity as echoing divine creativity. Thus we might generalize by saying that, under the continuing priority of rest and worship, towards which it perhaps aims, human activity (labour and work in Arendt's terminology) continues to rise in prominence throughout the medieval period, and is generally seen as in

participatory continuity with divine work. The most radical development of this line of thought comes in the philosophical tradition, where
St Thomas Aquinas expresses a long line of thinking when he argues
that work and rest cannot be understood in the usual oppositional sense
when we are speaking of God, who is always active and yet always at
rest.[11] This is perhaps the intellectual background to Meister Eckhart's
unusual reading (in German Sermon 86) of the story of Mary and
Martha, in which he gives priority to Martha, representing the active
life, although this remains an exceptional view.

The Reformation and Beyond

The Reformation marks a complex shift in the Christian tradition: on
the one hand it broadly continued the trajectory of according increasing value to worldly labour, undoing the division of labour which had
developed within monasticism and returning in some ways to the earlier ascetic tradition; yet at the same time it rejected the priority of
contemplation upon which the monastic life had been based as idleness
and paganism and was deeply suspicious of any analogy between divine
and human activity. Luther's insistence upon justification by grace not
works led to the depreciation of any talk of 'spiritual works', so that
we might even speak of a 'secularization' of work. Secular occupations
might be vocations allocated by God, but their goals were entirely this-
worldly (Lacoste 2005).[12] While there was some return to the earlier
tradition, which saw such work as a form of worship, rest was largely
reduced to a tolerated exception to work, rather than something which
might itself shed light on the hidden meaning of work.

It was, however, in the eighteenth and nineteenth centuries that the
rise of industrial labour and a new consciousness of the condition of the
'working classes' produced much reflection, from within and without
the Christian Church, on the problem or nature of labour. Here, especially in the political economists and in Marx, work becomes a serious
subject in its own right, and we can begin to discern what might be
called 'ontologies of labour', theories which attempted to understand
the very nature of labour, and often to make sense of humanity and
society through these labour theories. This is the situation to which
most modern theologies of work seek to respond. These labour theories
and the theologies which are responding to them build on aspects of the
Christian tradition which we have already explored: they continue the

late medieval and post-Reformation trend to accord increasing value to human work and the Reformation rejection of a division of labour based on the priority of contemplation. However the Romantic tendency to read all work through the lens of artistic creativity tends to undo the Protestant secularizing of work in favour of a more spiritualized perspective and one which is more comfortable with analogies between divine and human labour. If work is seen as the essence of humanity or even as divine, then it continues often to be identified with worship; yet virtually no place is left for rest in such views. Often these Romantic ontologies of labour can be useful in providing an ideal view of work which can be used to criticize dehumanizing forms of labour (as in Marx, and more theologically, Marie-Dominique Chenu, Miroslav Volf and John Paul II), yet they are perhaps less well equipped to question the exalted position that work holds in our society (Chenu 1963; John Paul II 1981; Volf 1991. See also Hughes 2007, ch. 1). Such a theological critique of the idolatry of work has been mounted in recent times upon a renewed theology of rest and the Sabbath (for example, by Karl Barth and Josef Pieper), but it usually entails the delimitation of a territory which is more fundamentally human beyond the realm of work, rather than any sense of how such a view of rest might be able also to critically transform the reality of work (Barth 1961; Pieper 1998. See also Hughes 2007, chs 1 and 6).

Concluding Remarks

I have tried to suggest that the opposition of work and rest is not so straightforward from a Christian theological perspective as common sense and ordinary usage might suggest. While there is certainly an important distinction and tension between the two (most clearly embodied in the Sabbath), nevertheless the New Testament itself problematizes this opposition. More fundamentally, its suggestion of an analogy of participatory cooperation between divine and human work points towards a possible ultimate convergence, beyond our temporal horizon, between work and rest. When this is taken into consideration, the exalted view of the dignity of human labour and creativity that has developed throughout the Christian tradition seems not just an accident, but rather an authentic outworking of these revolutionary insights. More specifically, the characteristically Christian notion that not only rest, but also work can be worshipful makes sense within such a participatory framework. To situate work within this theological tele-ology, against secularizing tendencies within and without the Church, so that it can be more or less worshipful, more or less participatory in God's work, provides the basis for Christian critical judgement of work, as we have seen.[13]

However, a number of dangers can be seen with this 'convergence' perspective on work, worship and rest, most obviously in its more extreme Romantic forms. Such a position can encourage an idolatry of work which succumbs to the Promethean temptation to see human value as self-made rather than a gift of grace; it can also lead to an over-realized eschatology, which thinks it can live beyond the diurnal rhythms of work and rest, but which in effect simply loses any sense of the value and meaning of rest other than self-interest; finally, it can also produce a spiritualizing idealization of work, which abolishes all proximate, this-worldly ends for working with the insistence that all work must be directly for God and like God's work, and is thus incapable of comprehending the necessary toil of subsistence, the post-lapsarian character of human work which continues to separate it from rest and worship.[14] These problems can become particularly acute when these ontologies of labour are secularized, as in Marxism for example. In such cases there is no sense of this idealization being kept in check by a more ultimate, as yet unattainable horizon, and the ultimate goal of work is immanentized as simply working for work's sake, or abstract profit, personal pleasure or something similar.

References and Further Reading

St Thomas Aquinas, 1964–80, *Summa Theologiae*, London: Eyre and Spottiswoode

Hannah Arendt, 1998, *The Human Condition*, Chicago, IL: Chicago University Press

St Augustine, 'Of the Work of Monks' (www.ccel.org/fathers2/)

St Benedict, 1936, *The Rule of St Benedict*, London: Chatto and Windus

Karl Barth, 1961, *Church Dogmatics III/4*, ET, Edinburgh: T. & T. Clark

Paul Beauchamp, 2002, 'Travail: Théologie Biblique', in Jean-Yves Lacoste (ed.), *Dictionnaire Critique de Théologie*, Paris: Presses Universitaires de France

André Birmelé, 2005, 'Work: Biblical Theology', in Jean-Yves Lacoste (ed.), *Ency-clopedia of Christian Theology, Vol. 3*, ET, Abingdon and New York: Routledge, pp. 1732–4

G. Johannes Botterweck and Helmer Ringgren (eds), 1975, *The Theological Dictio-nary of the Old Testament*, ET, Grand Rapids: Eerdmans

Malcolm Brown (ed.), 2011, *Crucible: The Christian Journal of Social Ethics*, January–March

Marie-Dominique Chenu, 1963, *The Theology of Work: An Exploration*, ET, Dublin: Gill and Son

Christine Fletcher, 2011, 'Restoring the Sense of Divine Vocation to Work', *Crucible: The Christian Journal of Social Ethics*, January–March, pp. 25–32

John Hughes, 2007, *The End of Work: Theological Critiques of Capitalism*, Oxford: Blackwell

Gerhard Kittel (ed.), 1964, *The Theological Dictionary of the New Testament*, ET, Grand Rapids: Eerdmans

John Paul II, 1981, *Laborem Exercens*, ET, London: Catholic Truth Society

Jean-Yves Lacoste, 2005, 'Work: Historical Theology', in Jean-Yves Lacoste (ed.), *Encyclopedia of Christian Theology, Vol. 3*, ET, Abingdon and New York: Routledge, pp. 1729–32

Josef Pieper, 1998, *Leisure as the Basis of Culture*, ET, South Bend, IN: St Augustine's Press

Eve Poole, 2011, 'Management as Sacred Trust, *Crucible: The Christian Journal of Social Ethics*, January–March, pp. 33–40

Esther D. Reed, 2010, *Work, for God's Sake: Christian Ethics in the Workplace*, London: Darton, Longman & Todd

Esther D. Reed, 2011, 'Lost Vocations', *Crucible: The Christian Journal of Social Ethics*, January–March, pp. 17–24

Alan Richardson, 1952, *The Biblical Doctrine of Work*, London: SCM Press

Miroslav Volf, 1991, *Work in the Spirit*, Oxford: Oxford University Press

Max Weber, 2001, *The Protestant Ethic and the Spirit of Capitalism*, ET, London: Routledge

Stuart Weir, 2011, 'Unwitting Workers of Grace', *Crucible: The Christian Journal of Social Ethics*, January–March, pp. 41–8

Notes

1 This can be done more subjectively, according to the subject's motive and intention, which seems to me more characteristic of the papers of Eve Poole (2011) and especially Stuart Weir (2011), in a more Protestant tradition [in the issue of *Crucible* in which this chapter was first published (Brown 2011)]; or more objectively, according to the form and end of the acts involved, under the common good, which is perhaps more characteristic of the papers of Esther Reed (2011) and especially Christine Fletcher (2011), in a more broadly catholic tradition. The latter strategy, which would be my own, requires some account of the specific qualities that make for good work, such as Dorothy L. Sayers and the Catholic Social tradition provide. This can be in terms of middle axioms or more traditional categories of natural law and metaphysics, and this in turn provides a way of overcoming Weir's problem about speaking of the good works of unbelievers.

2 For overviews of the perspectives on work in the Bible, see: Beauchamp 2002, Birmelé 2005 and Richardson 1952, especially pp. 25–9, for the views in Genesis. I am also grateful to Diana Lipton for conversations on the meaning of these texts.

3 For detailed philological analysis, see Botterweck and Ringgren, 1975, particularly Vol. VIII, pp. 325–31, for *ml'kh* and its primary sense of work as skilled artisanship, including cultic crafts, but also its later linking with manual labour

through opposition to the Sabbath; and Vol. X, pp. 376–405, for *'bd* and its wide range of meanings from slavery, through agricultural work and royal service, to cultic ministrations.

4 On the divine 'work' of creation, see Richardson 1952, pp. 14–16.

5 *ml'kh* is used of human work in all three cases, and an analogy between divine and human rest is made in the latter two cases, while only the Priestly author in Genesis uses *ml'kh* of both divine and human work in this context.

6 For *kopos* and its derivatives, see Kittel 1964, Vol. III, pp. 827–30.

7 In the majority of these cases the less negative *ergon* and its derivatives are used, for which see: Kittel, 1964, Vol. II, pp. 635–53. The Johannine usage in relation to divine works was probably building upon the Septuagint translation of the psalmic *m'sh* with *ergon*, while Paul's usage seems more indebted to post-exilic and Rabbinic language of works in terms of the keeping of the law. See also Richardson 1952, pp. 30–48.

8 Cf. Beauchamp 2002: 'L'agir cotidien rejoint le service liturgique, non finalise par le produit: "… le jour du sabbat, les prêtres dans le Temple violent le sabbat sans être en faute". Cet ordre nouveau n'est ni un état, ni a proprement parler une fin à atteindre, mais un commencement posé.'

9 See St Augustine, 'Of the Work of Monks' and St Benedict 1936, ch. 48, on 'Daily Manual Labour'.

10 See e.g., St Thomas Aquinas, *Summa Theologiae*, IIa IIae, q. 182. In the Greek philosophical tradition, Plato and Aristotle already regarded work in ways we might call 'proto-theological', by linking it with ontological teleology; see Kittel 1964, Vol. II, p. 636.

11 See his reading of the divine Sabbath in Genesis: *Summa Theologiae* Ia, q. 73, aa. 1 and 2.

12 See also Weber 2001 for a good account of the differences and similarities between Luther and Calvin and their successors.

13 It is my contention that these theological critiques of what makes for good and bad work, while often having a Romantic and Platonist flavour, can apply just as much to the service industries of advanced capitalist countries as to the mills of nineteenth century Britain or the sweat shops of the contemporary developing world. See Hughes 2007, ch. 7.

14 Reed 2011 offers an excellent critique of these dangers.

4

Work and Labour in Modern European Thought (2013)[1]

The 'question of labour' is a peculiarly modern one, describing a set of connected concerns, which arose in Europe through the processes of the industrial revolutions of the eighteenth and nineteenth centuries. The rapid changes in working conditions, due to new technologies, which encouraged mechanization and urbanization, led to the foregrounding of this question of labour, particularly in the thought of radical and progressive figures in Britain, France and Germany. For these thinkers, traditional ways of thinking about human work were too aristocratic and agrarian to make sense of the new realities of work, while these realities, the conditions of the newly emergent 'working classes', were the key to the future of Europe. Initially this debate happened largely outside specifically theological discourse and was often quite anti-theological in its desire to cast off more traditional ways of thinking (even if it was still shaped by earlier theological ideas). However, by the end of the nineteenth century, theologians had begun to engage directly with the question of labour which, with the rise of Marxism in the East, became a key philosophical concern in the early and mid-twentieth century. This theological engagement may be thought to have reached its high point in the various activities of liberation theologians, industrial missions, and Christian labour movements, and the development of normative principles for the ethics of work by ecclesiastical reports and other teaching documents. The discussion of labour in theological circles has quietened somewhat in the last twenty years, which some would attribute to the apparent triumph of capitalism since the fall of Communism in the USSR and the decline of manufacturing in the 'post-industrial' West. However, arguably, globalization and the ever-increasing virtualization of economic activity in contemporary capitalism can be seen as a fulfilment rather than refutation of some of the most important elements of the nineteenth century 'critiques' of labour, which are thus as relevant today as ever. Rather than confining myself to the narrowly and self-consciously theological, I will be drawing out some of the theological ideas implicit in or raised by the more mainstream approaches to the question of labour, before considering some of the explicitly theological responses. The discussion will be structured around the three headings of 'Utility', 'Politics', and 'Ontology'.

1. Utility: Political Economy and 'Natural' Labour

The British political economists of the late eighteenth and early nineteenth centuries, such as Adam Smith (1723–90), David Ricardo (1772–1823), Jeremy Bentham (1748–1832), Thomas Malthus (1766–1834), James Mill (1773–1836), and John Stuart Mill (1806–73), were the first significant modern theorists of labour. In differing ways, they shared a theory of labour as the principal source of the value of things, based upon a model of human labour in the supposed 'state of nature'. Behind them stood the 'labour theory of property and value' developed by John Locke in his *Two Treatises of Government* (1690). For medieval Christian thought, as can be seen for example in Thomas Aquinas (*Summa Theologiae*, IIa IIae, q. 66, a. 2), it was generally believed that communal ownership is natural and aligned with the use of things, while private ownership is secondary, concerns the management of things, and is only established by positive human law. Locke introduced a radically new way of thinking centred on a theory of labour, for which private property is something natural, linked with the appropriative usage of things. Locke argued that

> every Man has a *Property* in his own *Person* ... The *Labour* of his Body, and the *Work* of his Hands, we may say, are properly his. Whatsoever then he removes out of the State that Nature hath provided, and left it in, he hath mixed his *Labour* with, and joyned to it something that is his own, and thereby makes it his *Property*. (Locke 1988, II, §27)

Locke's repeated references to the situation in the New World ('Thus in the beginning all the World was *America*', Locke 1988, II, §49) indicate that it is the contrast between property rights in the Old World and the apparent lack of any formal division of ownership in the Native American societies which leads him to conceive of labour, in terms of appropriation-for-use, as the 'primitive' origin of ownership. Locke goes on to suggest that labour is not merely the origin of private ownership, but also, more radically, the origin of *value*: 'For 'tis *Labour* indeed that *puts the difference of value* on every thing' (Locke 1988, II, §40). While he admits that there may be some other element to value, with most things he claims it will be less than one hundredth part of that value. Locke's theory of labour as oriented to use and the principal natural source of value is still framed in the traditional Christian context of reflection on the divine command and cursing of work in the story of Adam and Eve, but it is these other novel elements, which make it particularly suited to the rising bourgeoisie, and which will be taken up without the theological context by the political economists. On the one hand this theory of labour has the radical quality of challenging all inherited and unequal claims to ownership, because if labour is the source of value then the world belongs to the 'use of the industrious and rational' not the idle (Locke 1988, II, §34). On the other hand, it also reflects the bourgeois desire for expansionist appropriation of supposedly 'idle' land, whether the enclosure of common land in England or the claiming of 'virgin' land in the New World. Beyond this, it embodies an elevation of individualistic private ownership over common ownership, as something more fundamental and natural, rather than merely artificial and secondary. Even more crucially, the claim that labour is the principle source of value has a curious twofold effect, which is particularly significant from a theological perspective: value is at one and the same time immanentized and paradoxically rendered pre-cultural. The value of things is no longer primarily something to be discovered, given by God in the ungraspable mysterious teleology of all things which establishes their right relations; rather it is something arbitrarily 'put into' things by human labour. Yet this sense of value as entirely man-made does not issue in a sense of the cultural mediation of value. Rather because this is presented in the context of the fictional pre-cultural 'state of nature', value is not something negotiated by the cultural processes of exchange. Instead the 'natural' processes of labour and consumption aim to provide an apparently fixed, universal, quantifiable, and morally neutral measure of the 'value' of things. Qualitative distinctions are flattened into one common quantitative scale. The Lockean theory of labour thus contributes to an anti-theological immanentizing and naturalizing of value, which will find its fullest expression in utilitarianism and free market economics. Labour is reduced to a matter of mere utility, an expression of our animal necessities.

With Adam Smith's *The Wealth of Nations* (1776), Locke's revolutionary theory of labour found its way into the heart of the founding text of political economy, which was also the birth of classical economics as a modern, ostensibly neutral, descriptive 'science'. 'Labour', says Smith, the Professor of Moral Philosophy and friend of David Hume, 'is the real measure of the exchangeable value of all commodities ... Labour was the first price, the original purchase-money that was paid for all things' (Smith 1991, p. 26). Smith qualifies this account of the state of nature somewhat when it comes to modern civil society where value in exchange, or 'price', consists of wages, profit and rent, but labour in the state of nature remains foundational for him. As for the later political economists, more complex civil societies are viewed as arising out of the state of nature for purely rational reasons of efficiency, such as increasing the capacity for production and consumption through the division of labour. The division of labour is celebrated not as in classical authors for its ability to bind humans together through their diverse needs, but rather through its capacity to increase productivity. The financial speculator David Ricardo, in his *On the Principles of Political Economy and Taxation* (1817), continued this way of thinking, insisting that 'The value of a commodity ... depends on the relative quantity of labour which is necessary for its production'. With Jeremy Bentham this emphasis on labour and production as the source of value shifts to a focus on utility as consumption, although this is now conceived not in terms of the right use of things, according to a received teleological perspective, but the immanent, naturalized and self-justifying utility of pleasure or pain.

Criticisms: The Neglect of the Soul, Morality and History

This labour theory developed by the political economists took various forms, but all of its proponents shared an immanentizing, naturalist perspective, viewing labour as an essentially morally neutral, quantifiable force, on the model of Newtonian physics. From this they manifest a sympathy for laissez-faire economics as leaving these forces to balance themselves out without intervention. These views were not without significant theological opposition, for their apparent 'egoism' and 'materialism', from the Cambridge Platonists, through William Law and Bishop George Horne's 'Letter to Adam Smith', to Samuel

Taylor Coleridge's Platonic–Kantian rejection of 'corpuscularism'. Yet it should be recognized that in addition to Hobbes and Locke, there were other Christian thinkers who paved the way for political economy, such as Dean Josiah Tucker of Gloucester, and many who wholeheartedly embraced it. The most notable of these was Thomas Malthus, a Church of England priest and the first professor of political economy, who rejected the perfectibilism of other Enlightenment figures while providing a theological gloss upon the egoism and agonism of political economy in terms of sin and theodicy: 'If Locke's idea be just, and there is great reason to think that it is, evil seems to be necessary to create exertion; and exertion seems evidently necessary to create mind' (Malthus 1993, p. 145).

Beyond theological opposition, the most penetrating criticisms of the political economists concerned their neglect of the element of historical contingency in the organization of labour and exchange so that bourgeois society and economy is made to seem the most superior and rational system. The desire to discover a rational science of political economy, comparable to the natural sciences, led to a neglect of the cultural and moral elements which shape the decisions as to what to produce and what to consume, making economics seem like a science of necessity. It was Marx who, following the more historical methods of German Idealism, made the claim that it is precisely because humans are *homo faber* that our socio-economic life has a history and is never just 'natural'. Arguably however, as we shall see later, even Marx held to a Whiggish naturalized view of history as having its own single rational immanent necessity which could be scientifically described. In this sense, it is perhaps Max Weber (1864–1920) whose greater emphasis on the sheer historical contingency of culture in shaping patterns of economics provided the more penetrating analysis of the relationship of political economy to modern capitalism. Weber's account in *The Protestant Ethic and the Spirit of Capitalism* famously linked the spirit of modern capitalism to specifically religious causes in the puritan ethos of work as proof of one's election combined with suspicion of luxury and consumption: 'Labour came to be considered in itself the end of life, ordained as such by God' (Weber 2001, p. 105). Far from being rooted in greed and gambling, specifically *modern* capitalism, according to Weber, derives from an ascetic and highly rationalized work ethos: 'Now [Christian asceticism] strode into the market place of life, slammed the door of the monastery behind it, and undertook to penetrate just that daily routine of life with its methodicalness' (Weber 2001,

p. 101). Weber also drew attention to how the anti-traditionalism and disenchantment of the world (*Entzauberung der Welt*) in Puritanism contributed to the pursuit of profit becoming the end in itself, sundered from traditional accounts of human flourishing or of the intrinsic and just value of things. 'The radical elimination of magic from the world', he claimed 'allowed no other psychological course than the practice of worldly asceticism' (Weber 2001, p. 97). If Weber is correct, the exclusion of moral concerns from political economy is not necessary at all, but is part of a particular theology of disenchantment. The spirit of utility which shapes modern working (the instrumental, rational, anti-traditional pursuit of profit, regardless of means) is the product of a particular theology, even if that theology generally no longer provides even the minimal restraint upon it which it once did.

2. Politics: Society, Labour and Cooperation

We have already seen that the theory of labour developed within the tradition of political economy was not without political consequences. The essentially bourgeois view of human nature which it embodies encourages a strong view of private ownership and a minimal role for the intervention of the state, although it can also, as we have seen, support a critique of 'idle' historic monopolies of land and capital. The primacy of the 'state of nature' in this view encouraged however a marginalizing of the social and political dimensions to work in favour of the paradigm of the solitary hunter-gatherer as more fundamental. Yet there were other traditions of reflecting on work, normally grouped together as 'socialist', for which the cooperative, social, and political dimensions were in no way secondary. In France, arising partly out of the experience of the Revolution and the subsequent re-imagining of the body politic, the utopian socialists such as Henri, Comte de Saint-Simon (1760–1825), Charles Fourier (1772–1837), and Pierre-Joseph Proudhon (1809–65) all stressed the cooperative, collective element to human labouring, even if they differed over whether this should be centrally organized or more genuinely democratic and anarchic. The most significant philosopher of labour in the nineteenth century, who certainly developed the socialist, political dimension of the question was Karl Marx (1818–83) who, with Friedrich Engels (1820–95), combined elements of the French radical political tradition with the economic analysis of the British political economists and the historical perspective of German Idealism to produce a synthesis which, at least on the surface, was hostile to religion and would dominate twentieth century discussions of labour. In Britain, coming out of the literary Romantic hostility to the conditions of the working classes under industrial capitalism, there was another more cultural–literary tradition of Romantic critics of capitalism, including Thomas Carlyle (1795–1881), John Ruskin (1819–1900), and William Morris (1834–96), who were not so anti-theological. These British authors shared sympathies for premodern traditional artisanal models of labour, encouraging freedom and responsibility among workers and patterns of cooperative labour oriented to real social and human goods rather than abstract profit.

These three traditions are characterized, in contrast with the political economists, by a newly critical perspective on the situation of industrial manual labour in the nineteenth century and a more or less utopian imagining of how things might be organized differently. This was primarily at the level of the political questions of the unjust distribution of wealth, which divided Europe into those who had no assets and had to work and those who had assets and did not, but it also extended to the very nature and quality of work itself, as we will see in the final section.

The French 'Utopian' Socialists

The theological dimension was more marked among some of the earlier French utopian socialists, even if it often took heterodox forms or was mixed up with positivistic elements. Saint-Simon illustrates this well, embracing science and industrialization as the greatest hope for the future wellbeing of humanity, but also affected by counter-revolutionary Catholic thought in rejecting the agonistic individualism of the Enlightenment and stressing that any social transformation will only be achieved by moral education and the rational coordination of industry and society by meritocratic leadership. Saint-Simon was influenced by political economy via Jean-Baptiste Say, and shared its suspicion of idleness. Despite his aristocratic background, his journal *Industrie* drew attention to the unjust situation of the working classes, although he believed that the interests of different classes were not essentially in opposition and so could be overcome by peaceful means of the reorganization of industry and society, rather than by violent revolution, for which view he earned Marx's scorn. In *Le Nouveau christianisme*, written in 1825 just before his death, Saint-Simon finally broke with Comte's positivism and his earlier more cynical use of religion to make his call for social reform explicitly Christian, identifying the heart of Christianity with fraternal affection and the obligation to help the poor, while also looking for a renewed Church, purged of corruption. Saint-Simon's followers generally took a more Comtean, positivist approach than their master, with some even forming their own quasi-religious cult, while retaining the stress on the collectivization and central coordination of industry and society. Similar emphases were found in the writings of Charles Fourier, who also rejected the political economists' ideas of trade, the division of labour and competition, in favour of the organization of society into cooperative 'phalanxes', living in *phalanstéres*. He believed that organized cooperation would increase productivity and ensure a decent minimum standard of living for all. Fourier looked for a more explicitly utopian future, in which humanity's natural desires were set free from oppressive codes of sexual morality, and our relations with nature were transformed beyond industrialism, when work itself would become pleasurable and like play. After his death there were a number of attempts to put some of his ideas into practice in communities in America, characterized by Marx as 'small experiments, necessarily doomed to failure'. A more significant legacy was Fourier's influence upon the *oeuvriers* and their demands for the right to work, which led to the establishment of state cooperatives for the unemployed after the Revolution of 1848. These movements were also influenced by Pierre-Joseph Proudhon's *What is Property?* (1840), which gave the famous answer: 'theft'. Proudhon shared the social analysis of other French socialists, looking to labour as the basis for the redistribution of wealth to create a more just society. In contrast to Saint-Simon, however, he possessed a deep suspicion of government and so took the cooperative thought of his predecessors in a more radically democratic and mutualist direction, tending at times towards anarcho-syndicalism. Together, these three French thinkers, with their stress upon cooperation rather than competition in labour and an egalitarian society with justice for the propertyless workers, influenced Marx and the British socialist tradition. Nevertheless, questions remain concerning the ultimate grounds of their critique and utopian visions, questions which are manifest in their ambiguous relation to the theological on the one hand, and which were articulated by Marx in his accusation that they were 'unscientific', on the other.

Karl Marx: Alienated Labour

It was the aim of the German thinker Karl Marx to overcome this deficiency by providing an account of labour which would be thoroughly 'scientific'. Marx became the most significant modern philosopher of labour, despite his limited recognition during his lifetime, when his ideas were taken up by various revolutionary workers' movements in the late nineteenth century, and then particularly when, following the Russian Revolution of 1917, 'Marxism' was made the official view of the USSR, and subsequently of China and Eastern Europe. This 'canonization' and systematization of Marx's thought, begun by his friend Engels who published many of his writings posthumously, generates its own problems with interpretation. Marx's originality and significance come partly from his innovative synthesis of apparently conflicting traditions: German Idealism, French political thought, and British political economy. While at university he had been influenced by the thought of the Young Hegelians, such as Ludwig Feuerbach, who offered a materialist account of history in which religious and metaphysical thought is seen as mere shadows of reality to be overcome. During the revolutionary 1840s he combined this with the French socialist concern for social and political justice, writing for a number of radical journals. At about the same time he began seriously to read the British political economists, in order to give his thought a more solidly 'scientific', economic foundation than his predecessors.

The foundation of Marx's thought was his labour theory, which constituted his anthropology: *'labour* is the *essence* of man' (Marx 1988, p. 50). Here he synthesized Hegelian ideas with political economy, enabling him at the same time to criticize both. Adam Smith's labour theory is accepted, but used to develop a radical historicist critique of Smith's naturalism. There is no state of nature, because humanity is irreducibly historical; our labour does not merely produce things, we also 'make' our world and ourselves. This sounds like a Hegelian account of history as auto-genesis, but it is important to notice that political economy has enabled Marx to transform this from a theory of intellectual history into socio-economic history, or historical materialism, beyond Hegel. The history of ideas is not, as for so many previous writers in the idealist tradition, the substance of human progress; rather it is epiphenomenal, the ideological 'superstructure' which merely expresses the material 'base' of real, socio-economic history. It is 'not consciousness that determines life', Marx argues, 'but life that determines consciousness' (Marx 1998, p. 101).

Marx develops this labour theory into a critique of capitalism through his account of alienation (*Entaeussern*), which blends insights from Hegelianism and political economy to describe how the 'surplus value' generated in all labour is not enjoyed by the labourer under capitalism, but rather is taken away to generate profit for someone else. The worker is alienated from his labour, and thus from himself. This alienation takes place because of the unjust distribution of capital within society, as the French socialists had claimed, with those who own assets (capitalists) using their capital to control and extract labour from the workers who do not (the proletariat). There is a genuine conflict of interests, competition, between these classes which cannot simply be harmonized through organization, as the utopian socialists had thought. Yet this class conflict is not eternal, but rather the product of a particular phase of history (capitalism) and will work itself out through the processes of history (dialectical materialism), which will lead to violent revolution and the establishment by the proletariat of the communist society, where the alienation of labour under capitalism will be overcome. For Marx this is not just a description of a necessary historical process, it is also, paradoxically, a call to action: 'The philosophers have only interpreted the world, in various ways; the point is to change it' (Marx 1998, p. 571); 'The Proletarians have nothing to lose but their chains; they have a world to win. Workers of the world, unite!' (Marx 1996, p. 30).

Two related questions occur about Marx's project: just how 'scientific' is his method? And, what is the real role of religion in his thought? Marx is famously an atheist materialist; religion, for him, is part of the superstructural realm of 'ideology', concealing the real truth of material relations, and to be left behind in the true communist society. More than this, Marx's account of the alienating surplus of labour began as an extension of the Young Hegelian critique of religion to intellectual production as such. Religion is the archetypical form of intellectual production for him, the original idolatrous 'fetishism' which precedes capitalist commodity fetishism. All ideology, it seems, is 'priestly'. Marx turns on the philosophy which had seemed to be the tool for critiquing religion and accuses it of being an equally alienating abstraction. Does this mean that thought itself is alienating and deceptive, and all ideas are ideology? Apparently not; *science* is Marx's preferred term for genuine knowledge as opposed to ideology: 'consistent naturalism', 'real, positive science'. At times this sounds like a crude scientistic positivism, as when Marx expects his historical claims to be 'verified in a purely empirical way', 'with the accuracy of physical science'. But at other moments, his historicism drives him towards a more pragmatist view of truth as realized in critical action, where it seems that the only thing that distinguishes proletarian truth from bourgeois falsehood is its capacity to bring its own predictions to pass. In this ambiguity we see Marx's rejection of any transcendent notion of truth, as much as any transcendent notion of ethics. His analysis claims to be thoroughly materialist and the rejection of the residual 'theology' even of metaphysics is part of this. Here, it seems Marx is not so far from the naturalism of the political economists after all, despite his historicism. Utility has been smuggled back in through the back door. Yet, given that his 'predictions' have not apparently been vindicated by empirical observation, it is far from clear whether Marx can actually sustain the critical political heart of his entire project on this purely immanent basis. Why should we be dissatisfied with alienated labour at all; and what possible ground could we have for hoping this might be overcome? Marx's determination to found his political critique on immanent, 'scientific' principles is problematic and involves a deliberate repression of theological–ethical aspects of his thought, such as the utopian vision of unalienated labour and the protest at social injustice, which may actually be more fundamental. As Walter Benjamin famously suggested, drawing upon the image of a 'robot' playing chess that was actually operated by a hidden dwarf, it may be that there is a theological dwarf operating the supposedly automatic Marxian puppet.

British Romantic Views of Labour

In Britain in the nineteenth century there was another tradition of cultural–literary critiques of capitalism, which did not attempt to justify themselves on purely immanent, scientistic grounds, but had more in common with the French socialists, including a more positive, though still not unambiguous relation to theology. This tradition grew out of the Romantic rejection of industrial utilitarianism and materialism. This found literary expression in William Blake's contempt for the 'dark Satanic mills' and in Dickens' character Mr Gradgrind, but took more precise form in Coleridge's Platonist hostility to the egoism of political economy, which denied the soul and any transcendent truth or goodness. After Coleridge it was Thomas Carlyle who became one of the most prominent spokesmen for this more Romantic criticism of capitalism.

Carlyle drew upon the Gothic sympathies developed by George Gilbert Scott and Augustus Pugin to contrast the avaricious pursuit of profit for its own sake without regard for the human or environmental costs in modern industry and trade ('mammonism') with the well-ordered society of the medieval monastery in *Past and Present* (1909). Influenced by German Romantic thought, Carlyle claimed that 'there is a perennial nobleness, and even sacredness, in Work'; for him, the monastic tradition was correct to think that *laborare est orare*, work is worship, because 'man perfects himself by working' and 'Labour is Life' (Carlyle 1909, pp. 202–3). He railed against the idleness of the leisured classes who lived off their capital, and idolized the 'Hero' or strong and virtuous leader who took courageous decisions for the sake of the common good. Following from this, Carlyle called for a new 'chivalry of labour' and a new 'aristocracy' of the captains of industry, admiring humane employers such as the great Quaker businesses. The example of the monastery obviously suggested a form of collective cooperation rather than individual competition, but Carlyle went further in insisting upon the need for an explicitly transcendent vision of the just society, such as that upon which the monastery was founded. Carlyle was not an apologist for Roman Catholicism (although even the choice of example was controversial in Protestant circles) and spoke warmly, for example, of Islam and Confucianism, as if the specificities of claims of revelation were largely a matter of indifference to him; but he clearly identified the egoism of mammonism with 'practical atheism' and the alternative hope for a renewed society with submission to divine justice and the restoration of the primacy of the soul over the stomach. Carlyle presents a critique of nineteenth century capitalism on the basis of a theological natural law view, combined with a remarkably strong account of the sacred dignity of labour, understood as heroic Herculean struggle.

Similar emphases can be seen in the art critic and social essayist John Ruskin. In *Unto this Last* (1860) Ruskin follows Carlyle in developing a very similar critique of political economy as a false 'science' which denies the soul and morality, reducing humanity to a 'covetous machine', constantly at war with itself. Likewise his solution is essentially the same as Carlyle: we must recover virtue and sacrifice and nobility in our working life, through the proper exercise of judgement in accordance with the divine law. The medievalist sympathy for the Gothic is developed by Ruskin in *The Stones of Venice* (1853), building upon Pugin, into an account of the medieval artisan as the exemplar of unalienated labour:

labour that is free, responsible, creative, intelligent as well as practical, and enjoying the fruits of its work. According to this view, beauty and pleasure are signs of just working conditions, while ugliness is a sign of enslaved labour. More than this, artisanal labour is not simply the highest form of human work; it is also the one that most properly resembles God's work: free, creative, delighting in its creation. Although Ruskin's own religious views were complex, moving from evangelicalism, through phases of biblical scepticism and spiritualism, towards a tentative return to a more open Christian faith, his social criticism was always expressed in Christian terms. More practically, Ruskin was involved in some of the beginnings of the cooperative movement and the working men's educational movement, and was connected with early Christian socialists such as F. D. Maurice.

William Morris developed Ruskin's account of the medieval artisan as the ideal of emancipated labour, overcoming the separation of beauty and usefulness and the division of labour into intellectual (free, responsible) work and manual (servile) work. Art, for Morris, was not about decadent ornament, but the 'element of sensuous pleasure' in the work itself, which is its only true reward (Morris 1993, p. 368). Following Ruskin, the ugliness of contemporary art was seen as reflecting the social injustices of its production. Morris combined this aesthetic account of true work with an analysis of history influenced by Marx, so that he looked for its realization through a revolution rather than education and moral transformation and regarded religion as part of the old order that would be swept away. Nevertheless, his aestheticism and medievalism saved him from the cruder positivism and hostility towards theology of other strands of atheist Marxism. Morris put his theories into practice with his own design firm, which played a key role in the development of the arts and crafts movement, and also through his involvement in the nascent British socialist movement. Through his youthful involvement with the pre-Raphaelites he exercised a considerable influence upon British ecclesiastical tastes, while his later writings were formative for what would become the British Labour Party. One of his indirect disciples was the Roman Catholic artist and essayist Eric Gill, who would develop Morris's social criticism in a much more explicitly theological direction.

The Christian Socialists

Although, as we have seen, many of the early nineteenth century writers about the question of labour employed theological frameworks of thought, whether consciously or not, it was not until the mid-nineteenth century that more explicitly Christian responses began to be developed. In France certain strands within the followers of Saint-Simon, such as Philippe Buchez, who was briefly president of the French Constituent National Assembly in 1848 and one of the founders of the worker-owned journal *L'Atelier*, held 'socialist' views clearly derived from Christian principles. This tradition of Christian 'socialism' migrated to Britain partly through the influence of John Ludlow, who with the theologian F. D. Maurice, and the authors Charles Kingsley and Thomas Hughes, formed the first significant group within the Anglo-Saxon theological world to identify themselves as 'Christian socialists' in the 1840s. They were responding to the rise of a mass workers' movement in Chartism in the United Kingdom and the influence of cooperativist views of labour deriving from the utilitarian factory reformer Robert Owen and his 'Owenite' followers. Theologically, however, the Christian socialists were more indebted to the Coleridgean Romantic rejection of utilitarianism. These Christian socialists were active in the early labour and cooperative movements and in promoting education among the working classes, establishing the Working Men's College in 1854 in London. Their vision of Christianity as essentially social against all forms of egotistical individualism and their refusal of the separation between the sacred and the secular led them to call for mutual collaboration rather than competition: 'by labouring strenuously in God's strength, that we may realise the true Fraternity of which this age has dreamed' (Morris 2005, p. 149). It is worth noting in passing that the dismissal of these more ethical and frequently Christian forms of socialism as 'utopian', purely derivative, bourgeois, and essentially quietist is due to the dominance of the self-proclaimed 'scientific' Marxist socialism in the twentieth century. If the 'scientific' nature of this perspective is called into question, particularly in relation to its view of history, then these alternative repressed socialist traditions emerge as at least as significant.

The Social Teaching of the Churches

The institutional Churches in Europe, with some exceptions, were initially suspicious of the revolutionary and sometimes anti-Christian intentions of the working-class political movements in mid-nineteenth century Europe, with the inclusion of 'socialism' and 'communism' among Pius IX's 1864 'syllabus of errors' being an extreme, but not unrepresentative example. By the late nineteenth century however, this situation had shifted significantly, with moves which would mark the beginning of the modern development of the Church's tradition of social teaching. Pope Leo XIII's encyclical *Rerum Novarum* on the condition of labour (1891) continued to reject the atheism, materialism, class warfare and revolutionary intentions of much of modern socialism and to insist on the necessity of private property, but it also applied traditional Catholic teaching on economic justice to the contemporary situation of the working classes in such a way as to draw some radical conclusions. The pope rejected the free market view that the supply and demand of labour should determine wages purely through the free contracting of employers and employees. Instead he pointed to concerns of natural justice to insist upon decent working conditions, just wages, and the duties of employers towards their employees: 'Workers are not to be treated as slaves' (Leo XIII 1983, p. 20). The encyclical insisted upon the duty of the state to intervene to protect the vulnerable and encouraged the organization of workers to defend their rights, although it looked for more corporatist models of collaboration between the state, employers and employees, rather than the confrontational model more common within the trade union movement. The encyclical had a wide influence and contributed to the development of Catholic workers' movements and political parties in Europe and elsewhere. This magisterial tradition of reflection upon social concerns continued in the Roman Catholic Church with *Quadragesimo Anno* (1931), the Second Vatican Council's document *Gaudium et Spes* (1965), *Populorum Progressio* (1967), and particularly with the encyclicals of John Paul II, who had spent most of his ministry in an officially communist country: *Solicitudo Rei Socialis* (1987), *Centesimus Anno* (1991), and *Laborem Exercens* (1981). The latter encyclical provides the most sustained account of labour within this tradition. The three objects of labour that John Paul II lists include the traditional production for self-preservation, but also the more modern concerns of the societal transformation of nature through technology and the transformation of self and society through cultural production. These two concerns indicate how much official Catholic teaching has been influenced by the more general discussion of the problem of labour. This does not mean that the pope succumbs to a relativizing progressivism, nor a naively uncritical attitude to modern technology. He insists that even the rapidly changing situation of modern labour 'remains within the Creator's original ordering' (John Paul II 1981, p. 4) and expresses concern that the increasing role of technology requires responsible ethical handling in order to avoid becoming dehumanizing. The pope sees this neglect of the human subjective dimension to work in both the free market ideology of the Right and the centralist collectivism of the Left, which are equally 'materialist' (John Paul II 1981, p. 7). We can see the familiar natural law emphasis on just wages and conditions of employment, complemented by the pope's own personalist philosophy. The generally positive Catholic view of natural human agency as a created good even after the fall is extended through a more unusual account of the cooperation of human labour with divine labour in the building of the Kingdom. This is combined with a spirituality of work, looking back to Christ the carpenter of Nazareth and suggesting that Christianity was responsible for a radical revaluation of manual labour in the ancient world. Again here we can see the influence of particularly modern views of labour as at least potentially salvific. These views had already been accepted by the magisterium at the Second Vatican Council, where *Gaudium et Spes* declared: 'By their work people ordinarily provide for themselves and their family, associate with others as their brothers and sisters, and serve them; they can exercise genuine charity and be partners in the work of bringing God's creation to perfection.' Beyond this, 'through the homage of work offered to God humanity is associated with the redemptive work of Jesus Christ, whose labour with his hands at Nazareth greatly added to the dignity of human work' (Flannery 1996, p. 246). We will return to these more ontological questions in the final section. While the Roman Catholic Church has offered the most developed ecclesial reflection upon labour, we can see similar approaches taken by other Churches, as in the report *Unemployment and the Future of Work*, produced by the Council of Churches for Britain and Ireland in 1997.

Liberation Theologies

Parallel to the official teaching of the Churches, during the last fifty years movements characterizing themselves as 'Liberation Theology' have arisen in academic circles and at more popular levels within the Churches, initially in Latin America, but spreading to the rest of the world, including Europe. These movements share a common sense of understanding the Christian message in terms of radical identification with the cause of the oppressed alongside the proclamation and practice of the gospel in terms of total liberation, including liberation from injustice, material poverty and oppression. Drawing upon earlier traditions of Christian social thought and arising out of the social and political upheavals of the 1960s and the *aggiornamento* in the Roman Catholic Church associated with the Second Vatican Council, the manifesto for 'Liberation Theology' was formulated by the Peruvian Dominican priest Gustavo Gutiérrez in Chimbote, Peru, in 1968, and developed into his seminal study *A Theology of Liberation* (1971). In this work Gutiérrez claimed that theology should be 'critical reflection on praxis', that 'liberation' should be the paradigm for contemporary understandings of salvation, and that the Church should stand in radical social and political solidarity with the poor and oppressed. Liberation theology found expression not only in academic and popular circles but also within the ecclesiastical hierarchy, especially at the Latin American episcopal conferences at Medellín, Colombia, in 1968, which spoke of the 'preferential option for the poor', and at Puebla, Mexico, in 1979. Some have seen Liberation Theology as in opposition to the social teaching of the Roman hierarchy, and it is certainly true that there have been points of friction such as the instructions from the Congregation for the Doctrine of the Faith in 1984 and 1986 and the censuring of some of the teachings of Leonardo Boff and Jon Sobrino, among others. Liberation theologians have at times accused the ecclesiastical hierarchy of being complicit with oppressive regimes and neglectful of the concrete realities of the poor; while the Congregation claimed that some liberation theologians had compromised the faith through adopting an essentially Marxist analysis of the social situation, which led to an excessively materialist and immanentist account of salvation and an overly conflictual view of class warfare, encouraging Christians to be dangerously politically partisan and even caught up in violent revolution. Despite these genuine instances of tension, it would perhaps be more plausible to follow Gutiérrez himself in seeing liberation theology and the Church's social tradition as not so far removed from one another and mutually informing. The original analysis of liberation theology arose out of the application of the Church's social teaching to the situation of Latin America and avoided the reduction of salvation to material prosperity and class warfare; while, as we have indicated, the liberation theologians' 'preference for the poor' and expectation of salvation as including real material transformation in this life seem to have been taken up by the magisterial tradition, particularly in the writings of Paul VI and John Paul II. Likewise, Gutiérrez and other liberation theologians have insisted that the preferential option for the poor does not exclude the universal nature of the Christian hope of salvation; while conversely papal teaching has affirmed the priority of labour over capital and reiterated the classical principle articulated by Aquinas and others that the rights of private property are secondary to the right to life, so that there are circumstances in which redistribution by expropriation is permissible. The view of labour at the heart of liberation theology is very similar to the post-Vatican II magisterial tradition, seen in *Laborem Exercens*, as in Gutiérrez's view that 'humanity fulfils itself by continuing the work of creation by means of its labour' or that 'to work, to transform the world, is to become a man and to build the human community; it is also to save', which he sees evident in the biblical narrative of the exodus from slavery into the Promised Land (Gutiérrez 2001, p. 158). Although at times this can sound as if humanity immanently saves itself through labour, as when he claims that 'faith "desacralises" creation, making it the area proper for human work', at other times he is careful to set this human labour within more participatory accounts of sharing in God's work: 'Salvation, totally and freely given by God ... is the inner force and the fullness of this movement of human self-generation initiated by the work of creation' (Gutiérrez 2001, pp. 157–8).

3. Ontology: Human and Divine Work and Rest

We have seen how the economic and political views of labour raise more fundamental ontological questions about human labour. Is labour the source of value or should it seek to correspond to the true value of things? Does labour operate according to morally neutral, quantifiable laws of necessity, like other physical forces, or is it always hermeneutical, cultural, and moral? Is human labour naturally self-interested and competitive, or can it be organized cooperatively? Are its ends purely material or are they also more spiritual? Is labour oriented towards the purely mundane ends of subsistence or to more ultimate ends such as human salvation? These last questions raise the possibility of some sort of analogy or participatory relationship between human and divine work and the relation of human work to rest, which has traditionally been seen within the Christian tradition as more 'divine' than labour, while the latter has been associated with the curse of the fall.

Ontologies of Labour

As we have seen, behind the Marxist categories, which have dominated so much political and economic discussion of labour, stand the philosophy of Hegel and German Idealism and Romanticism more generally. The question of action and practice had dominated these philosophical movements as they sought ways to develop more holistic philosophical systems on the basis of Kant's practical philosophy in the second critique, in order to overcome the dualism of the epistemological approach of the first critique and the tradition of Cartesian rationalism before that. Whether this was through Goethe's assertion that 'In the beginning was the Act', or the philosophies of will in Fichte or Schopenhauer, or more significantly the aesthetic philosophy of creation in Schelling and the philosophy of freedom in Hegel, there was an attempt among these philosophers to elevate *praxis* to the essence of humanity. These were *ontologies* of labour. Activity, labour, creation, were seen as essentially human: humans make themselves and their world. From these beginnings there has been a crucial ambiguity over this turn to the act: whether it should be conceived in a Promethean, nihilistic fashion as if humans have usurped God as the author of reality (as in Fichte and Schopenhauer), or whether this emphasis on *homo faber* should be seen as part of the *imago dei* by which humanity reflects, shares in, and continues the work of its Maker who is Pure Act (as perhaps is more the case with Schelling and Hegel). The former ontological position has, as we have seen, frequently coincided with a more materialist account of the ends of labour and a more agonistic account of the social relations implicit in labour. These ways of thinking about labour as ontological, rather than purely economic or political, more obviously connect directly with fundamental theological questions such as what it is to be human, and these quasi-theological debates were very much part of the milieu from which they emerged. However it was not until the twentieth century that explicitly *theological* ontologies of labour emerged (although we have noted traces of such a development in earlier strands of nineteenth century thought). These twentieth century 'theologies of work' were a significant influence on the development of the Church's social teaching and of liberation theologies in the last century. They embodied a transition from a purely justice-based concern with securing the minimum conditions for workers, towards a more potentially open-ended and qualitative transformation of the nature of human labour, so as more fully to participate in the divine labour of salvation.

Theologies of Work: Marie-Dominique Chenu and Miroslav Volf

Whether from a Catholic perspective, such as the Dominican Marie-Dominique Chenu writing in 1950, or from a Protestant background, such as Miroslav Volf, these theologies of labour share a desire to respond to the challenge of Marxism and to offer a positive account of human labour within the economy of salvation. Both move beyond natural law theologies of creation with their concern for justice, towards more Christological and pneumatological views of human labour as sharing in the building of God's Kingdom on earth. Chenu was part of the *ressourcement* movement in Catholic thought and looked to Maximus the Confessor to support a positive account of human activity transforming nature in cooperation with God. Despite some criticism at the time, Chenu's views were vindicated at the Second Vatican Council, where they found expression in *Gaudium et Spes*, as we saw previously. He also wrote at the time of the Dominican 'worker-priests' experiment, where French priests were exempted from parochial responsibilities and sent to work in the factories in order to reach the working classes who had become alienated from the Church. Chenu's desire to give a positive theological account of the dignity of human labour beyond mere subsistence and his sense of the radically changing nature of labour in modernity, leads him to make some very large claims for human work, perhaps influenced by the evolutionary thought of Teilhard de Chardin, such as that work achieves the 'synthesis of man and nature' which will lead to the 'complete assumption of the universe by man' (Chenu 1963, pp. 26, 73). Alongside Chenu and the French worker-priests, there were other movements and writers within the Roman Catholic Church which contributed to the development of a spirituality of work in the mid-twentieth century, from

Dorothy Day and the Catholic Worker Movement in the United States, which combined the promotion of distributivist political thought with direct action to help the poor, to the more conservative St Josemaria Escrivá, the Spanish priest who founded *Opus Dei* as a movement for the sanctification of the ordinary life of the laity. Within the Church of England, and from a more literary–aesthetic perspective, Dorothy L. Sayers developed an account of human creative work as analogous to the creative action of the Holy Trinity.

A similarly high view of human labour and its relation to salvation is found in Miroslav Volf's *Work in the Spirit* (1991). Coming from a Croatian Pentecostalist background, Volf is influenced by the political emphasis on eschatology in Jürgen Moltmann's *Theology of Hope* (1969) (itself influenced by the Marxist Ernst Bloch). Responding to Marxism, Volf sees the priority of contemplation over action in traditional Christian thought as an alien Greek philosophical denigration of labour, while he believes that the traditional Protestant theologies of work in terms of vocation (*Beruf*) are unsuited to the contemporary realities of labour. He would replace these ideas of vocation, which he claims are founded upon a backward-looking theology of creation, with an account of the gifts of the Spirit, which sets human labour in the context of collaborating with God in building the Kingdom through the eschatological *transformatio mundi*. This enables him to speak of a judgement of works ('All work that contradicts the new creation is meaningless; all work that corresponds to the new creation is ultimately meaningful', Volf 1991, p. 121), while also insisting that good work is not so integral to our salvation that it follows us into the eschaton (appealing to Rev. 14.13; Eph. 6.8; and 1 Cor. 3.12).

The Idolatry of Work and the Theology of Rest? Karl Barth and Josef Pieper

If twentieth century theologies of work have generally held these high views of human labour in relation to salvation and divine labour, the theological adoption of ontologies of labour has not been without its critics. Two of the most important have been the Reformed Swiss theologian Karl Barth (1886–1968) and the German Roman Catholic Thomist Josef Pieper (1904–97), who both criticized the modern idolatry of work as Promethean, against which they sought to recall the scriptural command to rest and the traditional priority of contemplation over action and divine action over entirely non-commensurate human responses. For Barth, work is essentially 'this worldly' (Barth 1961, p. 471) while the Sabbath commandment 'points [man] away from everything that he himself can will and achieve' (Barth 1961, p. 53). Pieper reiterates the Aristotelian principle that 'we work in order to be at leisure', while he sees the modern world of 'total work' as embodying the opposite ordering (Pieper 1998, p. 4). For Pieper 'the festival is the origin of leisure' and 'there is no festival that does not get its life from ... worship' (Pieper 1998, pp. 34, 51). While both Barth and Pieper argue from traditional premises for this caution towards idealizing views of labour, it is not insignificant that they wrote out of a wider cultural and philosophical context, which was more sceptical than the nineteenth century about human scientific and technological capacities to resolve all problems and establish the Kingdom of Heaven on Earth. These mid-twentieth century critiques of technocratic societies and instrumental and utilitarian modes of reasoning were themselves indebted to earlier strands of Romantic thinking which ran parallel with the more positive views expressed in Hegel and Marx. In Barth's case this meant that his commitment to socialism was closer to the spirit of Kierkegaard and the cultural pessimism of the West German socialists of the 1930s such as Theodor Adorno and the Frankfurt School rather than the naively optimistic view of science and progress expressed in Soviet Marxism. For Pieper, his Thomist concern with the classical hierarchical ordering of leisure and labour in Plato and Aristotle was sympathetic to the critique of technology found in Martin Heidegger's phenomenological analysis. For Heidegger, Western thought has been dominated by the 'equipmental' relation of *techne* which reduces things to tools to be used, as opposed to the organic shining forth of things which he sees in the work of art and other ways of relating to Being less concerned with mastery. This phenomenological approach to the question of work has been developed subsequently by Hannah Arendt and more explicitly theologically by Jean-Yves Lacoste.

4. Concluding Remarks

The theologies of work, deriving from nineteenth century ontologies of labour, can be seen not simply as a theological response to a new social situation and developments in secular thought, but rather as a genuine outworking of radical elements of the Christian gospel itself. Leaving aside the somewhat sentimental question of Christ's occupation as a carpenter in Nazareth, within the New Testament, particularly St John and St Paul, we can see how theurgic and liturgical elements of the Jewish Wisdom tradition are developed to speak of the collaboration of human works with the work of God. Such a collaboration can be seen as implicit in the logic of Chalcedonian Christology, while the divine kenosis and exaltation of human nature in the incarnation could encourage the anti-hierarchical elevation of traditionally servile activities. Such a view would fit with the apparent eschatological suspension of the opposition between work and rest on the Sabbath through the advent of the Christ: the eternal Sabbath has arrived in which all time and space is sacred and all work can become liturgy. At the very least, the New Testament could be said to problematize the conventional opposition between work and rest, work and worship, and slavery and freedom; while more fundamentally, its suggestion of an analogy of participatory cooperation between divine and human work points towards a possible *ultimate* convergence, beyond our temporal horizon, between work and rest, work and worship, human work and divine work. If this is so, then the exalted view of the dignity of human labour and creativity which has developed throughout the Christian tradition, from the early ascetic and monastic movements, through the Renaissance and into modernity, seems not just an accident, but rather an authentic outworking of these revolutionary insights. To situate work within this theological teleology, against secularizing tendencies within and without the Church, so that it can be *more or less* worshipful, *more or less* participatory in God's work, provides the basis for Christian critical judgement of work, as we have seen.

However, we have seen a number of possible difficulties with this 'convergence' perspective on work, worship and rest, most obviously in its more extreme Romantic forms. Such a position has been accused of encouraging an idolatry of work embodying the Promethean temptation to see human value as self-made rather than a gift of grace; it can also lead to an over-realized eschatology, which thinks it can live beyond the diurnal rhythms of work and rest, but which in effect simply loses any sense of the value and meaning of rest. Finally, it can also produce a spiritualizing idealization of work, which abolishes all proximate, this-worldly ends for working with the insistence that all work must be directly *for* God and like God's work, and is thus incapable of comprehending the necessary toil of subsistence, the postlapsarian character of human work which continues to separate it from rest and worship. These problems can become particularly acute when these ontologies of labour are secularized, as in Marxism for example. In such cases there is no sense of this idealization being kept in check by a more ultimate, as yet unattainable horizon, and the ultimate goal of work is immanentized as simply working for work's sake, or abstract profit, personal pleasure or something similar.

References

Theodor Adorno and Max Horkheimer, 1997, *The Dialectic of Enlightenment*, ET, London: Verso

St Thomas Aquinas, 1964–80, *Summa Theologiae*, London: Eyre and Spottiswoode

Hannah Arendt, 1998, *The Human Condition*, Chicago, IL: Chicago University Press

Karl Barth, 1961, *Church Dogmatics III/4*, ET, Edinburgh: T. & T. Clark

Walter Benjamin, 1999, *Illuminations*, ET, London: Pimlico

Thomas Carlyle, 1909, *Past and Present*, London: Oxford University Press

Marie-Dominique Chenu, 1963, *The Theology of Work: An Exploration*, Dublin: Gill and Son

Austin Flannery, 1996, *Vatican Council II: Constitutions, Decrees, Declarations*, Dublin: Dominican Publications

Eric Gill, 1983, *A Holy Tradition of Working*, Ipswich: Golgonooza Press

Gustavo Gutiérrez, 2001 (1971), *A Theology of Liberation*, ET, London: SCM Press

Martin Heidegger, 1993, *Basic Writings*, London: Routledge

John Paul II, 1981, *Laborem Exercens*, ET, London: Catholic Truth Society

Jean-Yves Lacoste, 2000, *Le Monde et l'absence d'oeuvre*, Paris: Presses Universitaires de France

Leo XIII, 1983 (1891), *Rerum Novarum*, ET, London: Catholic Truth Society

John Locke, 1988, *Two Treatises of Government*, Cambridge: Cambridge University Press

Thomas Malthus, 1993, *An Essay on the Principle of Population*, Oxford: Oxford University Press

Karl Marx, 1988, *Economic and Philosophical Manuscripts of 1844*, ET, New York: Prometheus Books

Karl Marx, 1996, *Later Political Writings*, ET, Cambridge: Cambridge University Press

Karl Marx, 1998, *The German Ideology*, ET, New York: Prometheus Books

Jürgen Moltmann, 1969, *Theology of Hope*, ET, London: SCM Press

Jeremy Morris, 2005, *F. D. Maurice and the Crisis of Christian Authority*, Oxford: Oxford University Press

William Morris, 1993, *News from Nowhere and Other Writings*, London: Penguin

Josef Pieper, 1998, *Leisure as the Basis of Culture*, ET, South Bend, IN: St Augustine's Press

John Ruskin, 1911 (1860), *Unto this Last and Munera Pulveris*, London: George Allen and Sons

Dorothy L. Sayers, 2002, *The Mind of the Maker*, London: Continuum

Adam Smith, 1991, *The Wealth of Nations*, London: David Campbell Publishing

Miroslav Volf, 1991, *Work in the Spirit*, Oxford: Oxford University Press

Max Weber, 2001, *The Protestant Ethic and the Spirit of Capitalism*, ET, London: Routledge

Suggested Reading

Hannah Arendt, 1998, *The Human Condition*, Chicago, IL: Chicago University Press

Oscar Arnal, 1986, *Priests in Working-class Blue: The History of the Worker Priests (1943–1954)*, New York: Paulist Press

Marie-Dominique Chenu, 1963, *The Theology of Work: An Exploration*, ET, Dublin: Gill and Son

Gustavo Gutiérrez, 2001, *A Theology of Liberation*, ET, London: SCM Press

John Hughes, 2007, *The End of Work: Theological Critiques of Capitalism*, Oxford: Blackwell

John Paul II, 1981, *Laborem Exercens*, ET, London: Catholic Truth Society

Nicholas Lash, 1981, *A Matter of Hope*, London: Darton, Longman & Todd

Michael Löwy and Robert Sayre, 2001, *Romanticism against the Tide of Modernity*, London: Duke University Press

Karl Marx, 1996, *Later Political Writings*, ET, Cambridge: Cambridge University Press

Josef Pieper, 1998, *Leisure as the Basis of Culture*, ET, South Bend, IN: St Augustine's Press

Pontifical Council for Justice and Peace, 2002, *Work as Key to the Social Question: The Great Social and Economic Transformations and the Subjective Dimension of Work*, ET, Vatican City: Libreria Editrice Vaticana

Esther D. Reed, 2010, *Work, for God's Sake: Christian Ethics in the Workplace*, London: Darton, Longman & Todd

Denys Turner, 1983, *Marxism and Christianity*, Oxford: Blackwell

Miroslav Volf, 1991, *Work in the Spirit*, Oxford: Oxford University Press

Max Weber, 2001, *The Protestant Ethic and the Spirit of Capitalism*, ET, London: Routledge

Notes

1 'Work and Labour', in Nicholas Adams, George Pattison and Graham Ward (eds), *Oxford Handbook of Theology and Modern European Thought*, Oxford: Oxford University Press, copyright © 2013. Reproduced with permission of Oxford University Press.

5

Bulgakov's Move from a Marxist to a Sophic Science (2002)

In this essay I hope to draw attention to the interest of Sergei Bulgakov as a philosopher of science. Bulgakov has become known in the last sixty years in English-speaking countries as an Orthodox theologian writing in exile in Paris, famous particularly for his controversy with Vladimir Lossky over the alleged unorthodoxy of his account of Sophia, or the divine wisdom. Recently more attention has been paid to his significance as a political thinker who, having abandoned his career as a Marxist academic economist, was briefly involved in Russian politics during the revolutionary period and subsequently attempted to think through an authentically Christian socialism. In seeking to argue that Bulgakov is also of interest as a Christian philosopher of science, I will be using a book, recently translated into English, from this period of his conversion from Marxism to Christian socialism. *Philosophy of Economy: the World as Household* was written in 1912, and forms part of his farewell to Marxism, while at the same time celebrating as truly theological some of its central insights, such as the significance of labour. Perhaps the central point of departure from Marxism for Bulgakov was his rejection of positivism, and this leads him to consider at some length within the philosophy of economy the nature of science.

Bulgakov's rejection of positivism can be seen as part of a pan-European reaction against mechanism and crude materialism, which took such diverse forms as the neo-Kantianism of the Marburg school, Freud's 'discovery' of the unconscious, or Saussure's account of language. Initially, in common with many other Russians of the Silver Age, Bulgakov turned to Kantian idealism to solve these problems, publishing *From Marxism to Idealism* in 1903. His argument in *Philosophy of Economy* could still be situated within a tradition of Kantian critique, seeking to delineate the proper limits of a field of knowledge and to insist upon the human subjective conditioning of all knowledge, yet he has by this stage significantly departed from Kant and especially the extreme Kantianism of the Marburg school. He rejects the possibility of 'pure' reason, insisting that philosophy cannot be the contentless circularity of logic without reference to life, but must be philosophy *of* something. This pushes his critique of science into a more radically historicizing direction, seeing knowledge as the product of specific socio-historical life situations. He then goes beyond a Marxist or Hegelian historicism, by contesting the possibility of obtaining a totalized knowledge of the whole, arguing instead for a plurality of perspectives arising from different practices, without a clear hegemony of one over the others.

Here his thought pushes in pragmatic, almost 'postmodernist' directions, anticipating in some ways Heidegger's critique of science. However, part of Bulgakov's interest is his drawing back from the abyss of utter scepticism and the denial of all truth. While providing a profound critique of the worldview of much modern science, and in particular the elevation of a method into ontology which he links with the rise of capitalism, Bulgakov does not abandon science altogether, arguing instead that science is founded upon a profoundly theological intuition – the rationality and interconnectedness of things – and that when this foundation is recognized as outside science itself, mysteriously inaccessible to comprehension, then a more 'tactful' science could be rediscovered, freed of its metaphysical hubris. This is what he calls, borrowing ideas from the Romantic Slavophile tradition, 'sophic science' in which this extra-scientific foundation of the rationality of the world is identified with the biblical divine wisdom or Sophia. Such a proposal is perhaps of particular interest to us for its attempt to mediate theologically between a crude dogmatic materialism on the one hand and a sceptical postmodern form of utilitarianism on the other.

Context

As already mentioned, Bulgakov's work did not arise in a vacuum, but was very much part of a wider current in Russian and European thought at the turn of the century: Across the continent in various ways a 'revolt against positivism'[1] can be detected, a persistent dissatisfaction with the crude materialism and scientific naturalism which for much of the latter nineteenth century had seemed to hold forth the promise of explaining everything and solving every possible problem. This rebellion was manifest in phenomena as diverse as Bergson's philosophy, the resurgence of neo-Kantian idealism in Germany, symbolism in art, the rise of psychology and anthropology, or Weber's social theory. There was then a renewed interest in those areas of life that a mechanistic or Darwinian account of human nature seemed to neglect, whether this took the form of a fascination with the moral, spiritual and rational, or with the cultural, artistic, mystical and irrational, and whether it sought to mystify the former or rationalize the latter. These various concerns echoed, often consciously, the agenda of the nineteenth century Romantic movement and its aesthetic–humanist protest against scientism.

Bulgakov drew in particular upon Schelling's philosophy of life and action in his move beyond the pure philosophy of idealism, and upon the more local Slavophile Romantic radicals such as Dostoevsky and especially Solov'ev in his efforts to translate this philosophy of life into an attack on the ethics of positivism and an alternative Christian socialist political programme. More narrowly, Bulgakov belonged to that group of intellectuals from the Russian Silver Age whose intellectual journeying began with the move 'from Marxism to Idealism'. This was perhaps not such a surprising journey as it might seem for, as his 1896 response to Rudolf Stammler's Kantianism indicates, Bulgakov's adherence to Marxism was already influenced by the Kantianism that he was here arguing against: the great strength of Marxism for Bulgakov seems to have been its rational monism, purportedly capable of explaining everything through iron laws, which fulfilled Kant's requirement of transcendental unity, albeit without leaving room for Kant's noumenal realm.[2] If Bulgakov's Marxism had always possessed a Kantian flavour, it was during the period 1900–03 that the Kantian idealism began to turn against the Marxism and take on a more critical and also more Russian socio-ethical stance. It is from this point that the argument of *Philosophy of Economy* begins.

Romantic Idealism Against Positivism and Marxism

Bulgakov's original idealist turn against Marxism has two typically Kantian moments: a scepticism about the limitless power of rationalism; and a humanistic attempt to rescue the ethical from the advances of mechanistic science. Both arose during his travels in Western Europe 1898–1900. The scepticism had its roots in the failure of his project to finish the work of *Das Kapital* by extending Marxist theory to provide a complete account of the development of agriculture in the West. The rediscovery of the ethical seems to have been stirred by epiphanies of transcendence: among the Caucasus hills and before the Sistine Madonna in Dresden. Comparisons could be drawn with Kant's Hume-motivated break from the rational dogmatism of Wolff, and his almost sublime experience of the 'starry heavens above and the moral law within'. The first expression of this transformation in Bulgakov's thinking, his lecture on Ivan Karamazov in 1901, while not yet precise in its thinking, already indicates his ethical dissatisfaction with Marxist positivism and his Slavophile turn to Dostoevsky and Solov'ev to counter the moral failure of the West. It is clear from this lecture that Bulgakov already recognized Marxism as more than just an economic theory but rather an entire *Weltanschauung* with its own hidden metaphysics despite its pretensions to have transcended metaphysics through science.[3] Bulgakov had abandoned belief in the dogma of necessary progress from religion to metaphysics to science, which dominated nineteenth century thought after Auguste Comte. This abandonment of faith in necessary progress, motivated partly by its inconsistency with the empirical data he had collected on the European tour, relegated scientism from being post-metaphysical neutral universal truth, to being one metaphysical stance towards the world among many others. Indeed, it is ironically one of the most 'dogmatic' and uncritical, despite its insistence to the contrary (Bulgakov 2000, p. 163).[4] The rejection of progress also took a powerfully ethical dimension for Bulgakov, following Dostoevsky and Solov'ev; he came to believe that, as the parable of the Grand Inquisitor so powerfully expresses, faith in progress actually means sacrificing freedom and the present for the sake of some supposed future happiness. Progress becomes a form of bizarre practical theodicy that deifies man in the process (Evtuhov 1997, pp. 58–9). This project is of course not just confined to positivism but has found expression in a number of forms of idealism, particularly Fichte and Hegel. Yet, as Bulgakov argues in *Philosophy of Economy*, idealism, in its attention to subjectivity, always contains the seeds of the deconstruction of its own pretensions to absolute knowledge as well as those of science. For idealism never quite forgets that knowledge belongs to human beings, and thus it should never totally succumb to the delusions of escaping this and attaining a 'God's eye view' of thought 'from nowhere' (p. 59). Kantian transcendental idealism can make room for human and ethical concerns because it 'reveals the truth that *science is constructed by people*' (p. 164), a truth which '*humanizes* knowledge' (p. 166). This means that even those, such as the Marburg school, who endeavour to unite Kantianism with positivism to demonstrate the *a priori*, logical necessity of science, unwittingly demonstrate the very contingent, instrumental and approximate nature of particular sciences (pp. 164–5).

Transcendental idealism provided Bulgakov with a means of humbling and restraining the pretensions of science within its own proper limits, making room for freedom, ethics and the soul. Science itself leads one back to the 'mystery of man', because 'Man is the creator of science, ζωον μαθηματικον' (p. 166) not vice versa. Yet Bulgakov did not rest content with Kantian transcendental idealism.

Pragmatism Against Idealism

Bulgakov became ultimately dissatisfied with Kant's system because he believed it remains too ideal, an artificial 'armchair' abstraction divorced from reality and practice (p. 179). Kant's account of reason is too 'theoretical, inactive', finally just an 'absorbing game of the logical imagination' (pp. 178, 177). This is manifest in the familiar problems of the unknowability of the *ding an sich*, and the possible unreality of the phenomenal. The gap that Kant creates between the subjective and objective and then endeavours to solve, is never quite bridged; the reality of the external world is only known 'theoretically', because *theoria* is conceived not as in some way a form of relation to and in reality, but as a mirror outside life, reflecting it (p. 193). Existence is something incidental for Kant, as can be seen in his discussion of the ontological argument where he insists that existence is not a predicate: conceptually a real tree and a fictional tree are no different (p. 179). Thus Bulgakov insists that the very terms in which Kant poses his central problem, doomed him to a 'labour of Sisyphus, a constant chase after the ever-escaping shadow of reality' (p. 178).

How then are we to escape this dreamy solipsism? Bulgakov's response to this problem is thoroughly Romantic: at once experiential – we must 'feel' the reality of nature (p. 179) – and pragmatic – we must leave our armchairs and 'act' in this arena of life where our theories will be tested against reality. Bulgakov makes clear his debt to Romantic *Lebensphilosophie*, in particular Schelling, who he acknowledges as the only one 'able to tear the spider web of Kantian epistemology' with his 'breakthrough to reality' (p. 180). This is a theory of the integration of knowledge and action, a 'praxeology' rather than an epistemology (p. 178). Yet it is not just a naive apolitical and anti-scientific aestheticism of 'feeling' the reality of life. It is also, politically, a rejection of quietism and a call to action, and a powerful endorsement of technology at a phenomenological level. For technology, *techne*, has the power to convince us that 'science is not erecting a phantasmagorical world but is somehow related to reality' (p. 179), it is a form of labour by which subject and object, humanity and nature, are united and transformed, as Bulgakov makes clear elsewhere in *Philosophy of Economy*. This turn to a pragmatic philosophy to counter the uselessness of transcendental idealism, also transforms further the perspective with which scientific knowledge is viewed: for technology now reveals that science is not truly a form of pure absolute thought, removed from any connection with life, but rather is itself practical, caught up in specific circumstances, projects, presuppositions and goals. Thus despite its positivist self-forgetting delusions, the secret truth is that science is always already practical and connected to life: 'Scientific knowledge is active or, to put it differently, it is technological ... *logic is technological*' (p. 177). Even more boldly: 'in reality there is no such thing as purely theoretical knowledge; it is an abstraction, for knowledge exists only as a moment of an action's concrete unity' (p. 180).

This is crucial to the overall argument of *Philosophy of Economy*, as its name suggests. Bulgakov insists that philosophy is not separate from life, but a part of it, and that therefore human thought is never pure thought thinking itself, but is thought '*about something*' (p. 58), reflecting upon and arising out of some part of life: 'Thought is intrinsically "oriented" rather than independent' (p. 58).[5] This decision as to the orientation of scientific thought is a moment of 'freedom' at its very foundation, a somewhat arbitrary selection of some things over others, and some modes of investigation over others. This decision is also driven by questions of utility which then imprint a pragmatic nature upon the whole scientific endeavour: science is 'born of practical need' and so in Bulgakov's terms is 'economic' in character: 'the labour of research is directed towards the satisfaction of needs dictated by life', even if more is discovered than was originally intended (pp. 181, 170). All of life is economy, labour for Bulgakov, yet it is important to note that he thoroughly resists any attempt to put philosophy or science outside this process, as had been implicit in much nineteenth century thought. Science, the theoretical orientation towards the world, is a 'necessary tool' in that economic relation to the world which is life. The pragmatism and instrumentalism of science and of all knowledge in Bulgakov's view is particularly clear here, as when he boldly insists 'the sciences have their *raison d'être* in utility rather than in Truth' (pp. 167, 174). Even mathematics, which is often seen as the most pure of sciences, is not immune from this pragmatic and economic deconstruction: Bulgakov cites the philosopher of science Jules Henri Poincaré on the equal validity of non-Euclidean geometries, insisting that axioms are only 'conventions' and that the question 'Is Euclidean geometry true?' has no more meaning than 'Is the metric system true?' (p. 173). Here pragmatism has penetrated to the innermost citadel of scientism.

This is a thoroughly socio-historical account of science, sensitive to its political and economic implications, indicating how much Bulgakov still shared with his Marxist heritage. A sentence such as, 'Science is a social process involving *labour* and directed towards the *production of ideal values*, that is, of knowledge, which are necessary and useful to man for various reasons' (p. 168) could well have been written by a much more 'orthodox' Marxist than Bulgakov had become by this stage. Indeed Marxism is openly accredited by Bulgakov with recognizing the economic nature of knowledge and the centrality of the problem of economy.

Yet this historicizing and economizing of knowledge is different from Marxism in a number of ways. We have already encountered Bulgakov's rejection of the predictive powers of Marxist science; this was linked to his rejection of its claims to provide a single unified account of things, one unified science. No doubt despairingly at first, given it was this promise of a monistic unity of total knowledge that had originally attracted Bulgakov about Marxism, he came to contest this rational absolutism which Marx had inherited from Hegel. The finitude of the human subject that does the knowing, and the limitations imposed by the selection of object and method, prevent knowledge from ever being total. This is a consequence of the freedom present in the moment of embarking on science: 'geometers deal not with all theoretically possible geometries but only with those that contribute to the understanding of our three-dimensional space' (p. 58). Therefore it follows that 'given a multiplicity of initial orientations, we must also acknowledge a multiplicity of paths for thought' (p. 58).

The pictures of the world arising out of different practices cannot claim to contain the totality of truth, but are also not without their own 'local' truthfulness; rather they are like different views of the same mountain. Yet these different views are themselves radically contingent. Discursive thought, whether science or philosophy, is a human temporal activity, and so is 'pluralistic by nature' (p. 59). Bulgakov insists that 'there can thus be no single scientific picture of the world ... each science yields its own picture of the world ... Each creates its own cosmos ... each has its own style, and stylizes reality in its own way' (p. 161). In this rejection of a total science synthesizing all knowledge as a utopian delusion, Bulgakov is rejecting the Hegelian–Marxist absolute historical science, the positivist evolving synthesis through classification of all sciences dreamed of by Comte and Herbert Spencer, and the hope of a reconciliation of all the sciences through mathematics that bewitched Hermann Cohen and other neo-Kantians. This hope of a scientific synthesis is utopian because, unassisted, 'science has no way out of the empirical world, where all is multiplicity' (p. 161). If then, we have no access to a 'God's eye view', science and philosophy are transformed into sciences and philosophies, something more like 'working hypotheses' (pp. 60, 160). This radical pluralizing of scientific knowledge is, Bulgakov claims, supported by recent science itself which has a more modest account of its task than positivist philosophies and, we might add, resembles the later 'postmodern' accounts of science that have followed such works as Thomas Kuhn's *The Structure of Scientific Revolutions.*

The Phenomenology of Scientific Method

Having argued that knowledge is pluralistic and arises out of specific practical life situations and needs, Bulgakov now proceeds to ask what is the specific situation out of which science arises, what is the spirit, phenomenology, or *sitz im leben* of the scientific method in general. His answer is to argue that science arises as a specific moment in life where, for an instant, life temporarily forgets itself. If life is to be understood, according to Bulgakov's definition, as the process of the subject's penetration and synthesis with the object, then science is the prior moment of 'preparation for action' when the subject 'makes ready, taking aim like a tiger before it leaps on its prey, and freezes for an instant in this pose' (pp. 185, 182). During this brief moment, the subject is so completely focused upon the object that all sense of self, all subjectivity, is temporarily forgotten. At this time, the object appears to be all; so great is its 'hypnotizing influence' that we can say that 'before being conquered the object temporarily conquers its conqueror' (p. 188). Science therefore is the moment of life's self-alienation. This is why the scientific method can never 'see' freedom or the soul: by its very method it necessarily perceives the entire world as objects, lifeless 'facts' and things, so that it can be said that '*a scientific relation to the world is a relation to the world as a mechanism*' (p. 183). Borrowing Hegel's idea of the 'cunning of reason', Bulgakov describes this moment of forgetfulness as the 'cunning of economy': that is, to assume nature is a machine in order to penetrate its secrets (p. 184).

This moment is in itself both necessary and good within the life process of economy for Bulgakov. However he believes that it becomes problematic when instead of being a moment within life, this is taken as an orientation for the whole of life, the most truthful account of reality, the only real world. This is the origin of the various dogmatic scientisms and positivisms which, as we have seen, Bulgakov rejects: the ontologizing of scientific methodology into a pseudo-scientific *Weltanschauung*. He writes: 'An *ontological* interpretation is frequently ascribed to science's contingent–pragmatic mechanical worldview ... the world is seen as a totality of things, whereas the knowing reason ... appears as a passive schematism of the world' (p. 186). Bulgakov attacks Comte in particular for believing that 'scientific reality is true reality and science is above life because it is its quintessence' (p. 163). To this belief he responds with the question: 'Which is more real: my impression of music and colour, or the corresponding mathematical formulae of aural and visual waves?' (p. 162). Naive experience is more real, and more true to life, of which science is only a part. The geometer is unable to differentiate between a marble statue and its original – sciences cannot even comprehend questions outside their field (p. 186). Thus Bulgakov insists: 'scientism is but a pose assumed by life ... it cannot and should not legislate over life, for it is really its handmaiden. *Scientia est ancilla vitae*' (p. 182). Bulgakov offers some hints as to why this situation has become disordered in modernity, with science often assuming the role of tyrannical lord of life rather than *ancilla*: It is the 'high value of science as a tool', its enormous achievements in modernity, which has led to 'the expansion of its field beyond its real limits and has provoked an effort to use this key to unlock locks that it does not fit at all' (p. 188).[6] More specifically, he argues these scientististic views have their roots in the philosophies of Locke, Hume, Bacon and Mill, and blossom in the nineteenth century due to the 'terrible intensity of economic energy' that was the triumph of capitalism, as Marx and Werner Sombart both recognized (pp. 187–8). Positivism's view of the world shows reality 'as it appears to the calculating proprietor' (p. 166).

In describing the disastrous consequences of this metaphysical hubris of science, Bulgakov waxes lyrical and vitriolic: 'Mephistopheles, the spirit of scientific rationalism, produces a table of logarithms with a flat sneer and with the words *eritis sicut dei scientes bonum et malum*, and maliciously looks on as God's world is ground at this mill' (p. 187). Why is his contempt so intense? This is because he believes that science has in its very nature a murderous eye, an orientation towards death. As we have already seen, the scientific 'moment' consists in the subject's self-forgetfulness, the perception of all as objects, a relation of 'alienation and mutual impenetrability' between life and dead matter (p. 181). While this might be a necessary moment in the process of economy, to absolutize this into metaphysics, making an ontology of it, drains the universe of life, making of everything a 'dead desert ... an anatomical dissecting room ... a kingdom of shadows, of subjectless objects' (p. 183). The objectivity and impersonality which are even virtues in their proper place of the scientific 'moment', now constitute nothing less than a 'murder of the world and of nature' in order to examine its corpse, seeing everything as nothing more than lifeless mechanism (p. 183).

The deathly metaphysics of this positivist materialism is described in some depth: Although it treats everything as dead and endlessly dissectable into unconnected pieces, it also thinks it can obtain a total overview of these unconnected things. This entails a denial of the mysteriousness of temporality, which of course is what makes knowledge inherently discursive, finite and impossible to totalize; things must be frozen and fixed, unable to change, in order to be completely knowable. Thus there can be no memory of the past, or any hope for the future (pp. 184–5). There is here a law of conservation, of the stasis of matter and the impossibility of anything new, that resembles the Nietzschean 'eternal return'. Miracles, let alone any form of true eschatology, are automatically rejected, as 'the possibility of any new creation, any enrichment or growth of the world, is excluded in advance' by this worldview (p. 185). In its place we have the simulated novelty of the rearrangement of other evolutionary scientisms which claim an 'unlimited capacity for prediction', precisely because they believe the world can be known as a whole, like 'one immense system of simultaneous differential equations' (p. 185).[7]

Yet this is not Bulgakov's final word on science. He is not content to leave science as a purely pragmatic activity without any relation to Truth, nor as a purely murderous practice opposed to life. We will now turn to his positive alternative philosophy of science.

Sophia Beyond Pragmatic Relativism and Death

It is in fact science itself that refutes scientism and points towards a more positive philosophy of science. This is because science is incapable of comprehending itself in its own terms (p. 192). Science may view the world as lifeless things, but it can only exist as a product of life, an activity undertaken by the living; it may view the world as a deterministic mechanism, yet it is itself the product and expression of freedom. Science is not self-founding, but must look beyond itself for its ground; science leads beyond itself towards not a science of sciences, but a philosophy of science that can describe its situation in life. In this sense, science is 'an answer to a question that precedes science' (p. 170) and scientism is self-refuting. The very horror that the scientific orientation can arouse, the recognition of recognition of the non-ultimacy of this perspective: 'the dead is not conscious of itself as dead, and pure mechanism is not conscious of its mechanicity. The horror of death can appear only in the living' (p. 191). Hence Bulgakov agrees with Henri Bergson that even mechanism presumes life, the 'economic cunning' which is science is only a means to an end, and that end is life (p. 189). Bulgakov then carries this further towards a radical vitalism that rejects any ultimate Manichean dualism, in a manner similar to Augustine's theory of evil as *privatio boni*: ultimately, he claims, 'there is only life, and that which is taken for death and for lifeless mechanism is damage or discontinuity in life' (p. 191). This is what provides the assurance of the hope that the final victory in the economic struggle of life and death belongs to life.

In this great metaphysical drama of the cosmic struggle of life and death, science has its own crucial role to play. While it can become the servant of death, when it exceeds its proper place and seeks to establish itself through metaphysical hubris as the ultimate reality and the final court of appeal, nevertheless it can and should act instead as the servant of life. The world perceived scientifically as mechanism is experienced as a nightmarish boundary of life, but also as an opportunity for transformation, 'actively recognized as the possibility of organism ... of the victory of the conscious over the unconscious in nature' (p. 190). Bulgakov's description of this vivifying role for science is as impassioned as his earlier descriptions of its deathly potential: science is the 'flaming torch of knowledge' in the hand of economic man; like a miner or sculptor it 'calls the scientific cosmos forth from the meonic twilight, awakens dreaming meonic being to life' (pp. 166, 169). Bulgakov's thought here is heavily indebted to Schelling, Hegel and German Romanticism generally. Science, we are told 'introduces the light of differentiation and regularity into the dark chaos of inert matter ... it ideally organizes the world as an object and permeates the chaos of phenomena with the light of ideas, of universal and rational laws' (pp. 194–5).

At times these claims about the transformative power of science can sound almost Nietzschean in their constructivist vision of man creating an ordered world for himself by imposing his will on chaotic reality. Yet while Bulgakov certainly makes large claims for human creativity, comparing science and philosophy to art or a 'poetry of concepts', this is significantly different from Nietzsche. Even his boldest claims – as when he says science is 'the restoration through labour of the ideal cosmos as an organism of ideas' – are significantly qualified, here by the use of the term 'restoration' and the definite article to indicate his belief that there is one ideal cosmos.

These qualifications also point us towards the reasons why Bulgakov rejects pure pragmatism in science, despite all that we have already seen. For Bulgakov insists that it is deeply wrong to make utility the sole criterion of truth, because while science is born of life and is technological and economic, it cannot be equated with the latter, as 'science does not only serve economic needs, and man does not live by bread alone' (p. 172). Science, while it might not have a transcendental view from nowhere, does possess intimations of transcendence, an excessiveness which, like all arts, exceeds mere utility. Sciences may be *born* of life, but 'once generated, [they] develop according to their own laws and lead an independent existence' (p. 172). Pragmatism cannot account for this; its radically arbitrary fictive nature cannot make sense of the logical consciousness, of the necessity of certain conclusions following from certain premises. Science, correctly, presumes that there is a certain rationality about the cosmos rather than arbitrary chaos, a certain 'objective and logical connectedness – the logic of ideas inevitably based on the logic of things'. Science presupposes some sort of connection between being and consciousness, between ontology and thought, so that one can say '*reality is logical*; it is coherent', and this is what makes science truly scientific, rather than 'arbitrarily subjective or voluntaristic' (p. 175).

This 'trans-subjective connection' of all with all, is according to Bulgakov in a Kantian turn of phrase, the condition of possibility for science or economy. This unified truth may not be available to us as an object of immediate knowledge (the mistake of the various scientisms), yet it nevertheless really exists, constituting and being present to discursive thought, as an 'ideal of knowledge', to use Kantian terms again (p. 157). Hence thought and language are not alien impositions upon a dumb and deathly world, but rather the reawakening of that world from its deathly slumber, a world which is always already ontologically grounded in thought and speech, which is of course none other than the divine Logos, the Word or reason which speaks creation into being. Thus the danger of a Faustian gnostic constructivism is overcome by a thoroughly Platonic account of the pre-existence of all things in their ideal form in the divine nature, as thoughts in the divine mind. Human creativity is not an arbitrary and wilful imposition upon nature, but a participation in the divine creativity manifested in nature, which is its necessary precondition and ground. Our creativity is not so much *ex nihilo*, but rather more of a recollection of these divine ideas, a 'prophetic and creative anamnesis' (p. 194). This anamnesis depends on the mysterious unity of subject and object, so that we can say, again in highly Platonic terms, 'I find the starry sky within myself, otherwise I would not see it above me' (p. 193).

The unity of all things exists then, as the positivists and idealists claimed, but not in a general ideal as they thought, but rather in the 'mysterious and immeasurable depths' of reality, at a 'supralogical rather than logical' level, united in the analogy between the creator of science and the 'womb of life' from which he came: 'there is a Logos of the world that in turn sets up a logic of things, a logic of sciences, a logic of actions ... For the world in its positive basis is not chaos but Sophia' (pp. 162, 176). Bulgakov here identifies the mysterious depth of rational interconnectedness in creation with the divine Sophia, popular in Russian piety and with the Slavophiles, and raised to philosophical significance by Solov'ev. Hence this is Bulgakov's final answer to dogmatic positivism on one hand, and sceptical pragmatism on the other: '*Science is sophic* ... a tool for reviving the world, for the victory and self-affirmation of life' (pp. 176–7).[8] Sophia mediates between transcendence and worldly needs, giving birth to ideas and reality by a kind of 'erotic inspiration' quite different from mirroring or accounting (p. 194). In action, in the service of life, sophic science attains a unity of the ideal and the real that overcomes the antinomies of pure idealism or pure pragmatism, neither of which can exist in reality.

Science Grounded in Sophia

We have seen how Bulgakov began by rejecting the pretensions of Marxism to be 'scientific' rather than metaphysical, and then moved on to criticize all pseudo-scientific positivist worldviews for their failure to recognize themselves as metaphysical. He uses arguments from idealism and pragmatism to show that these worldviews represent an extrapolation of the scientific method into a worldview or ontology, and one that is at best partial with many blind spots, and at worst sinister and destructive. He offers an explanation for this extrapolation that combines a phenomenology of science as the necessary moment of the subject's self-forgetting and the object's triumph, with a historical account that links scientism with the success of capitalism. The almost Wittgensteinian approach of seeing science as one language or perspective upon reality among others, which cannot perceive let alone answer questions outside its own territory, is both radical and clever. It saves faith from competing on the same territory as science, a familiar tactic that leaves God and the soul to retreat into the gaps left by science's ignorance. Bulgakov's approach instead argues that they are simply different and incommensurable (although not incompatible in life) orders of looking at reality: 'Even if science could understand the entire universe in mechanistic terms, life would be no more threatened than a landscape's beauty is by maps and surveys' (p. 163). And yet, as we have seen, this does not dissolve Bulgakov's position into purely relativist perspectivism or constructivism. Rather Bulgakov offers an account of a more 'tactful' science which knows its place as the handmaiden of life, not its master. This science is not an idle hobby, but is crucial to the fundamental human task of the transformation and vivification of the world. This transformative practical science is erotic and creative, yet it is grounded in the always already creative divine wisdom, which is the mysterious foundation of the rationality of nature that makes science a possibility. Science reveals this Sophia, and so is truthful without possessing an overview of the totality of truth. Such a science can certainly recognize and even aim for genuine progress, but without being deterministic or capable of irrefutable predictions. This is a vision of science as both pragmatic and ideal, neither dogmatic nor sceptical, and it is founded in a metaphysics of the 'real–ideal', which as such seems to correspond to the logic of the doctrine of the incarnation. In all these ways Bulgakov offers much promise for the development of a more detailed theological philosophy of science today.

References

Sergei Bulgakov, 1979, *Karl Marx as a Religious Type: His Relation to the Religion of Anthropothesism of L. Feuerbach*, ET, Belmont, MA: Notable and Academic Books

Sergei Bulgakov, 1993, *Sophia: The Wisdom of God*, ET, Hudson, NY: Lindisfarne Press

Sergei Bulgakov, 2000, *Philosophy of Economy: The World as Household*, ET, New Haven, CT and London: Yale University Press

Catherine Evtuhov, 1997, *The Cross & the Sickle: Sergei Bulgakov and the Fate of Russian Religious Philosophy, 1890–1920*, Ithaca, NY: Cornell University Press

Notes

1 H. Stuart Hughes' phrase.

2 See Evtuhov 1997, pp. 30–1.

3 This belief, that there is no such thing as a person truly without a religion, and that Marxism and positivism are as much religions as those they condemn, is evident in another of Bulgakov's early essays from 1907: *Karl Marx as a Religious Type* (Bulgakov 1979).

4 All subsequent references to Bulgakov 2000 will be by page number within parentheses in the main body of the chapter.

5 Cf. Heidegger's account of thought as always already 'thrown', and possessing a 'mood'.

6 He gives the example of Bentham's ridiculous attempts to devise a 'moral arithmetic' as particularly illustrative of this mentality.

7 The words are those of Emil du Bois-Reymond. Bulgakov finds similar sentiments in Kant, Pierre Laplace and Thomas Huxley.

8 For a more detailed account of Bulgakov's mature views on sophiology and its relation to other doctrines such as creation, incarnation and the Trinity, see Bulgakov 1993.

PART 2

Theology, Church and Society

6

Proofs and Arguments (2011)

John Hughes argues that 'modern' apologetics often seems at once both too modest and too arrogant. It is too modest in thinking that the question of Christian faith is just another question, about some more 'facts' within an otherwise self-evident world, rather than something that changes the way we think about everything. And it is too arrogant in thinking that we can attain 'proof' of these ultimate matters, as if we could step outside the limitations of our human reason. For Hughes, this modern approach to apologetics is complicit with an ahistorical, uncritical and anti-Christian account of reason. To illustrate this, and help us find a way out of this cul-de-sac, he recounts the history of how we got here, arguing that such narratives and genealogies of thought are an important part of the apologetic task. For Hughes, beyond both modernist foundationalism and postmodern relativism, faith may be incapable of proof in the narrow sense, but it is no less rational for that.[1]

If apologetics is partly about arguing or persuading people to believe the Christian faith, then it is worth stopping first of all to think about what we mean by 'argument', 'proof' and 'persuasion'. This touches on some of the big questions of what is sometimes called 'fundamental theology' or philosophical theology, questions such as: the limits of reason, the nature of faith, arguments for and against the existence of God. For reasons that will become clear in a moment, I would like to explore these questions by way of a little historical story, before leading into some more general contemporary conclusions.

This story begins not so long ago, perhaps twenty or thirty years past. In those days, perhaps especially in the English-speaking world, everyone seemed to have enormous confidence in reason and common sense. Whether they were believers or atheists, they shared a common set of basic assumptions about what was reasonable and so were able to meet each other on this safe, common playground. This made philosophy of religion very easy: you could simply line up arguments for and against questions like the existence of God, the problem of evil and all the rest, and simply make up your own mind on the balance. Down at street level, this overflowed into the more confessional business of popular apologetics. There was quite an industry of popular books of apologetics that aimed to prove the things of faith to ordinary people on the basis of simple rational arguments. If you were Roman Catholic, these things would normally begin from 'natural theology', and the so-called 'proofs' for the existence of God, usually based upon the *quinquae viae*: the five ways of St Thomas Aquinas. Any sensible person could observe motion, causation, contingency, teleology and hierarchies of excellence in creation, and so they could deduce from this their Origin and Goal, *quod omnes dicunt Deus*, 'which everyone calls God' (*Summa Theologiae*, Ia, q. 2, a. 3, rep.). If you were Protestant on the other hand, your apologetics would usually begin by demonstrating the rationality of revelation, whether this was proving the Bible's authority from prophecies that have been fulfilled, or its authenticity from biblical archaeology, or the evidence for the resurrection of Christ, often considered in the manner of a legal trial. Both these traditions can be seen merged in the figure of the former Nolloth Professor of Philosophy of Religion at Oxford University, whose influence continues to be disturbingly widespread. Richard Swinburne famously claims to calculate the statistical probability of the existence of God and the resurrection of Christ (Swinburne 2003, 2004). It is worth pausing to consider this for a moment. This is problematic, to put it mildly, not only in that these calculations clearly fail to resolve the matter (or else why would there still be atheists), but also absurd in suggesting that the existence of God and the resurrection of Christ are things whose probability can be measured like any other ordinary 'thing' in the world, in the same way one might wonder about the existence of an ancient Greek battle or another planet in our solar system, rather than something *much* more fundamental which alters one's entire view of *everything*. Swinburne's efforts, and many similar attempts were of course honourable in intent, building on a long tradition, and various people continue them today (Alvin Plantinga among Protestants, and Scott Hahn among Roman Catholics), but they reached some quite curious and problematic conclusions as we have suggested.

We can trace the origins of this project of proofs back through history to understand where it came from, before we go on to see how it may have run aground. This project of proving the foundations of faith by reason goes back into the nineteenth century, where we find the First Vatican Council affirming on the basis of neo-scholastic philosophy that the existence of God is a truth that can be known by reason unaided by grace or faith. In Anglican circles a similarly confident rationalist natural theology was represented by William Paley's famous analogy of the watch found on the beach, from which one can deduce the existence of a watchmaker, which remained a staple of Anglican textbooks well into the twentieth century. But the project goes back before Pius IX and Paley, enjoying its heyday in the eighteenth century, with such supremely confident rationalists as Leibniz and Wolff, and arguably taking off even earlier, in the seventeenth century with the so-called 'founder of modern philosophy', René Descartes. Descartes famously sat alone in his boiler room, stripping away all potentially doubtable beliefs founded upon traditional authorities such as Scripture or the Church, in order to find a common, neutral, indisputable rational foundation upon which everyone could agree. This 'Cartesian method', of using doubt to find certainty, supposedly born in reaction to the European Wars of Religion, was to become classically modern. This is what people sometimes call 'foundationalism', the quest to find a rational foundation 'behind' all the different views people have, upon which they must all agree (see Toulmin 1992 and Nagel 1986).

The point to be made here is that the project of trying to 'prove' God's existence and the truth of the Christian faith, according to supposedly 'pure' reason, while it might have precursors, is not so ancient as we might think, but actually belongs to this particular philosophical project, which we call modernity and the European Enlightenment, and more specifically to rationalist foundationalism. If this is so, then we might well have good reasons for being more than a little suspicious of its hidden agendas and unseen consequences.

The first thing to note is that it simply does not seem to work. Hume and Kant in the eighteenth century famously spelled out the problems with the cosmological and teleological 'proofs' of God's existence: Why could there not just be an infinite regress? Why does someone have to start causation and motion off? Is it legitimate to argue from patterns within a series to explanations for the entire series itself? The order in the universe is at least as susceptible to being read in terms of organic generation or chance as it is in terms of design. And so on. This debate was summed up by the famous encounter between Bertrand Russell and Fr Frederick Copleston, when Russell insisted that the universe needed no explanation beyond itself but 'just is'. There is nothing to prevent the atheist sidestepping the argument's premises in this way. If these are 'proofs', then they seem to have failed.

The second thing to notice seems to me to be more important for apologetics today, but less frequently commented upon. This is the pernicious consequences of this rationalist foundationalism for faith. It was some of the Romantics in the late eighteenth and early nineteenth century who first noticed that if you made the Christian faith into something that could be proved by reason, one effectively placed reason above faith, belittling faith in the process. In the twentieth century, Karl Barth made a similar point in his attack on natural theology which, he argued, required God's revelation to be squeezed into the meagre categories of our human reason. For this rationalist foundationalism, faith now seems to be characterized as dealing with the most *uncertain* things, rather than the most important. Belief in God is presumed to be self-evident, so no longer requires the will to be combined with the intellect as in ancient accounts of faith, so it is no longer really a free response. Other beliefs, which are still based on faith, such as those deriving purely from revelation, now look rather vulnerable by comparison. Most crucially God himself is reduced to just another, very big 'being' among others, on the same plane as everything else, and subject to the same laws, such as probability. The mysterious timeless, simple, unchanging God of the Fathers and medievals has become the 'Supreme Being' or the 'Ultimate architect' of the eighteenth century rationalists. This rationalist, foundationalist project of proving God's existence has unwittingly smuggled the Christian God out of the back door and replaced him with the cheap imitation god of the deists. Such a *deus ex machina*, a god of the gaps, is largely useless and readily dispensable, so from here it is but a short further step to atheism, to Laplace's famous remark to Napoleon, 'I no longer have need of that hypothesis.' Michael Buckley has brilliantly traced these developments from natural theology through deism to atheism in his book *At the Origins of Modern Atheism* (1990). Much more could be said about this sub-Christian view of God, particularly in relation to the voluntarism that made him seem like a capricious tyrant. It is arguably *this* god, not the Christian God, whom John Robinson wanted to leave behind in his *Honest to God*, and whom Heidegger rejected under the term 'ontotheology'. Some have traced him back before Descartes to Duns Scotus and his doctrine of the univocity of being. But that is another story (see Pickstock 2005).

The point that should be grasped is just that the rationalist project of proofs has sold out the Christian faith to deism and turned the God of Jesus Christ into an idol of human reason. There is a crucial issue here about our fundamental views of the world, which applies just as much to secular worldviews as religious ones: the foundation of one's belief cannot, by its very nature, be based on some other foundation without that becoming the more ultimate instead. So if one proves God on the basis of reason then secretly one establishes reason as the more ultimate foundation and thus the real object of worship. The other consequence of this is that worldviews are essentially incapable of proof, because the only possible premises come from within the system itself. The views themselves determine what would even count as evidence; one's ultimate stance affects the significance of every possible 'fact'. *All* ultimate questions, our positions or existential stances upon them, are therefore suprarational, incapable of proof. They are more than empirical; they are properly hermeneutical, questions of interpretation. How important it is to remind secularists of this, again and again!

But to return to our historical story, foundationalism has not only been rejected in terms of religion, it has now come under considerable attack in all areas of knowledge. Beginning with Nietzsche's attack on the notion of one absolute truth in the nineteenth century, this critique of rationalism has gained strength throughout the twentieth century, first in Continental philosophers such as Heidegger and Derrida, to become mainstream in the last thirty years in what people loosely call 'postmodernism' (see Ward 1997). It is easy to get caught up in debates over definitions here, but if we can see modernism as characterized by the assertion of human freedom and scientific reason against tradition and authority, an era which climaxed with the enthroning of the pagan cult of Reason in Notre-Dame during the French Revolution, then much of this era seems to have come to an end. Now, it seems, the rationalist attempt to establish consensus through an appeal to universal reason has been deconstructed and unmasked as in fact just one particular way of looking at the world (Western, scientific, male, dominating, and so on). Science is no longer the paradigm of all knowledge, and indeed many philosophers of science point out that even science does not have the universal ahistorical certainty that some have pretended for it. All knowledge is embedded in time and space. Our knowledge always begins not with some universal foundation but 'in the middle of things'. So now, the tools of deconstruction, questions such as 'where did these ideas come from?', 'whose interests do they serve?', 'what voices are being silenced here?' are no longer simply used against theology, but are turned back upon the secular rationalism that had attacked it. Theology may be in a strong position here, as the first area of human knowledge to face up to these challenges, the limitations of its own certainty. The ball has now returned to the rationalists' court. We may no longer be able to prove God, but perhaps proof and the particular sort of rationalism that went with it has had its day more generally. We are no longer quite so sure about the infinite progress of the march of reason, sweeping away all other traditions and authorities before its advance.

Does this mean that we are all postmoderns now? Has reason had its day? It sounds like all we are left with is deism, the arbitrary decision, the leap of faith. Some existentialist Christians and Barthian Protestants, and non-realist postmodern theologians such as Don Cupitt, have found they could make themselves at home in the postmodern world in this way, but at what cost? Disturbingly, it sounds as if there can be little point in apologetics, in any discussion and conversation with other people, on this account, because after all everybody has their own particular view and nothing could persuade them to change it. If we cease to believe in rationalism, do we throw out all belief in reason and truth? If so, we are left with nothing but the bleak self-assertion of millions of different perspectives; Nietzsche's will to power. This is the anarchy of complete moral, theological, political and philosophical relativism.

This sort of postmodernism seems after all to be not so different from modernism, just an extension of its basic premise of individualistic freedom to fit with the more extreme forms of consumer capitalism that have developed in the last fifty years or so, as Terry Eagleton and others have argued (Eagleton 1996). It is not surprising then that we treat our worldviews just as we treat everything else, like commodities to be purchased from our global pick 'n' mix and consumed until we grow bored with them. This sort of postmodernism is not only politically sinister, it is also contrary to basic Christian beliefs such as the idea that God is Truth and that the Christian faith is not just a private language, but can and should be shared with everyone. More fundamentally, we can argue that this sort of postmodernism is internally incoherent. Inasmuch as it claims that there are no truths, only perspectives, it reveals the hidden truth that it does actually have its own fundamental belief which positions all the others; and insofar as it still bothers even to engage other positions in dialogue, it shows a commitment to the very possibility of communication and changing one's mind, which can only be understood as a hangover from the belief in something like Truth. We would be foolish to sell out to postmodernism after all.

It is not simply that we can use deconstruction against modernist rationalism, we can also deconstruct the irrationalism of the postmodernists. This was the strategy of Alasdair MacIntyre in his books *After Virtue* (2003) and *Three Rival Versions of Moral Enquiry* (1990). MacIntyre proposes that we take on board the postmodern critique of rationalist foundationalism, but that we should not abandon reason altogether. He points to the practices of the medieval university as embodying a commitment to ultimate truth, mediated through specific socio-historical traditions and authorities, yet precisely because of this belief, open to dialogue with all seekers after truth. In this situation there may no longer be room for proofs, because there are no longer common foundations upon which everyone agrees; the starting points may be many and various. But there is still the possibility of real debates and discussions, more modest and pragmatic arguments, based on the partial and provisional acceptance of certain non-ultimate premises. MacIntyre demonstrates this method in the way he plays the rationalism of the Enlightenment off against the irrationalism of the postmodernists. He has no knock-down proofs against them, but he can employ a complex series of attacks: situating them genealogically, unmasking their agendas and inconsistencies, allowing them to deconstruct themselves and one another. And because we are creatures of flesh and blood rather than pure intelligences, these arguments will persuade us not by some irrefutable logic, but also by all the powers of persuasion, by their goodness and even their beauty. They will be arguments that must be enacted in our lives as well as in our words. But if they are authentic then their rhetoric will persuade by virtue of their *inherent* beauty and goodness, rather than because of some added spin or window-dressing. Form is not accidentally related to content: the medium must fit the message. It may well be that these are the sorts of arguments that will be appropriate for a twenty-first century apologetics: not proofs, but critiques, genealogies and explorations, persuasive and attractive narratives that help us to make sense of our intellectual and cultural situation and inspire us to participate in them. For those today who would be teachers and preachers of faith, we must learn again the importance of rhetoric, and not as mere wordmongering, but as the art of faithfully performing our proclamation of the faith.

Many of the more ancient arguments for the existence of God, whether Anselm's or Aquinas', can be rehabilitated within this more modest rationalism: not as unquestionable proofs, but as arguments that draw out the logic of a certain position or line of thought, that lead people from particular phenomena, such as contingency or degrees of excellence, towards the idea of God. Many have taken Anselm's famous phrase to describe this more modest project of apologetics: *fides quaerens intellectum*, 'faith seeking understanding'. Faith is not completely irrational after all: reason and faith can collaborate together. Faith can deploy a more modest reason in its service, and this more modest reason may well even lead people to faith, without being able to 'establish' it. Indeed, one of the most powerful arguments that might be made in favour of faith is that the common-sense notions of reason that we take for granted are historically derived from and only really make sense in relation to faith in a God who has rationally ordered creation. Nietzsche here can help us see that if people are going to be consistent in abandoning God then perhaps they should abandon belief in truth and goodness as we have known them as well.

Perhaps particularly in the last ten years or so, we have seen a revival of Christian philosophy, of a certain modest Christian rationalism beyond secular rationalism and postmodern irrationalism. The encyclical *Fides et Ratio* can be read in this way, as can the more general revival of interest in metaphysics (see John Paul II 1998, Candler and Cunningham 2007, and Long 2009). Some have even argued that faith and reason belong so closely together that they are more or less indistinguishable: reason is always a certain leap of faith, while faith is always a certain sort of rationality (Milbank 2005). If this is so, then the old boundaries between apologetics and dogmatics begin to fall down. Whereas thirty years ago, we might have been convinced by the postmodern relativists that we had heard the last of apologetics, it now seems that *everything* is apologetics! Christian faith can articulate itself only through an engagement with culture. *All* God-talk, from formal theology, to the liturgical proclamation of the word, to the conversations in pubs and cafes, should be apologetic; not in the sense of establishing common neutral foundations for faith, but in setting forth the Christian faith in a way that engages with, criticizes and responds to the other views that are current in our world, and that is attractive and persuasive in itself.

References

Michael J. Buckley, 1990, *At the Origins of Modern Atheism*, New Haven, CT: Yale University Press

Peter M. Candler Jr and Conor Cunningham (eds), 2007, *Belief and Metaphysics*, London: SCM Press

Andrew Davison (ed.), 2011, *Imaginative Apologetics: Theology, Philosophy and the Catholic Tradition*, London: SCM Press

Terry Eagleton, 1996, *The Illusions of Postmodernism*, Oxford: Blackwell

John Paul II, 1998, *Fides et Ratio*, ET, London: Catholic Truth Society

D. Stephen Long, 2009, *Speaking of God: Theology, Language, and Truth*, Grand Rapids, MI: Eerdmans

Alasdair MacIntyre, 1990, *Three Rival Versions of Moral Enquiry*, Notre Dame, IN: University of Notre Dame Press

Alasdair MacIntyre, 2003 (1981), *After Virtue*, London: Duckworth

John Milbank, 2005, *The Suspended Middle*, London: SCM Press

Thomas Nagel, 1986, *The View from Nowhere*, Oxford: Oxford University Press

Catherine Pickstock, 2005, 'Duns Scotus: His historical and contemporary significance', *Modern Theology*, Vol. 21, Issue 4, October, pp. 543–74

Richard Swinburne, 2003, *The Resurrection of God Incarnate*, Oxford: Clarendon Press

Richard Swinburne, 2004, *The Existence of God*, Oxford: Clarendon Press

Stephen Toulmin, 1992, *Cosmopolis*, Chicago, IL: University of Chicago Press

Graham Ward (ed.), 1997, *The Postmodern God: A Theological Reader*, Oxford: Blackwell

Notes

1 Andrew Davison's abstract in Davison 2011, p. 3.

7

What is Radical Orthodoxy?
With Matthew Bullimore (2002)

Geneses

Radical orthodoxy is not exactly a movement or an ideology. Like any serious political and academic endeavour, it is characterized by a lack of homogeneity among its proponents. It refuses to prescribe answers, and so sustains a certain open-endedness. As a loose association of the like-minded, it can be seen as a common project, both in terms of its origins and its shared concerns.

Radical orthodoxy emerged as an academic intervention into what its proponents saw as a stale theological and philosophical environment. However, it is not a voice from nowhere. It has its roots in the Cambridge theological tradition, with its strongly philosophical emphasis (as opposed to purely systematic or ploddingly biblical approaches). This tradition was shaped by such diverse currents as the Anglican pacifist philosophy of Donald MacKinnon; the postmodern forays of Don Cupitt; the revisionary Thomism of Nicholas Lash; and the work of Rowan Williams, which mixes (among other things) the radical politics of Gillian Rose's Hegel and the conservative patristic and medieval theology of Hans Urs von Balthasar.

Who are the proponents of radical orthodoxy? The intellectual progenitor of radical orthodoxy is John Milbank, a philosophical theologian, now a professor in Nottingham, schooled in intellectual history, who gave up studying for the Anglican priesthood when his tutor, Rowan Williams, persuaded him that his calling was to an academic ministry. Williams also introduced him to von Balthasar's work, whose Christian orthodoxy Milbank found refreshingly akin to postmodern critiques of secular modernity, and yet as providing an opening to be strangely more critical. Milbank's major work develops a critique of the violence inherent in modernity's secular social theories by blending the voices of Alasdair MacIntyre, Gilles Deleuze, Friedrich Nietzsche and St Augustine (Milbank 1990). While at Cambridge, Milbank met Graham Ward, a soft-spoken priest from Manchester, with a background in literary criticism and a doctoral dissertation that suggested likenesses between poststructural linguistics (Jacques Derrida) and an orthodox Christian theology of revelation (Karl Barth). In the early 1990s, Milbank spotted Catherine Pickstock, a doctoral student in liturgy with an interest in philosophy and radical politics, whose first book developed a startling critique of Derrida's reading of the *Phaedrus* and a critical analysis of the non-liturgical politics of modernity (Pickstock 1997).

Along with other sympathetic theological voices and some of their students, in 1999 these three issued an academic manifesto that proclaimed the bankruptcy of the secular and the urgent necessity of the return of the theological afresh (Milbank, Pickstock and Ward 1999). The ripples it caused spanned the Anglo-American theological establishment, provoking both vicious and sympathetic reactions, but never lukewarm and not always considered.

The 'Difference' of Radical Orthodoxy

As indicated by its very name, radical orthodoxy, they insist that only Christian orthodoxy is truly radical. For only here can the root of secularity be reached (after all, it is nothing other than Christian heresy). The unwillingness to ignore paradox allows for a slipperiness, which makes radical orthodoxy difficult to categorize in terms of contemporary positions, be they philosophical, political, or theological, and thus leaves it open to hostility from opposing camps. Liberal theologians object to their obstinate conservatism; while conservative theologians bewail their fraternization with the dangerous continental *rive gauche*.

Is this then just the typical grey fudging characteristic of non-offensive and compromising Anglicans? Radical orthodoxy proclaims that theological mediation, rather than mere positivism or crude dialectics, is the only critical position – a conviction instantiated in their unapologetic rhetoric of critique and persuasion. This rhetorical strategy is employed to proclaim their common convictions regarding: 1) the diagnosis of modernity/postmodernity; 2) philosophical dualisms; 3) radical politics; and 4) the Christian theological tradition.

These convictions are as follows:

1. Is the project modern or postmodern? Or, in terms of philosophy, is it more indebted to Descartes or Nietzsche? Perhaps neither, because it is critical of 'modernists' while employing 'postmodernist' arguments. Yet, the proponents of radical orthodoxy are not simply postmodernists in the usual sense, because ultimately they regard postmodernism to be merely an undesirable intensification of modernism, with all the same problems. Likewise, the project could not be categorized as either naive realism or anti-realism, either crude rationalism or anti-rationalism. Neither the obsession with order nor the celebration of chaos, neither absolute homogeneity nor arbitrary relativist flux, neither spurning of the flesh nor its orgiastic divinization will suffice. The modern and the postmodern are united in their secularity and capitalist logic.

2. Deconstructing 'dualisms': Radical orthodoxy frequently employs a conscious strategy of resisting familiar modernist oppositions by seeking to expose their 'secret' dialectical identity and common foundation. This is evident particularly in its approach to the relation between reason and faith. Here, it rejects *both* the rational 'proofs' of theism, and blind fideism, *or* some sort of two-tier compromise that keeps them both hermetically sealed from one another, yet operating in parallel. If anything, this is *the* distinctive and original strategy of radical orthodoxy, which leads to its endlessly interdisciplinary 'parasitic' style. This strategy is based on a rejection of the idea of the 'secular', that is, an inert, value-free realm of the *factum*, somehow imagined as subsisting outside any relation to God, autonomous and self-defining. Instead, radical orthodoxy believes that *everything* that exists mediates transcendence and always exceeds itself. This is not, however, an original insight, but rather an attempt to think through the consequences of Henri de Lubac's revolutionary work on grace and nature (for example, de Lubac 1984). Nor could it be wholly original, for the project is radical in its commitment to the roots of the tradition. Yet, for it to be *orthodox* it has to proclaim the Christian *logos* anew, made strange once again. Thus, this antipathy to entrenched dualisms is further extended. For example, there is no dualism of body and soul; no priority of the modern subject or the premodern object; no possibility of the theocratic, for there can be no coercive *dominium* of the *ecclesia* over and above a semi-autonomous and manipulable extra-theological *saeculum*.

3. This rejection of the secular is motivated by a radical political concern manifest in a definite commitment to Christian socialism. But not the recent *pastiche* of socialism offered in England by the centralized, technocratic, Blairite 'Third Way'. Instead, this political concern is enhanced by a rediscovery of the organic and aesthetic dimension of social and political life through the vision of a liturgical *polis*, in the face of the dehumanizing processes of modern mechanization. A sustained critique of mainstream secular liberal political thought, with its language of formal democracy, rights, and property, underwriting the violence of capitalism, has characterized the project throughout.[1] This political radicalism rests on the adoption of two strategies: genealogical reconstruction, and the retrieval of a metaphysical vision alien to metaphysics in its decadent modern guise.

a. Genealogy: This historical and cultural approach provides a truly radical angle, yielding a more fundamental critique of the most basic assumptions usually taken for granted. Two genealogies are blended: the standard Left critique of the Cartesian legacy, and the von Balthasar-influenced Catholic recognition that this critique must extend further back to the theological problems inherent in late medieval nominalism and voluntarism. Radical orthodoxy mourns the loss of the participatory metaphysics of Aquinas, which was abandoned in favour of the representational account of language in William of Ockham, and the wilful God of Duns Scotus. The advent of nominalism and voluntarism opened up the horizons of the project of modernity, culminating in the Fichtean *ego*, the abyss of the Kantian *Ding-an-sich*, and the textual nihilism of poststructuralism – all of which inevitably dissolve into apolitical nihilistic construals of the world in their common denial of the theological. Radical orthodoxy offers instead, not a nostalgic romantic reaction, but a 'resuming the thread' with the help of a counter-modern repressed romantic tradition. The patristic and medieval tradition is wedded to the best in Luther, Kierkegaard, the meta-critiques of Hamann and Jacobi, and the tradition of Christian socialism opened up in various ways by S. T. Coleridge, F. D. Maurice, and J. H. Newman.

b. Metaphysics: Radical orthodoxy is committed to philosophy after its rejection by postmodernists and pietists, so offering a more radical critique. This includes a rehabilitation of the Platonic legacy (which is seen to be not about dualism or totalitarian rationalism, but rather a mystic moral realism) and in particular its Christian form after Dionysius the Areopagite. This recovery of metaphysics emphasizes: the priority of *ekstasis* without loss in any authentic theological anthropology; apophaticism as a recognition of the transcendence of the divine and the objectifying hubris of any self-present account of rational meaning; participation as the key to an analogical understanding of the suspension of the material always from a donating transcendent source; and St Augustine's theory of evil as the *privatio boni*, such that there can be no positivist or deterministic account of evil. Such doctrinal and philosophical renewal, however, cannot be regarded as a simple hankering after the lost Eden of the Middle Ages. Indeed, this theological cosmology is seen through the lens of the contemporary, radically linguistic worldview, offering a new rendering of the Christian narrative free from the essentialist problems of the premodern metaphysics of substance, and open to the ubiquity of the cultural in the present.

These genealogical and metaphysical strategies lead to a return to the Christian tradition, especially as embodied in the thought of St Augustine, St Gregory of Nyssa, St Anselm, and St Thomas Aquinas. The best of contemporary scholarship on such thinkers is combined with a respect for the living tradition that thus refuses a simple conservatism. Indeed, these thinkers are read in novel ways: thus, St Augustine is seen as neither a proto-Cartesian, nor a Calvinist obsessed with sin, flesh and fear; and St Thomas does not appear as an Aristotelian rationalist whose theological preoccupations are subordinated to a philosophical starting point.

The Shape of a Non-Systematic 'Systematics'

The radically orthodox approach to key Christian doctrines has yielded insights into traditional themes of Christian dogmatics. These insights form no mere descriptive encyclopedic systematics, but follow from the political realization that theology must, to be theology, open the possibility of living a truly ethical life. Such insights include:

1. The Trinity: Radical orthodoxy has assisted the recovery of the Eastern concept of *epektasis* in which God is not to be seen as an infinite positive quantity, but as forever ecstatically giving more and more. This is a dynamic God of depths unknown, whose beauty makes a mockery of the sterile God of Scotus who marks the infinite point of extension within a univocity of being. Moreover, a 'linguistic' interpretation of

the Trinitarian relations occasions an emphasis on the temporal mediation and interpretation of the *logos*, now also embodied as *ecclesia*, back to the Father by the power of the indwelling Spirit. This is allied to a 'relational substantive' model of Trinitarian personhood that subverts both a bland social Trinity and a now troubled ontology predicated on natures and substances. Finally, radical orthodoxy rejects a two-tier, immanent-economic Trinity, such that God is only as he presents himself in and through the cultural and material processes of life (in the sense in which Engels would render the material: social, political, religious and economic). In short, God is cultural. Not reducible to culture, but only understandable through its mediations.

2. Christology: A 'high' Christology of the cosmic Christ as *logos* is allied to the necessity of the particularity of the humanity of Jesus of Nazareth. Indeed, *this* Jesus Christ presents a unique scandal as *the* exception to human norms. Christ is the *homo sacer* rejected by all forms of the human *socius*, be it the Roman *imperium*, the Herodian tribal monarchy or the democratic mob. Christ's kingdom as first proclaimed is Other and opened through Christ's non-identical return in resurrection *despite* human sin. This returned body of Christ is transfigured and requires a thinking through of the dispersal and proliferation of the now various analogical bodies of Christ, and in so doing subverts essentialism. The Church as the multigendered body of Christ is analogically related to individual, social and political bodies, and feeds on the eucharistic body of Christ. Responding to postmodern discussions of 'lack', radical orthodoxy also provides a new interpretation of *kenosis* Christology. Here, the procession of the Son from the Father, and the Spirit from the Son and Father, opens up difference through an unqualified giving.

3. Atonement: Christ's 'sacrifice' is seen as the end to all sacrifice, subverting a traditional logic of sacrifice in which a part is given up in lieu of the whole. Christ is returned as Christ, scarred but transfigured and whole. The scars only persist as a sign that evil has effects which are simply absurd. The scars are healed, for in God there is no evil or knowledge of evil. Instead, an ontological priority of the Good implies that evil is always reactionary, and good is always a continuation of what has always been (against all masochistic ethical systems, be they liberal or Levinasian).

4. Ethics: A radical ethical vision has been a constant component of the project of radical orthodoxy, emphasizing resurrection over and above either the positivism of death (as in Blanchot and Derrida) or

a secular vitalism (as found within liberal discourses). Beauty and the particular are set against the empty legal universalism of the Kantian legacy; similarly, *eros* and *agape* are set over and against either Kant's notion of duty or the place of the accusation of the wholly Other in the Levinasian and Derridean tradition. Yet, radical orthodoxy does not replace these concepts with a Left-bank dandyism, nor does it have recourse to a postmodern fascination, after Bataille, with a Dionysian abandonment to a chaotic flux now read as 'festival.' Instead, radical orthodoxy has sought to point towards a joyful socialism based on the freely given gift, against so many theologies that have sought to hypostasize a notion of the tragic. Ethics stands at the centre of the project, for here the political, the social and the aesthetic all coalesce theologically.

5. Ecclesiology: Following Stanley Hauerwas, the Church is seen as both intrinsically political and ethical. The Church is part of a narrative that uniquely seeks peacefulness and refuses coercion. The Church must use persuasion and innate credibility to present itself in a postmodern marketplace, standing or falling on how beautifully it narrates itself. With the collapse of the rational justification of any metanarrative, theology, *like any other discourse*, can only present itself persuasively. Unlike any other discourse, however, theology has at its heart an ontology of peace. Only theology can truly subsume difference without either exalting the same or hypostasizing otherness and difference. It does this by providing the spatio-temporal analogy of a musical consensus (after St Augustine) in which difference is harmoniously related through time. This peaceable kingdom subverts the violence of other discursive articulations and, following the traditional convertibility of the classical transcendentals, the most beautiful vision is, of course, also the most truly good.

6. Eucharist: Radical orthodoxy has developed a sacramental semiotics, and this is essential as it informs and lies at the heart of Christian practice. In the performance of the eucharistic mysteries, Christ promises that this bread is his body, and that this cup is filled with his blood. Belief in this reference allows for a faith in all representation. However, this is a semiotics with depth that embraces presence and absence. God is at once the God who draws near in the Eucharist, satisfying man's desire, and the God whose apparent absence is a drawing away that opens up the space of relation and provokes further desire.

7. Eschatology: Ends remain as problematic as beginnings in much recent philosophy and critical theory. Radical orthodoxy does not

espouse the utopian dialectics of Marx or Hegel, or an existentialist absolutizing of the present moment, or the ennui of Beckett's eternally unfulfilled *Waiting for Godot*. Instead, it seeks to think a partially realized eschatology, which always exceeds prediction. It works within the purview of a determinate end that will come but is still not yet, and so must be constantly re-imagined. The resurrection of the body remains central to the radically orthodox vision, for here is found the irreducibility of the particular within the realization of perfect community, and also the retention of transfigured materiality in all its depth as that originally created as good. Radical orthodoxy holds to the hope of *apocatastasis*, in which all is eventually redeemed. With eschatological community comes the prayer for and prayers of the dead, the interrelation of the analogically coextensive bodies of the Church, the intertwining of the eternal and the temporal (where the latter, as suffused with a dynamic ethical 'density' is, after all, simply the image of the eternal).

Future

As Christian practice, radical orthodoxy is an ongoing project. It is also relatively new, as are the projects of the main proponents. In time it will pass away as new and stranger practices of the Christian *logos* further those practices that attempt now, with integrity and vitality, to live theologically. The reception of radical orthodoxy is also ongoing. Radical orthodoxy has injected new life into theological debates, attracting criticisms from liberals and conservatives, from modern realists and apparently postmodern non-realists. It has, however, also attracted the interest of others seeking a way out of the postmodern impasse that infects the present. Radical orthodoxy has used and furthered the insights gleaned from so many other currents of thought, and can only gain from an active engagement with other projects. Despite its sometimes rhetorical belligerence, it proclaims no hubristic ownership of truth. It is to be hoped that radical orthodoxy may again reinvent itself in relation to other projects that seek a rejection of the secular, and by so doing remain faithful to the logic of the Christian *logos*.[2]

References

Daniel M. Bell, Jr, 2001, *Liberation Theology After the End of History: The Refusal to Cease Suffering*, London and New York: Routledge

Stephen D. Long, 2000, *Divine Economy: Theology and the Market*, London and New York: Routledge

Henri de Lubac, 1984 (1980), *A Brief Catechesis on Nature and Grace*, ET, San Francisco: Ignatius Press

John Milbank, 1990, *Theology and Social Theory*, Oxford: Blackwell

John Milbank, Catherine Pickstock and Graham Ward (eds), 1999, *Radical Orthodoxy: A New Theology*, London and New York: Routledge

Kyle Nicholas, 2015, 'The Progress and Future of Radical Orthodoxy', 22 October, www.telospress.com/the-progress-and-future-of-radical-orthodoxy/

Catherine Pickstock, 1997, *After Writing, On the Liturgical Consummation of Philosophy*, Oxford: Blackwell

Notes

1 This has more recently been extended by the attempts of D. Stephen Long and Daniel M. Bell, in the series of volumes under the banner of radical orthodoxy, to offer a friendly critique of liberation theology, where they deepen its theological and psychological sophistication and help prevent its collapse in the daunting face of the apparent global triumph of the market (Bell 2001; Long 2000).

2 (Nicholas (2015) offers a short (and positive) assessment of the 'progress' of radical orthodoxy over the years since our article was written in 2002 and looks as we did to its future prospects. He praises its present diversity and also its critical influence.)

8

Anglicanism as Integral Humanism: A de Lubacian Reading of the Church of England[1] (2013)

Background: What is 'Anglicanism' and why should one think of it in terms of 'integralism'?

I should start with a confession: I've always been rather suspicious of the study of Anglicanism. This is not because I'm a post-denominationalist, who thinks that such distinctions are no longer of any importance; nor because I'm the sort of Ultra-Catholic that in Eric Mascall's famous poem of the same name regards the Church of England as in 'heresy and schism'; nor because I'm simply uninterested in the history and traditions of my own Church. On the contrary in fact, I would be more likely to find myself as something of a 'militant Anglican' (if this is not an oxymoron) in relation to these three positions, all of which can be found within the Church of England itself.[2] My scepticism about Anglican studies is rather because my ecclesiology precisely *as* an Anglican means that I don't think being an Anglican is something of ultimate significance.

I am particularly sceptical of the view, unsurprisingly widespread in secular discourse but also more common in Anglican churches outside England and Wales, which sees Anglicanism in denominationalist and confessional terms, as a particular 'brand' of Christianity. Such a view normally says that 'Anglicanism' was invented in the sixteenth century as a state Church which would embody a pragmatic compromise between more conservative and radical elements of the Reformation. According to this view, being an Anglican is often identified with Erastian latitudinarianism, with pragmatic compromise, with the addition of Reason to Protestant Scripture and Catholic Tradition in its sources of authority. It is also identified with a certain doctrinal light-weightedness, whether this is viewed positively as inclusion and tolerance, or negatively as fuzziness. But this is seriously to betray our own ecclesiology. To be an Anglican is not the same as being a Lutheran or a Calvinist, nor to idealize one rather Machiavellian moment, however significant, in our own history. As the name itself indicates, we are not a Church defined by a confession or founder, but by geography and culture. In the words of *The Revised Catechism* of 1962, 'The Church of England is the ancient Church of this land, catholic and reformed. It proclaims and holds fast the doctrine and ministry of the One Holy Catholic and Apostolic Church.' (*The Revised Catechism* 1962, §19) The Church of England understands herself to be simply that, and to teach no peculiar doctrines of her own, but simply the universal Christian faith as she has received it. Anglicanism is then in relation to being Christian not like Leninism is to Socialism, but more like French in relation to literature, Creole in relation to cuisine, or more obviously Greek Orthodox in relation to Christianity. Such a position can help us I think in understanding the complexity of Anglicanism, because it is an evolving historical tradition, which can be read in different ways, rather than a fixed essence. Similarly this position enables us to understand its relationship to other Christian traditions in a properly ecumenical fashion. For, if the Church of England has no peculiar doctrine that is essentially its own, then it is both free to learn from other Christian traditions, and also to offer the particular insights of its own historical experience to other churches.

This is all by way of methodological preface to say that, when I speak of Anglicanism I am speaking in this way of a historical tradition, open to various interpretations, rather than some fixed denominationalist essence. I shall return to this at the end. The claim of this paper is that the category of 'integral humanism', drawn from the debates of mid-twentieth century Roman Catholicism is surprisingly helpful in making sense of certain distinctive features of the Anglican tradition, or at least some of its prominent strands. In this paper I will give a brief account of the origin and meaning of the phrase 'integral humanism' drawing on Henri Cardinal de Lubac, but also looking at Jacques Maritain, before moving on to see how this category might be used to interpret a number of key theological writers in the Anglican tradition and whether there might be deeper significant reasons for this, which tell us something about Anglicanism.

Before I do that, however, I think it's only fair to explain how I came to this rather strange proposal. Twenty years ago the name Henri de Lubac was not particularly well known in Anglophone theological circles, especially outside the Roman Catholic Church. The fact that this has changed, with him now having an entire article devoted to him in recent editions of David Ford's *Modern Theologians* (the ultimate test of becoming mainstream in British theology ...) and introductory guides to his work appearing, not to mention many articles, is in no small part due to the attention given to him by John Milbank, who has claimed that the account of theology and philosophy, faith and reason, which is at the heart of the radical orthodoxy project is a development of de Lubac's account of nature and grace. Milbank offers a few hints here and there as to why such an account of nature and grace might particularly appeal to Anglicans of a catholic sensibility. While I do not wish to discuss radical orthodoxy further here, this was how I got onto the scent of this idea, which I originally experimented with in relation to Anglican social thought and am only now attempting to extend to Anglicanism more generally.

What is meant by 'integral humanism'?

For the origins of this phrase we must go back to 1930s France and to another figure, whose works were rapidly translated into English and as such have had a much longer reception in Anglican thought, the lay Roman Catholic philosopher and theologian Jacques Maritain.[3] Maritain was, as you probably know, a convert to Catholicism, influenced by Charles Péguy and Henri Bergson, who advocated a renewed Thomism. In his work *Humanisme Integral*, translated into English as 'true humanism', written in 1935–6, Maritain developed an account of integral humanism as a proposal for the renewal of Christianity in the light of the contemporary historical and social situation. What is perhaps particularly striking here is that the category of integral humanism is developed largely in response to external challenges to Christianity, especially in response to the atheist and socialist humanisms of Nietzsche and Marx. Maritain develops a particular genealogy of modernity and the Christian origins of the humanist rejection of Christianity in order to argue for a renewal of Christianity that both criticizes these secular humanisms and also embraces all that is true in their positions.

'Integral' here is being used by Maritain primarily in contrast to a secular naturalist humanism which, according to his perspective is truncated or distorted by excluding the spiritual element of human nature and its transcendent goals. Maritain notes that for many the very idea of humanism is fundamentally opposed to religion which, according to Ludwig Feuerbach and others, debases the human through dependence and idealist projection. Instead Maritain argues that the springs of Western humanism are both classical and Christian and, because the order of medieval Christendom was 'of unity of flesh and spirit, a regime of incarnate spirituality', it embodied a 'virtual and implicit humanism' (Maritain 1996, p. 154). Humanist ideas of 'human dignity, of liberty and of disinterested values' are a 'heritage of ideas and sentiments once Christian but today little loved' but which are therefore ripe for being reintegrated, or brought back to the fount of truth. This integral humanism will have 'no standards in common with "bourgeois" humanism' and will be 'all the more human because it does not worship man' (p. 155). Integral humanism, for Maritain, is not anthropocentric, but a 'theocentric humanism, rooted where man has his roots ... [the] humanism of the Incarnation' (p. 197). According to Maritain's genealogy, the attempt to enthrone humanity without God over the last five centuries in the West has had the opposite effect of destroying the human. Anthropocentric humanism is a contradiction that deconstructs itself into pure naturalism.

While 'integral humanism' is for Maritain understood primarily against secular, naturalistic, anthropocentric humanism, yet there are also indications that something further is intended by the idea of 'integralism' which corresponds to a particular position within intra-Christian theological debates on grace and freedom. For Maritain, naturalism and anthropocentric humanism are the outworking of a series of mistaken positions in these debates. Once the classical orthodox position, which holds onto the paradox of divine grace and human freedom, breaks down then human agency seems to be in competition with divine agency so that one can only secure the value of the human by denigrating the divine. If on the contrary the classical view is held then the only true humanism will be a theocentric, integral humanism; integral, that is, precisely because the human and divine are *integrally* related rather than extrinsically or dualistically opposed. Integralism is not therefore simply the name for a theological as opposed to secular anthropology, it also describes a particular account of the relationship between the human and the divine, grace and nature, from which many other things follow, such as particular accounts of the relation between faith and reason and the Church and the world. The connection between these two senses of integralism is clear for Maritain: non-integral, extrinsicist or dualist accounts of the relationship between God and humanity pave the way for anthropocentric humanism and ultimately for naturalism.

Integralist understandings of the human and divine break down in the medieval period according to Maritain, so that both Protestant and modern Catholic positions reflect, in different ways, this new dualism. For Protestantism the doctrine of total corruption means that human nature and freedom are understood as essentially nothing. Maritain sees Karl Barth as repeating the mistake of Luther and Calvin in thinking that 'grace does not vivify' (p. 196). For Catholic Molinism on the other hand there is a semi-Pelagian human initiative prior to grace, leading to a 'Christian naturalism' for which grace is 'a simple ornament capping nature', a sort of 'supernatural varnish' (p. 165). From here it is a short step until 'grace has been reabsorbed in nature' and we are left with a *'freedom without grace'* (pp. 165–6). In both cases an integralist perspective has been replaced by an extrinsicist and dualistic one. Maritain sums up the alternative to integralism with bitter sarcasm: 'Thus, by a sagacious division of labour which the Gospel has not foreseen, the Christian will be able to serve two masters at once, God for heaven and Mammon for the earth' (p. 166). If Calvin and Molina represent the anti-integralist or even 'Manichaean' theologies of grace and freedom, it is, unsurprisingly, to Thomas Aquinas that Maritain looks for the resources for an integralist alternative, a *'rehabilitation of the creature in God'* (p. 198). This is not simply a reactionary project of reconstruction, for this integralism will be 'progressive', a 'new humanism', a 'deeper synthesis' (pp. 195, 198, 199). Building upon the Thomist principle that 'man is at once a natural and a supernatural being' with one natural–supernatural end, this new integral humanism will draw out fresh aspects of the mystery of how created freedom is 'traversed, imbued even to its slightest actualization by [God's] creative causality' (pp. 158, 199). This is the basis for Maritain's claim that 'that which I call integral humanism is capable of saving and of promoting, in a synthesis fundamentally different, all the truths affirmed or glimpsed by socialist humanism, by uniting them in an organic and vital manner with numerous other truths' (p. 208). 'Christian humanism, integral humanism', he says, 'is capable of assuming all, because it knows that God has no opposite' (p. 210). It is worth noting the metaphysical non-dualism underlying this argument, and that Maritain's position here resists being characterized as straightforwardly conservative or liberal. Maritain proceeds to develop an account of the unity in distinction of spiritual and temporal authorities and realms in a 'new Christendom', which I have described in more detail elsewhere (see Chapter 9).

Maritain has moved then from using the phrase 'integral humanism' to describe a 'theocentric humanism' opposed to atheistic humanism, towards using 'integralism' to speak of a particular theological anthropology, with an integralist account of grace and nature, opposed to more dualistic and extrinsicist versions found among such diverse groups as medieval Averroists, early modern Cartesians, Calvinists and Molinists. This is the sense of integral humanism that we find in Henri de Lubac's writings, although as with Maritain it is clear that this account of grace and nature and all that flows from it is developed in dialogue with atheist humanism. In his *Catholicisme* of 1937, de Lubac uses 'integral humanism' in the sense of a theocentric humanism opposed to an atheistic humanism, yet the work as a whole offers an account of the Church as truly 'catholic', unfolding through history to embrace the entire world, a sign of the unity which God desires for the human race (de Lubac 1988, pp. 353–6). We can see here an integralist account of the relationship between the Church and the world, opposing more Manichaean views in ways that will become very influential at the Second Vatican Council. In his 1946 book *Surnaturel*, de Lubac developed a more technical and radical theological and philosophical account of this integralist position on the supernatural, grace and nature, building upon the philosophy of Maurice Blondel and including the controversial claims that there is no pure nature and that Thomas Cajetan and Francisco Suárez misread Aquinas on this question. The censuring of de Lubac on suspicion of modernism that followed, before his subsequent rehabilitation, makes it clear that integralism was not only opposed to atheist humanism, Molinism and Calvinism, but that it also stood in opposition to much of the dominant Leonine Thomism of the early twentieth century with its 'two-tier' account of the relationship between grace and nature. Thus despite Maritain's invocation of Aquinas as the integralist theologian par excellence, it became clear with de Lubac that this was a more Platonic–Dionysian Aquinas than the early modern Aristotelian reading provided by Suárez and Cajetan, for whom grace does come to seem like an ornamental varnish in its extrinsic relation to nature.

De Lubac's vindication came with the Second Vatican Council, which can I think not implausibly be described as the integralist Council. De Lubac was one of the theological advisors at the Council and along with others played a significant role in shaping the dogmatic constitution on the Church (*Lumen Gentium*, Paul VI 1964) and the pastoral constitution on the Church in the modern world (*Gaudium et Spes*, Paul VI 1965). His considerable influence has been acknowledged by Hans Urs von Balthasar and Joseph Ratzinger. Key theological claims of these documents from the Council reflect an integralist account of the Church in the world: 'the Church is in Christ like a sacrament or as a sign and instrument both of a very closely knit union with God and of the unity of the whole human race' (Paul VI 1964, 1:1). Or again, variously:

All men are called to be part of this catholic unity of the people of God which in promoting universal peace presages it. And there belong to or are related to it in various ways, the Catholic faithful, all who believe in Christ, and indeed the whole of mankind, for all men are called by the grace of God to salvation. (Paul VI 1964, 2:13)

The joys and the hopes, the griefs and the anxieties of the men of this age, especially those who are poor or in any way afflicted, these are the joys and hopes, the griefs and anxieties of the followers of Christ. Indeed, nothing genuinely human fails to raise an echo in their hearts. (Paul VI 1965, Pref.: 1)

The Church holds that the recognition of God is in no way hostile to man's dignity, since this dignity is rooted and perfected in God. (Paul VI 1965, I:1:21)

The truth is that only in the mystery of the incarnate Word does the mystery of man take on light. (Paul VI 1965, I:1:22)

The Church ... goes forward together with humanity and experiences the same earthly lot which the world does. She serves as a leaven and as a kind of soul for human society as it is to be renewed in Christ and transformed into God's family ... The earthly and the heavenly city penetrate one another ... The Church believes that she can contribute greatly toward making the family of man and its history more human. (Paul VI 1965, I:4:40)

Christians, on pilgrimage toward the heavenly city, should seek and think of these things which are above. This duty in no way decreases, rather it increases, the importance of their obligation to work with all men in the building of a more human world. (Paul VI 1965, II:2:57)

The Gospel of Christ constantly renews the life and culture of fallen man. (Paul VI 1965, II:2:58)

It is worth noting the ambiguity of this integralist position of Vatican II: some have read this celebration of the human as an uncritical embrace of secular humanism, whether this is seen as positive by liberals, or disastrous, as by ultra-conservative Roman Catholics. But surely a more faithful interpretation is provided by Rowan Williams in his address to the Synod of Roman bishops in 2012, echoing similar claims made by Pope Benedict. Williams speaks of a 'renewal of Christian anthropology' at the Council which 'in place of an often strained and artificial neo-scholastic account of how grace and nature were related in the constitution of human beings ... built [instead] on the greatest insights of a theology that had returned to earlier and richer sources – the theology of spiritual geniuses like Henri de Lubac' to proclaim that 'the Catholic and Christian faith is a "true humanism", to borrow a phrase from another genius of the last century, Jacques Maritain' (Williams 2012, §3). Williams goes on to spell out that this is not to give up on evangelization in favour of humanization, because for integral humanism there can be no humanization separate from Christ, for 'to be fully human is to be recreated in the image of Christ's humanity' (Williams 2012, §4, 5).

In what sense is the Church of England characterized by an 'Integral Humanism'?

I have spent more time than I ought trying to explain what I mean by 'integral humanism'; Rowan Williams provides a good point to turn to the Church of England to see what currency such an idea might have here and how it might fit or illuminate some of our practices and traditions. Part of the problem with asking if the Church of England can be characterized by 'integral humanism' relates to my initial claim that the Church of England is not defined by any one confession or figure, so to make a claim such as this runs the risk of being as generalizing and impossible to establish as making claims about the particular character of English literature. It will necessarily involve selecting certain examples from our traditions that hopefully have an informally canonical status, as well as making some very provisional observations about our organizational life and practices. I am not claiming that every Anglican is an integral humanist, indeed many counter-examples could be found, including Anglican Calvinists, neo-scholastics, and semi-Pelagian latitudinarians such as William Paley. I am claiming that there is at least a strong, perhaps dominant, tradition of integral humanism in the Church of England. I am also not claiming that this is something uniquely Anglican; as we've seen I think that it characterizes large swathes of Christianity, both historically and today. Despite my initial comments about the Church of England not coming into existence in the sixteenth century, my examples are drawn from the post-Reformation Church, although as will hopefully emerge, these examples are chosen because they embody a continuity with an earlier and more universal tradition. Indeed in relation to the Church of England's unusual ecumenical position as in its own words 'catholic and reformed', I want to suggest that this may be one reason why, along with the Orthodox Churches, the 'integral humanism' of the patristic period is less obscured by the post-Reformation polemics on grace and freedom that Maritain and de Lubac describe. If this is so then one relatively peculiar feature of the Church of England as being a *via media* between Rome and Geneva can be understood as something fruitful, as Eric Mascall suggested, not in the sense of pragmatic compromise, but rather in terms of holding onto some of the paradoxes of orthodoxy (Mascall 1956, pp. xi–xiii).

In order to try and illustrate this claim I will turn first to a number of key texts to look at the doctrinal hearts of the integralist question: the doctrine of creation and anthropology with its consequent account of grace and human nature and freedom. The thirty-nine articles may seem a surprising place to begin, not least because they are often seen as part of the high-tide mark of Calvinism in the Church of England. However, notwithstanding my earlier comment about the Church of England not being a confessional Church, we must recognize that these articles were the expression of the resolution of that time of upheaval that led to our being a Church that is 'reformed as well as catholic', so that they continue to be a significant part of our theological inheritance. I think we can discern here in articles 9 to 14, something approaching an integralist account of grace and freedom in the form of a minimalist reformed restatement of the Catholic Augustinian-Thomist position against both the Calvinist view and the late medieval semi-Pelagian, proto-Molinist reading of Aquinas which was used to justify the Roman theology of works.

According to Oliver O'Donovan's interpretation, article 9 on original sin takes a clearly anti-Pelagian view, even if it reflects the late medieval theological worldview which 'had lost its hold on a strong doctrine of creation, the belief in the primordial goodness of all nature' and thus 'was careless about defining itself against tendencies towards Manichaeism', without actually becoming Manichaean (O'Donovan 2011, pp. 70–1). Beyond this, article 10 on free will, in insisting that 'we have no power to do good works pleasaunt and acceptable to God, without the grace of God by Christ preventyng us, that we may have a good wyll, and working with us, when we have that good wyll' is affirming – in a thoroughly Christological integralist way – the Thomist doctrine that grace is not purely juridical or extrinsic, but rather vivifies both as 'prevenient' and 'cooperative'. Here, according to O'Donovan, Cranmer draws 'on the tradition of Saint Thomas to ward off the influence of late medieval voluntarism on the one hand and early Calvinist predestinarianism on the other' (O'Donovan 2011, pp. 73–4). Likewise articles 11 to 14 on justification and good works, even if their emphases are clearly reformed, can be understood in an integralist way as rejecting the proto-Molinist position of good 'works done before the grace of Christ' in favour of a thoroughly Christological account of grace. Similarly article 17 refuses the language of double predestination, insisting that 'predestination to lyfe, is the everlastyng purpose of God'.

Moving on from the articles of Cranmer and Parker to the writings of perhaps the defining Anglican theologian of the post-Reformation period, Richard Hooker, we find a similar conservative integralism in relation to soteriology and more explicitly in relation to creation. In book 5 of *The Laws of Ecclesiastical Polity* we find what Rowan Williams calls 'a beautifully lucid summary of patristic Christological teaching, designed to bring out as fully as possible the fact that the incarnation is not an isolated fact about Jesus but the ground for a renewing of the entire human race' which is a 'renewing, not a total alteration of human nature' (Williams 2004, p. 27). In the context of developing his sacramental theology Hooker offers a more positive account of creation than the articles, as well as stressing the vivifying nature of grace in Christ, and the integral relation of Christ to creation and the Church. 'All other things that are of God have God in them and he them in himself likewise', we are told, so that 'he likewise actually is *in them*, the assistance and influence of his Deity is *their life*' (V:56:5.

Hooker 1907, pp. 226–7). Not only is God integrally related to creation in this way, but similarly so is Christ to the Church: 'Christ is whole with the whole Church', so that 'the life which we live according to godliness is his' (V:56:10. Hooker 1907, p. 232). This is not purely something extrinsic or juridical, because 'we participate Christ partly by imputation ... partly by habitual and real infusion' (V:56:1. Hooker 1907, p. 232). Others have written or are writing about the language of participation and deification in Hooker, but hopefully from these brief glimpses you can see something of the outlines of a recognizably integralist rather than dualistic account of Christology, soteriology, anthropology and creation in this most Anglican of authors, where nature is always already oriented towards supernatural grace and where grace does not destroy nature but fulfils and perfects it.[4]

We can also detect here something of how these doctrinal positions might be reflected in a particular piety and sensibility which could be seen as characteristically Anglican: a sense of all creation being in God and God being in all creation, through Christ. One final brief example from the period of classical Anglicanism can illustrate this. As Rowan Williams notes again, the poems of George Herbert indicate a rejection of the view that 'God can only be honoured by a kind of dishonouring of the human' (Williams 2004, p. 71). In 'Providence' he writes,

> thou art in all things one, in each thing many
> for thou art infinite in one and all

while 'Love (III)' suggests an integralist account of the relationship between creation and redemption: 'Who made the eyes but I?' Likewise in 'The Pulley' Herbert develops an image of humanity as the only creature who naturally desires a supernatural end, manifest in our restlessness:

> When God at first made man,
> Having a glass of blessings standing by
> ...

> ...
> When almost all was out, God made a stay,
> Perceiving that, alone of all his treasure,
> Rest in the bottome lay.

For if I should, said he,
Bestow this jewell also on my creature,
He would adore my gifts instead of me,
and rest in Nature, not the God of Nature:
So both should losers be.

These examples of an 'integral humanism' in classically Anglican authors have been all too few and underdeveloped, but I think a similar case could be made in relation to, for example, Thomas Traherne, John Wesley, S. T. Coleridge, John Keble, John Henry Newman, F. D. Maurice, B. F. Westcott, Michael Ramsey, C. S. Lewis, T. S. Eliot, Austin Farrer and Rowan Williams (there is clearly a book that could be written here!). If all these authors have at the least a family resemblance to the 'integral humanism' of Maritain, de Lubac and Vatican II, is this just an insignificant coincidence? Or could it be rather that, as Williams suggests, it is because they both draw on the same patristic sources (more Platonist and Augustinian–Thomist than Aristotelian or voluntarist) to avoid the theological and philosophical dualisms of the late medieval and early modern period. Beyond this, there may also be particular ecclesio-political reasons why the structures and organization of the Church of England are particularly conducive to integralism. The rediscovery of the dignity of the laity in the Reformation and the suspicion of the clericalism which had developed in the medieval West from the Hildebrandine reforms of the eleventh century onwards, meant a return in the Church of England to the more non-dualist, integralist ecclesiology of the first millennium, combined with a more Byzantine or Carolinian view of the priestly nature of 'secular' authority, which was recovered in the Reformation and remains today in the role of the queen as anointed supreme governor. The establishment of the Church of England can be seen here not merely as civil religion or a state Church, but a contemporary version of the integral humanism that shaped the whole of Christendom. More could be said about this, but that will have to wait for another day.

In conclusion I want to briefly ask, what use is this category of 'integral humanism' if I have managed to persuade you that it can be seen as applying to the Church of England? I suggest that it offers a way of reading our particular ecumenical situation, as well as the characteristic but not unique elements of our tradition and identity that is more theologically interesting than the customary Erastian and latitudinarian lines about pragmatism, compromise, empty inclusion and not having to believe very much. 'Integral humanism' provides a way of understanding our relation to culture and society, including very concrete material practices such as our policy of baptizing any children, or crowning the monarch and being represented in the House of Lords, or marrying and burying anyone, or running church schools, or having lay representation in our synods, or being committed to everyone in a locality through the parish system, as not being a liberal secularizing humanism that sells out on the Church's central task of making new disciples of Christ, but rather as flowing from and to him, who is the Alpha and Omega of all things.

References

Henri de Lubac, 1988 (1937), *Catholicism: Christ and the Common Destiny of Man*, ET, San Francisco, CA: Ignatius Press

Richard Hooker, 1907, *Ecclesiastical Polity Book Five: Volume Two*, London: J. M. Dent & Sons Ltd and New York: E. P. Dutton & Co. Inc.

Jacques Maritain, 1996, *Integral Humanism, Freedom in the Modern World, and A Letter on Independence*, ET, Notre Dame, IN: University of Notre Dame Press

Eric L. Mascall, 1956, *Via Media: An Essay in Theological Synthesis*, London: Longmans

Edmund Newey, 2002, 'The Form of Reason: Participation in the Work of Richard Hooker, Benjamin Whichcote, Ralph Cudworth and Jeremy Taylor', *Modern Theology*, Vol. 18, Issue 1, January, pp. 1–26

Oliver O'Donovan, 2011, *On the Thirty-Nine Articles: Conversations with Tudor Christianity*, London: SCM Press

Paul VI, 1964, *Lumen Gentium*: A dogmatic constitution of the Church solemnly promulgated by His Holiness Pope Paul VI, 21 November, ET, www.vatican.va/archive/hist_councils/ii_vatican_council/documents/vat-ii_const_19641121_lumen-gentium_en.html

Paul VI, 1965, *Gaudium et Spes*: A pastoral constitution on the Church in the modern promulgated by His Holiness Pope Paul VI on 7 December, ET, www.vatican.va/archive/hist_councils/ii_vatican_council/documents/vat-ii_const_19651207_gaudium-et-spes_en.html

The Revised Cathechism, 1962, Authorized by the General Synod of the Church of England, London: SPCK

Rowan Williams, 2004, *Anglican Identities*, London: Darton, Longman & Todd

Rowan Williams, 2012, The Archbishop of Canterbury's address to the Synod of Bishops in Rome, 10 October. rowanwilliams.archbishopofcanterbury.org/articles.php/2645/archbishops-address-to-the-synod-of-bishops-in-rome

Notes

1 A paper delivered to the Anglican Studies Research Seminar, Department of Theology and Religion, Durham University, 5 February 2013.

2 (That is, John's 'militant Anglicanism' would criticize the notions that we are in a post-denominational situation (although he describes Anglicanism as a tradition defined by geography and culture and not as a denomination), that the Church of England is a heretical sect, or that the Church of England no longer needs to pay attention to its historical roots and development.)

3 (In a footnote to himself John lists some examples of Anglicans whom he regards as being influenced by Maritain: William Temple, T. S. Eliot, possibly Michael Ramsey (he left himself a note to do some more research), Eric Mascall, Rowan Williams and John Milbank.)

4 (See, for example, Newey 2002.)

9

Jacques Maritain: Pre-Conciliar Conservative or Thomist Liberal Democrat?[1] (2010)

To a contemporary observer, Jacques Maritain's political writings appear to contain remarkably contradictory political worldviews. On the one hand, we have Maritain the anti-modernist, anti-liberal, raging against Descartes and Rousseau and the Revolution, looking to medieval Christendom as his political ideal, defending the high papalist views of ecclesiastical intervention in political spheres, and not without some sympathy for the semi-fascist restorationist views of the *Action Française*; on the other hand we have Maritain the champion of the free world, passionate democrat, believer in progress, pluralism, freedom and equality, one of those who contributed to the drafting of the Universal Declaration of Human Rights, no less.[2]

What are we to make of these contradictions? Did Maritain simply change his mind from his early days in the anticlerical Third Republic to his later days in America reacting to the rise of Nazism? While Maritain's emphases are expressed differently according to context, I will argue that there is actually much greater continuity in his thought than the above opposition might indicate. Both his earlier 'conservatism' and his later 'liberalism' are more nuanced than they appear, not quite fitting the conventional categorizations, and as such are not so inconsistent.

I begin with some elements of Maritain's thought which sound most offensive to modern liberal sensibilities. Writing in 1927 in his first major work of political philosophy, Maritain develops the critique of modernity that he had already begun in his philosophical writings *Anti-moderne* and *Trois Reformateurs*. The book – in English *The Things Which Are Not Caesar's* – arose out of the controversy surrounding the papal condemnation of *Action Française*, the conservative political movement which had sought the restoration of a Royalist Catholic political settlement as an authoritarian counter to the anarchy of modern secularism and liberalism. Maritain reveals moments of sympathy for *Action Française*, but the book is an unqualified acceptance of the papal position and a strident defence of the papacy's right to intervene in political affairs, a sensitive point in France with its history of Gallican sensibilities of independence from Rome. This defence appeals to traditional Catholic doctrines of obedience and the primacy of the spiritual over the temporal realms (the French title of the book is *Primauté du Spirituel*). 'Liberalism', he tells us in this book, 'is a condemned error' (Maritain 1930, p. 133).[3] He appeals to the tradition of papal condemnations from Gregory XVI's *Mirari vos* and Pius IX's *Syllabus* through to Pius XI, and describes the core of liberalism as the Kantian–Rousseauian axiom: 'Obey nobody but yourself.' Following the teaching of Leo XIII, Maritain sees this as operating in various degrees, from the refusal of all authority and law, divine and human, to the rejection merely of divine authority in the public realm, but insists that 'every form of liberalism tends to absolute liberalism as to its perfect type' (p. 137). He opposes this formal, arbitrary, empty modern notion of liberty to the classical account of Aquinas, which stresses the orientation of freedom to goodness and truth and the consequent subordination of arbitrary potential freedom of choice to the acquired freedom of the virtuous life. Maritain spells out the various 'errors' of liberalism: independent morality, which is said to imply the 'parity of truth and falsehood, of justice and injustice, good and evil' (p. 137); denying 'the right of the spiritual power to intervene in temporal matters' and the 'subordination of civil society to the Church of Christ'; denying that civil society has a moral as well as material end (p. 138); belief in the 'liberty to practice any religion whatsoever indifferently (as though the civil power were under no obligation, to the best of its ability and without claiming any jurisdiction over consciences, to do homage to truth), liberty to express any opinion, liberty to print anything, liberty to teach any doctrine' (p. 141); believing that political authority derives not from God but from the masses (p. 146); believing that we are not conscience-bound to obey civil laws.

Moving on from the core of the issue, we find Maritain condemning 'democratism' as 'the dogma of the Sovereign People, which, combined with the dogma of the general will and Law as the expression of Number, constitutes, in the extreme, the error of political pantheism' (p. 132). Maritain's preference for the medieval sacral polity of Christendom is evident in his narration of the historical roots of modern problems and the way he poses the solution:

> The homicidal ideas informing the world which issued from the Reformation and the Revolution, perverting therein normal developments which pursue their course elsewhere, are the *cadaverous forms* of the corruption of the Christian world, progressively destroyed by the claim of modern politicians and philosophers, kings and nations, to absolute independence (*aseity*). It was five hundred years ago that we began to die.

Rebellion against the pope is virtually equated by Maritain with rebellion against the Church, which is itself identified with rebellion against God and morality and thus effectively suicide. France's problems, he claims to the members of *Action Française*, predate the Revolution, going back to the Gallicanism to which they appealed in defence of their resistance to the pope. Secularism, or any claims of political autonomy from ecclesiastical authority, seem to be ruled out.

The practical political consequences of these ideas are worked out in his defence in the same book of the 'indirect power' of the papacy in temporal affairs. This position begins from the hierarchy of ends: the end of the state (the common good) is subordinate to the ultimate end of human life (God) and so, as Aristotle recognized, 'the subordination of politics to ethics is absolute and even infinite' (p. 2). But there is another supranational state which is oriented to this ultimate end, namely the Church. Hence 'we must', he says, 'assert as a truth superior to every vicissitude of time the supremacy of the Church over the world and all earthly powers'. Many Christians might agree thus far in principle; however, this is not just a theoretical supremacy but a practical one:

> the Church must lead the nations to the ultimate end of human life, which is also that of States, and must therefore, in virtue of the spiritual interests entrusted to her, direct governments and nations and bend before God the stiff necks of the powers of flesh. (p. 74)

And when he says the Church, it is rapidly clear whom exactly Maritain means: 'The Pope is living authority' (p. 79). 'Kings [should] be subject to the Supreme Pontiff' as the body is to the soul (p. 14). This, according to Maritain, somewhat glossing over the debates between papalists and conciliarists, is the unanimous teaching of the Church through the ages on political authority from St Bernard, St Thomas Aquinas, Bellarmine and Suarez, Innocent III and Boniface VIII – the 'doctrine of the two swords' as it is sometimes known: Christ possesses the fullness of all spiritual and temporal authority, he holds both swords. The Church (that is, the ecclesiastical hierarchy) wields the spiritual sword directly, has direct authority over spiritual matters, but is said to operate the temporal sword 'indirectly', not wielding it normally or personally, but possessing the right to direct its use when spiritual matters are at stake. 'The special interventions of the spiritual power in temporal matters are motivated by one object only,' Maritain tells us, 'the avoidance or repression of sin' (p. 12). Yet this remains a considerable, if indirect, power: the right to 'quash and annul laws promulgated by a State, it can extend to deposing kings and emperors, if the danger to which they expose souls is too great, and set their subjects free from their oath of allegiance' (p. 15). Such claims are familiar from the history of the papacy, and yet to hear them being expressed in the early twentieth century remains startling, not least because they are no longer heard from even the more conservative voices of the Roman magisterium in the last fifty years.

We have seen how it is certainly possible to see Maritain's views on theology and politics in the twenties as embodying a conservative papalist anti-modernism. But when we look more closely, the picture becomes more complex. It is worth noting again the occasion of Maritain's writing: he is seeking to persuade an authoritarian nationalist political movement that they should not put their political nationalism before their Christianity, their loyalty to the political movement or the nation above their loyalty to the Church, which they regarded as 'sliding to the left'(!) (p. 81). Hostility to liberalism and democracy and sympathy for the Middle Ages are thus the common ground Maritain can assume his audience shares from which to build his argument. It is also worth recalling that the trauma of the papal condemnations of 'modernist' Catholic intellectuals was still recent enough to explain something of Maritain's slavish closeness to the recent documents of the magisterium.

Even then these positions are importantly qualified. Under his discussion of liberalism, for example, it is absolute freedom from all authority and obedience that is rejected. Maritain does appear to defend a certain account of freedom of religion, at least in terms of the limits of the state's power, if not absolutely, decades before *Dignitatis Humanae* made this view normal in the Roman Catholic Church. He cites Leo XIII with approval:

> man in the State has the right to follow the will of God according to the dictates of his conscience and to fulfil his commandments, and ... no hindrance should be offered to him. This true liberty, worthy of the children of God and gloriously protecting the dignity of human personality, is superior to all violence and oppression; it is particularly dear to, and has always been desired by, the Church (p. 141, n. 2).

Thus it is possible to read Maritain's rejection of liberalism as the recognition, shared by most political theorists, of the practical impossibility of *absolute* freedom of religion and expression, on the one hand and, on the other, the more fundamental refusal to make freedom the ultimate value above truth and goodness, a position which would be shared by most Christian thinkers and indeed by most people other than absolute relativists. In keeping with this distinction between the ultimate untruth of liberalism, and its practical negative usefulness in the political sphere, Maritain notes Aquinas' view that the 'republic' or mixed system of government, enshrining political liberty, while not the most ideal form of government, may be the least evil and therefore the one most useful to the Church (Maritain already points to American democracy as an illustration of this). 'Every liberty must be accounted legitimate,' claims Maritain, following Leo XIII again, 'to the extent that it increases the power of doing good' (p. 143). Here we see the somewhat embryonic beginnings of Maritain's later views on freedom.

On democracy similarly, Maritain's position, even in this early work, is more subtle than simple rejection. He consistently, again following the encyclicals of Leo XIII, distinguishes 'democratism', the 'religious myth' of 'political pantheism' that makes the people the ultimate source of sovereignty and law, which he identifies with Rousseau and condemns, from democracy as a political system (in the sense used by Aristotle and Aquinas), which he regards as a legitimate form of government, although not the only one. These are then distinguished in turn from what he calls 'Christian or social democracy' or 'demophily', 'democracy as a social tendency'. This is the desire to transform the conditions of the working classes according to the principles of justice and charity, which he strongly commends. Here we see the beginnings of Maritain's later passion for democracy and social justice.

While Maritain does look to medieval Christendom as an ideal, he regards it as a more just and anti-authoritarian society than the absolutist states of the seventeenth and eighteenth centuries.[4] He refuses to identify Christendom with European civilization in the nationalist and authoritarian fashion of the *Action Française*, stressing its internationalism ('Europe is not the faith', p. 95) and its inner spiritual life, rather than external coercion. He looks for inculturation of the Church in China and the East in a way that is ahead of his time. He even points to Gandhi as a representative of the primacy of the spiritual. He is not uncritical of the abuses of clerical power and the use of force in the Middle Ages (p. xvi). He protests that he is accused of being 'anti-modern' simply for opposing eternal truths to the errors of the present day (p. xviii). Maritain does not look simply for a restoration of the Middle Ages, but speaks of a new 'modern Christendom' in which there will be a diversity of religions and in which the Church would voluntarily choose not to exercise any of its authority in the political sphere other than 'a merely moral influence' (p. xvii).[5] The popes have already, wisely mindful of the different historical situation, elected not to exercise their indirect power in recent years, he notes (p. xv). It is possible, then, to argue that the doctrine of the 'indirect power' is primarily a negative definition of the limits of the state's authority and even of the pope's. The state must not seek to subjugate ultimate ends to its own uses, but must leave room for other bodies to represent these ultimate ends to which it nevertheless remains open and by which it is itself capable of being judged. Likewise the pope does not have direct rule over temporal things but can only exercise his teaching authority in these areas insofar as spiritual things are also bound up with them. We are left with a much more careful and qualified position, which sounds more similar to the later Maritain, looking for a truly Christian society, rather than one with merely external ecclesiastical privileges and power.

I want now to sketch briefly the direction these elements of Maritain's thought took in his later more obviously democratic, even 'liberal' writings, arguing that he never abandons his earlier critique of secular immanentism, and that against such a position he remains committed to the 'primacy of the spiritual' which had been the keynote of his earlier writings.

During World War Two, Maritain was living in the United States and published two key texts intended as contributions towards the post-war rebuilding of Europe: *The Rights of Man and Natural Law*

(1942) and *Christianity and Democracy* (1943). The contrast between European totalitarianisms of the Right and the Left and the democracy of the free world seems to have developed Maritain's interpretation of modernity's relationship to Christianity.[6] He writes with what he confesses might seem like optimism but what he believes to be hope of the 'path to a new civilisation and a new democracy', whose 'inspiration' will be Christian, but which will embrace not only the parts of the world historically influenced by Christianity but the whole world, drawing upon what he calls the 'moral forces of the naturally Christian soul' (Maritain 1986, p. 8).[7] He describes the current war as the end of modernity, which he traces through the familiar lineage of Machiavelli, Luther, Descartes and Rousseau, seeing the capitalism and nationalism that led to war as the conclusion of this immanentist trajectory of humanity believing it can save itself. But now he stresses that 'this world was born of Christendom and owed its deepest living strength to the Christian tradition' (pp. 14–15). More than this, he claims that the *liberté*, *égalité* and *fraternité* of the Revolution and its consequences are 'secularized Christian idealism' (p. 15), that modern notions of reason, justice, human dignity and progress, all of which were turned against Christianity, are essentially and inescapably Christian. 'One would have to have the soul of a slave', he tells us, 'to wish for the destruction of this very sense of freedom and justice on account of the suffering and disorder it may have occasioned' (p. 16). This is the basic structure of his argument in these later works; claiming the most exalted aspects of liberal democracy as the fruits of the Christian tradition, while arguing that they become distorted when they forget this origin and are isolated from this living source.

Maritain retains his criticisms of immanentist liberalism and democratism, the 'heavenly Jerusalem of Godless Man' (p. 133) or bourgeois individualistic liberalism, as he now often calls it. But now these errors are seen as distortions of the democratic ideal, paving the way to totalitarianism, and to be cast aside by the emerging 'new democracy' (p. 60). Facing the 'pagan empires' of Europe, he now realizes that 'freedom's chances coincide with those of the evangelical message' (p. 32). In *The Rights of Man and Natural Law*, he lays out the four philosophical foundations for this new civilization of free men. It is *personalist*, which means that the person is part of society and subordinate to it in relation to its ends, against liberal individualism, but also superior to society in relation to the ultimate end of man, against communism and fascism. It is *communal*, which means humans are naturally social and

political, oriented to life together, and yet, against fascism and totalitarianism, this coming together is for the purpose of an end *beyond*
the community itself, the common good. This common good, unlike
its bourgeois liberal shadow, is redistributive, authoritative and intrinsically moral, not a positivist aggregate construction (the derivation
of rights from the eternal law via the natural law demonstrates this
ultimately ontological nature of Maritain's political theory).[8] These
first two points are straightforwardly derived from Thomist anthropology and political thought, although formulated in terms specific to
the contemporary international clash of ideologies. His third characteristic of this civilization is that it is *pluralist*, by which Maritain means
it recognizes the freedom for people to form groups with ends inferior
and superior to those of the state, without seeing them as dangerous
rivals to its loyalty. Here we see how Maritain's earlier hesitant pragmatic acceptance of religious liberty in the state has developed from
the limitation of temporal authority by the doctrine of indirect power
into an anti-totalitarian theological defence of freedom and account
of the state's inability to control conscience. The fourth and perhaps
most controversial characteristic of this society is that it is '*theist* or
Christian', not in the sense that it expects every member to be Christian
or believe in God, but:

> in the sense that it recognizes that in the reality of things, God, princi-
> ple and end of the human person and prime source of natural law, is
> by the same token the prime source of political society and authority
> among men; and in the sense that it recognizes that the currents of
> liberty and fraternity released by the Gospel ... are the internal energy
> which civilisation needs to achieve its fulfillment. (pp. 104f.)

This assertion of the Christian nature of his vision of democracy is where
the primacy of the spiritual continues to be most evident in Maritain's
later work. He is quite unapologetic on this point: 'not only does the
democratic state of mind stem from the inspiration of the Gospel, but
it cannot exist without it' (p. 49; cf. p. 20). Roosevelt is quoted with
approval here, as is Maritain's old teacher Henri Bergson: 'democracy
is evangelical in essence' (p. 54). However much the accidents of history
may have made the gospel seem opposed to democracy, he can now say
that the democratic ideal is simply the secular name for Christendom!
The origins of this position go back though to Maritain's distinction of
the three senses of democracy. Rousseauian democrat*ism* is still con-

demned, although now it is seen as an aberration rather than the ideal type; democracy as a political system is now endorsed as not merely a legitimate option, but the teleologically final of the three elements of Aquinas' mixed polity, superseding and subsuming within itself monarchy and aristocracy. And now Christian/social democracy as desire for justice for the poor is seen as the deepest and truest sense of the word and comes much more to the fore. This elevation of the ordinary working person is seen as distinctively Christian and one of the greatest achievements of the modern world. Maritain's account of rights, unlike those of many liberals, is one third given over to the social rights of the worker, including the right to a just wage, the right to unionize and so on. The liberal civic rights of equality before the law and universal suffrage mean very little without these social and economic rights or transformations. While rejecting the communist idea of a dictatorship of the proletariat, Maritain has now come to believe that in the face of the spiritually bankrupt elites of Europe, the leadership and authority that will be necessary for the construction of a new world must come from the ordinary people, the 'heroism of the plain man' (p. 81).[9] Similarly he now insists, developing his earlier critique of the authoritarian restorationist hopes of the *Action Française*, that the Christian nature of a society will consist not in what he calls a Pharisaic, 'clerical or decoratively Christian state' based upon ecclesiastical privileges and compulsion, but in a 'vitally Christian society' (pp. 107–13) where the living spirit of faith animates the social life of the people.

In conclusion, there is something attractive about Maritain's attempt to articulate a universal Christian social democratic civilization, embracing the best fruits of modern political thought as rooted in the Christian tradition and offering a critique of secular immanentist liberal democracy as incoherent precisely in that it tries to deny or isolate itself from this vital source. His call to the Church not to cling to 'ornamental' Christian civilization but to take up the task of being the vital life of a society is a bold challenge.

Two critical lines of questioning remain for me however. The first one is typically Barthian, de Lubacian, or Hauerwasian: for all the obvious apologetic and strategic attraction of consensus-building strategies appealing to a natural law which appears at least relatively autonomous from the theology which is supposed to undergird it, is such a strategy ultimately unsustainable? Have we not seen in the sixty years since the UN Declaration of Human Rights that these rights have been predictably cut away from their theological roots and have been conceived in precisely the immanentist, positivistic way that Maritain feared?[10] Likewise, there are real questions about whether his interchangeable use of 'Christian' and 'theist' is really satisfactory. We may need to be even more clear than Maritain about the specifically *Christian* nature of any proposals we might make. We might also ask, as an aside, whether in fact Maritain was too quick to accept the entire language of rights as an essential part of the Christian natural law tradition when, as Joan Lockwood O'Donovan has suggested, the very language of rights already indicates a decadent shift within the natural law tradition away from notions of justice in real relations towards justice as a proprietorial possession, necessarily in competition with that of others. So despite all Maritain's efforts to insist upon rights as dynamic and transcendentally grounded, perhaps the very language was working against him.

Finally and following on from this, if we should want to follow Maritain in affirming against the closed immanentism of the secular some sort of 'primacy of the spiritual' over the public realm, which seems to be one of the challenges of our time, how might we go about this, without locating it, as he seems to, in the authority of the papacy, understood in an absolutist and positivist fashion? Does Maritain conceive of this primacy too much according to a static Aristotelian hierarchy where the spiritual sits on top of the temporal like tiers of a wedding cake? To put it another way, could an even more integralist vision of the relation between the spiritual and the temporal help us to locate this primacy, as Maritain begins to at certain moments, as much in the vital Christian life dispersed through a society, as in any one locus of authority, magisterial or juridical?

References

Ralph McInerny, 2003, *The Very Rich Hours of Jacques Maritain: A spiritual life*, Notre Dame, IN: University of Notre Dame Press

Jacques Maritain, 1930, *The Things Which Are Not Caesar's*, ET, London: Sheed and Ward

Jacques Maritain, 1938, *Integral Humanism*, ET, London: Centenary Press

Jacques Maritain, 1940, *Scholasticism and Politics*, ET, London: Centenary Press

Jacques Maritain, 1954, *Man and the State*, ET, London: Hollis and Carter

Jacques Maritain, 1986, *Christianity and Democracy and The Rights of Man and Natural Law*, ET, San Francisco, CA: Ignatius Press

Notes

1 This paper was originally delivered at the 2008 Society for the Study of Theology conference in Durham and I am grateful for the feedback from various people on that occasion. (John's abstract for this chapter read: This article traces the development and contrasts between the early and later political thought of Jacques Maritain, arguing that, beneath the superficial appearance of a radical move from papalist monarchical conservatism towards democratic liberalism, we can see deeper continuities: a consistent qualified support for democracy and religious freedom on the one hand, and an affirmation of the primacy of the spiritual over and against secular liberalism on the other.)

2 For a somewhat hagiographical account of Maritain's life, see McInerny 2003. For Maritain's comments on the UN Declaration, see Maritain 1954, p. 70.

3 Further references by page number in the main body of the text will be to Maritain 1930 until indicated otherwise.

4 He would later develop this critique of early modern absolutism and its roots in the mistaken notion of political 'sovereignty' through Bodin, Hobbes and Rousseau (Maritain 1954, pp. 25–48, especially pp. 45–7).

5 This distinction of a 'new' Christendom, more pluralist, even 'secular', was developed more extensively by Maritain as soon as 1934 in his *Integral Humanism* (Maritain 1938), especially pp. 132f., and also in 1938 with his *Scholasticism and Politics* (Maritain 1940).

6 Although the development of this trend of thought in Maritain began much earlier and can be followed in its earlier stages from *Integral Humanism* through *Scholasticism and Politics*, where he is already developing a critique of politics of the Left and Right and arguing in favour of a new 'pluralist' Christendom.

7 Further references to Maritain 1986 will be by page number in parenthese in the main body of the text.

8 This is made even more explicit by the later Maritain (Maritain 1954, pp. 76–97).

9 There does appear to be something of a shift here in Maritain's thinking on the question of the derivation of political authority: in 1938 he is still insisting primarily on its divine origin (Maritain 1940, pp. 82–6), while after the war this is considerably attenuated as only *through* the people and not in the image of God or representing him, in explicit contrast to the spiritual authority of the papacy (Maritain 1954, pp. 118–19).

10 Maritain does partially recognize this problem of the tendency towards a false autonomy, in *Man and the State* (Maritain 1954, pp. 73–6), but remains optimistic about the possibility of a purely *practical* consensus (Maritain 1954, pp. 69–73).

10

Integralism and Gift Exchange in the Anglican Social Tradition, or Avoiding Niebuhr in Ecclesiastical Drag (2011)

Introduction

In this paper I would like to begin by asking what, from an Anglican perspective, is particularly interesting about *Caritas in Veritate*, before exploring what resonances its key theological ideas of 'integral development' and charity as reciprocal gift exchange have within the Anglican social tradition(s). My argument will be that, first, Anglicans have been at the forefront of the recovery of Augustinian notions of charity as reciprocal gift exchange and the associationist application of such ideas to the social and economic sphere; and second, that, despite some recent evidence to the contrary, Anglicanism has particular ecclesiologico-political reasons to be sympathetic to this integralist social agenda and indeed may have some of its own resources to offer in understanding this position in the modern world.

A Conservative Encyclical? Development, Sex and Religion

First, what is significant in Benedict XVI's encyclical *Caritas in Veritate*? In terms of the international development agenda, this encyclical may well receive a negative reception in liberal Western circles. If one wishes to paint Benedict as a social conservative, undoing all the 'advances' of Vatican II and pulling up the ecclesiastical drawbridges, then it is easy to focus on the way the encyclical introduces a significant new element upon the work of its predecessor, Paul VI's *Populorum Progressio*, whose anniversary it marks, by linking social and economic development with what in liberal society are usually seen as more private concerns such as sexual ethics, questions concerning reproduction and the beginning and end of life (contraception, abortion and euthanasia) and even with explicit Christian belief.

On this interpretation, the encyclical marks a withdrawal of the collaboration begun in the 1960s between the Roman Catholic Church and other development and aid organizations on the grounds that such organizations are now pursuing more aggressively secular agendas, which are incompatible with Catholic moral teaching. Claims such as *'openness to life is at the centre of true development'*, or 'The Church forcefully maintains this link between life ethics and social ethics' may seem reasonably uncontroversial in themselves (Benedict XVI 2009, para. 28, emphasis original; para. 15). But when this is followed by appeals to *Humanae Vitae*, with its rejection of artificial contraception, and *Evangelium Vitae*'s analysis of the contemporary 'culture of death' (supposedly evident in IVF therapies, embryo research and euthanasia), alongside renewed papal condemnation of 'the spread of an anti-birth mentality' (para. 28) by certain development agendas through the promotion of contraception and abortion as forms of demographic control, liberal alarm bells start to ring.

Similarly, few should be surprised by *Caritas in Veritate*'s grounding of the Church's social teaching in Christian faith and doctrine, as in claims such as *'God is the guarantor of man's true development'* (para. 29, emphasis original). But when this is accompanied by the claim that the Church's social teaching and commitment to development is part of evangelization, or by the renewed rejection of religious indifferentism, syncretism or 'practical atheism', it may seem to some that Benedict is allowing the question of development to be subordinated to his more usual concerns about the rise of relativism and its erosion of the uniqueness of Christian claims (see paras 15, 55, 29). More explicitly, when the pope refuses the 'exclusion of religion from the public square', cites John 15.5 ('Apart from me you can do nothing') and insists that 'A humanism which excludes God is an inhuman humanism' (para. 78), it sounds to many liberals as if he has abandoned the Second Vatican Council's willingness to collaborate with all people of good will, regardless of their beliefs.

While some Anglican ethicists have been sympathetic to the papal analysis of the culture of death and contemporary relativism and secularism,[1] it would be true to say that many Anglican commentators, perhaps influenced in this respect as much by the recent ecumenical *froideur* between Anglicans and Roman Catholics as by substantive differences such as the question of contraception, share a broadly liberal, unsympathetic reading of *Caritas in Veritate*. At best, such liberal Anglicans may see it as an unhelpful muddying of the waters of Christian social teaching, by dragging in a number of highly divisive and not necessarily relevant questions of life-ethics or religious confession. At worst, it may be seen as the return to an authoritarian, isolationist, and exclusivist social agenda, which is founded upon the belief that it is the Catholic Church's job to rule the world, and which promotes policies that oppress the reproductive rights of women and encourage a dangerously irresponsible neglect of contraception, worsening both the AIDS epidemic and the approaching demographic crisis.[2]

Charity Beyond Justice: The Radical Agenda

But, if to many European liberals (including many Anglicans), *Caritas in Veritate* looks like a typical piece of conservative Catholic carping about sex and religion when it should be talking about poverty, this is not the whole story. For, across the Atlantic, to many neo-liberal and neo-conservative Roman Catholics, this encyclical looks like a confused muddle, a papal sell-out to leftist European social democratic ideals (see, for example, Novak 2009 and Weigel 2009). It is important not to overlook this social and economic radicalism in *Caritas in Veritate*, which arguably goes further than any previous papal encyclical in this direction.

Markets, Ethics and the Environment

Caritas in Veritate starts from the (traditional Christian) presupposition that the economic sphere is not a neutral realm unconnected with theology and morality. 'The economic sphere', we are told, 'is neither ethically neutral, nor inherently inhuman and opposed to society' (para. 36). This insistence that '*every economic decision has a moral consequence*' (para. 37, emphasis original) may seem uncontroversial in Christian social teaching, but it is of course in direct opposition to neo-liberal free market ideas of the market as a morally neutral, self-regulating force for good (para. 37). Profit, according to the pope, cannot be an absolute end in itself, but must serve the common good, without which it 'risks destroying wealth and creating poverty' (para. 21). If the market must not be allowed to become 'the place where the strong subdue the weak', then the 'economy needs ethics in order to function correctly' and examples of socially responsible businesses, 'fair-trade', consumer cooperatives, and 'ethical' banking and finance are commended (paras 36, 66, 45).

Traditional policies of Catholic social teaching are reiterated: the encouragement of unionization to protect the dignity of workers, the desire for stable employment for all, the insistence upon 'food and access to water as universal rights of all human beings, without distinction or discrimination' (paras 24 and 64, 32 and 63, 27). The pope endorses the need to care for the world's resources and to recognize our 'responsibility towards creation' to ensure that our natural environment can sustain life into the future (paras 48–51). The political principle of subsidiarity, or encouraging responsible decision-making at the most local level, is reasserted against bureaucratic state centralism in welfare provision and neo-colonial models of aid and development, which are both accused of encouraging disempowering dependency; while at the same time collaboration is encouraged at every level, right up to the establishment of a new international global consensus (paras 58, 67).

Beyond these traditional planks of Catholic social thought, the encyclical seeks to bring up to date the agenda of *Populorum Progressio* by responding to contemporary crises, environmental and economic, and it is here that *Caritas in Veritate* is particularly radical. On the question of ecological concerns, particularly in relation to energy consumption and the damaging effects of this upon our planet, the pope moves beyond simple platitudes about the need to care for God's creation. Philosophically, he rejects both the technocratic optimism, which characterized much of the domination of nature in the last two centuries, and the more recent neo-pagan rejection of humanity's unique position as the crown of creation (paras 68–71). Practically, he insists (to the horror of American neo-conservatives!) that the 'technologically advanced societies can and must lower their domestic energy consumption' and that we also need 'a worldwide redistribution of energy resources, so that countries lacking those resources can have access to them' (para. 49).

Globalization and the International Regulation and Redistribution of Capital

In response to the international financial crisis, the pope condemns 'badly managed and largely speculative financial dealing' and economic short-termism, and looks for the 'regulation of the financial sector, so as to safeguard weaker parties and discourage scandalous speculation, and experimentation with new forms of finance, designed to support development projects' (paras 21, 32, 65). He recognizes that many of the problems of the recent crises have arisen out of the new situation of globalization with the deregulation and rapid international movements of capital and labour. The analysis of globalization is balanced, acknowledging that 'globalization, *a priori*, is neither good nor bad. It will be what people make of it', while also recognizing that 'inequalities are on the increase' (paras 42, 22). The task, therefore, as the encyclical sees it, is the moral ordering of the ever-increasing international flows of trade, capital and labour 'to promote a person-based and community-oriented cultural process of world-wide integration that is open to transcendence' (para. 42). While some have seen globalization as the end of the role of the state, the pope argues instead that 'in terms of the resolution of the current crisis, the State's role seems destined to grow' (para. 41) and that greater international cooperation is needed.

Here the pope is reviving one of the more radical proposals of his predecessor John XXIII (again to the horror of American neoconservatives): the 'urgent need for a true world political authority', beyond merely the reform of the United Nations and international financial organizations, so that 'the concept of the family of nations can acquire real teeth' (para. 67). Here the pope speaks also of the need for 'disarmament, food security and peace' (para. 67). In terms of global inequalities, the pope raises the question of the waste of international aid through corruption and excessive bureaucracy and, in keeping with much post-colonial development thinking in the past thirty years, calls for aid which encourages the recipients to be able to participate themselves in the international economy, rather than simply to become permanently dependent upon aid (para. 58; cf. 60, 47).

It is in this context, however, that the pope raises again one of his most challenging calls to the wealthy nations of the world: 'The processes of globalization, suitably understood and directed, open up the unprecedented possibility of large-scale redistribution of wealth on a world scale' (para. 42; cf. 37, 49). This will involve opening up the protectionism by which the rich nations maintain their dominance over the poorer ones, such as high tariffs and 'an excessive zeal for protecting knowledge through an unduly rigid assertion of the right to intellectual property, especially in the field of health care' (paras 33, 22).

New Forms of Social Enterprise and Civilizing the Economy

As if talk of local and international regulation of finance, protection of the environment and even large-scale redistribution of wealth were not quite upsetting enough for the neo-conservatives, the encyclical goes on to speak sympathetically of new models and forms of business enterprise. These new models are based upon fraternal solidarity and the gratuity of reciprocal giving, and belong neither purely to the realm of the market and the logic of pure profit alone, nor to the sphere of state control and public duty (paras 38–40). These new models often seem most at home in civil society, but they are not confined to it. They are often 'based upon mutualist principles' and can encourage forms of greater 'economic democracy', such as cooperativist stakeholder ownership, rather than purely shareholder ownership (para. 38). Here the traditional distinction of profit and non-profit organizations seems to be breaking down. In an important passage, the encyclical notes the emergence in recent decades of an intermediate area, which is not just a third sector but is having an impact upon the two traditional models of public and private enterprise:

> It is made up of traditional companies which nonetheless subscribe to social aid agreements in support of underdeveloped countries, charitable foundations associated with individual companies, groups of companies oriented towards social welfare, and the diversified world of the so-called 'civil economy' and the 'economy of communion'. (para. 46)

The pope endorses these 'hybrid forms of commercial behaviour', with their renewal of responsibility and ethics, fraternal solidarity and reciprocal gratuity in commerce and industry as 'civilizing the economy' (para. 38). This stress on mutualism and new forms of social economy rooted in solidarity and reciprocal gift exchange is not without some precedent in Catholic social thought, but the renewed emphasis on them in *Caritas in Veritate* is quite striking. In the light of this radical social and economic agenda, it simply will not do to continue to paint Benedict XVI as an economic conservative on the basis of his past conflicts with liberation theologians.

Charity as Gift-Exchange and Integral Human Development: The Theological Heart of *Caritas in Veritate*

While some have argued that *Caritas in Veritate* is just a hopeless mixture of conservative and radical views (thus Weigel's ridiculous claim (2009) that one can separate all the 'gold' bits written by Benedict, which of course he likes, from those written by the supposedly dreadful 'red' liberals at the Pontifical Council for Justice and Peace), it is my claim that the 'conservative' and 'radical' elements of the encyclical are part of a thoroughly consistent outworking of a theological perspective which, while building upon much of the tradition of Catholic social teaching, also develops a distinctly Augustinian theological voice which is very much Benedict's own. We can summarize this as the belief in charity as gift-exchange and integral human development.

Charity as Gift-Exchange

Benedict XVI has already laid out his views on Christian charity in what we might think of as his manifesto encyclical *Deus Caritas Est*, to which he refers repeatedly in *Caritas in Veritate*. Benedict's view of charity is thoroughly Augustinian and Johannine in stressing the social, public and reciprocal nature of charity as a supernatural participation in the divine Trinitarian life, against more modern and Protestant individualistic notions of charity as unilateral, private, interiorized and sentimentalized. 'Charity', he tells us, 'is love received and given' and 'has its origin in God' (paras 5, 1). It cannot be confined to 'subjective emotions and opinions' but is 'gift, acceptance and communion' and therefore concerns the 'macro-relationships (social, economic and political ones)' just as much as the personal (paras 3, 2).

As gift, charity goes beyond the opposition of obligation and self-interest: 'Gift by its nature goes beyond merit, its rule is that of superabundance' (para. 34). 'Love – *caritas* – is', according to the encyclical, 'an extraordinary force which leads people to opt for courageous and generous engagement in the field of justice and peace' and 'the principal driving force behind the authentic development of every person and of all humanity' (paras 2, 1). From all this it follows that 'Charity is at the heart of the Church's social doctrine', but this is the first time Benedict has spelled out what this means in concrete political and particularly economic terms (para. 2). This vision of charity as reciprocal gift-exchange is the basis of the encyclical's rejection of dependency models of welfare and aid, but also of its support for radical sharing and redistribution of international resources and wealth. This is not just a private matter for individual believers: 'in commercial relationships the principle of gratuitousness and the logic of gift as an expression of fraternity can and must find their place within normal economic activity' (para. 36).

Generosity and communion, the gratuitous actual sharing of real goods, is at the heart of the gospel message about economics and development and this is a central theme of *Caritas in Veritate*. Here, 'charity goes beyond justice, because to love is to give, to offer what is "mine" to the other' (para. 6). Yet at the same time it 'never lacks justice'; rather, 'charity demands justice' which is the 'minimum measure' of charity (para. 6). More precisely, we can say 'charity transcends justice and completes it in the logic of giving and forgiving' (para. 6). In this account of the supercession of justice by the gift of charity, Benedict is making a particular argument which brings us on to the question of his 'integralism'.

Integral Human Development

When Benedict writes that 'the logic of gift does not exclude justice, nor does it merely sit alongside it as a second element added from without', he is manifesting his Augustinian 'integralism', against the dualism of what has been called the 'distinction of planes' model of Christian social thought (para. 34).[3] In doing this he is also subtly developing the tradition of his predecessors John Paul II and Paul VI. While he does not of course accuse them of this, it is certainly possible to see a slightly different tendency in the social teaching of these earlier popes.

Acting perhaps out of an admirable desire to find common ground with non-believers, but also building upon the neo-scholastic distinctions of reason and faith, nature and grace, previous encyclicals had often spoken with two voices: first setting forth the demands of natural justice which should be evident to all reasonable people regardless of their faith, and second describing the supererogatory works of charity to which Christians might be particularly called over and above these minimal demands of justice. We can certainly see the attraction of this 'distinction of planes' strategy in seeming to enable a minimal consensus for international collaboration across religious and cultural divides upon questions of poverty and development.

Yet at the same time such a model, with its naive optimism about the ease of global consensus and its relegation of the heart of the Christian faith to an optional supplement, now seems dated at best. This is not least in response to a more militant secularism that seeks to exclude religious viewpoints from the task of development altogether, while at the same time being left with a minimal account of justice incapable of negotiating the complexities of contemporary problems.

This is what leads the pope to make the following claim: 'The sharing of goods and resources, from which authentic development proceeds, is not guaranteed by merely technical progress and relationships of utility, but by the potential of love that overcomes evil with good' (para. 9). Once again, we can see that it is the *same* integralist theological reasoning that leads the pope to insist that faith is indispensable for development *and* that leads to the most radical distributivist and mutualist elements of his economic vision.

Integralism and Charity as Gift-Exchange in the Anglican Social Tradition

We turn now to see how this distinctive theological agenda of Benedict, driving his social and economic thinking, compares with Anglican social thought. Here we have to speak of 'thought' or 'tradition/s' rather than capitalized 'Teaching' because, significantly, there is no one voice which could claim to speak authoritatively and finally on social matters for the Church of England, let alone the Anglican Communion, in the way that the Roman magisterium does for the Roman Catholic Church. Yet this is not to say that Anglicanism has no social thought. On the contrary, it has a substantial body of writings, some from representative or authoritative bodies, such as Synodical reports or official statements by Church leaders, and some from respected Anglican thinkers, whose authority is more organic than formal. This polyphonic tradition certainly contains different voices, but we can also discern commonalities and developments, and in this we might note that our earlier analysis has suggested that such diversity and development can be detected even within the Roman magisterial tradition.

To focus our attention on the last half century or so of British Anglican social thought, we might well come to the conclusion that the dominant strand was closer to the 'distinction of planes' model than to Benedict's integralism. We can call this strand of Anglican social thought 'conservative liberalism' and its heyday was the period from

the 1960s to the 1980s (Sedgwick 1997, p. 290). The most significant figure for this tradition is William Temple (1881–1944) who was
successively Archbishop of York and of Canterbury and whose book
Christianity and Social Order (Temple 1956) was enormously influential, although it is unclear whether Temple himself should be completely
situated within this tradition which claims him.[4] The William Temple
Foundation, based in Manchester, has been one of the strongholds of
this tradition, particularly through the work of Ronald Preston, professor at Manchester University, and John Atherton, at Manchester
Cathedral (for example, Preston 1993 and Atherton 1992). We could
also however include the work of John Habgood, Archbishop of York,
David Jenkins, Bishop of Durham, Peter Selby, Bishop of Worcester,
Peter Sedgwick, Principal of St Michael's College, Cardiff, and Richard
Harries, Bishop of Oxford, as well as many of the publications of the
national Board for Social Responsibility in this 'conservative liberalism'
category.[5]

All these authors are characterized by a basically liberal (Kantian–
Weberian) analysis of modernity, with its increasing secularization
and pluralism, while at the same time, in varying degrees, wanting
to hold on to something of the Church of England's historic claim to
be the conscience of the nation. As a result all tend to offer comment
on contemporary politics and economics which seeks to speak in the
categories of 'natural reason', independent of specifically Christian
claims, and therefore supposedly acceptable to all, regardless of their
beliefs; while at the same time they end up offering at most only very
modest critiques of the status quo. The appeal is to a certain form of
English common sense, against what is seen as the pietism and absolutism of more integralist alternatives such as Catholic liberation theology
or evangelical communitarian thought.

It is difficult to miss the episcopal, establishment nature of this strand
of Anglican social thought, and it has often been expressed through
responses to government reports and interventions in the House of
Lords. Among the many theological influences, the principal figure
seems to be Reinhold Niebuhr and his 'Christian realism'. It is not
difficult therefore to see why Stanley Hauerwas has nicknamed this
strand of Anglican social thought 'Reinhold Niebuhr in ecclesiastical
drag'.[6]

'Conservative liberalism' was not however the only show in town.
We can trace a second strand of thought with more in common with
the radical integralism of Benedict XVI, more at home in the academy

than on the episcopal bench, which has perhaps risen to ascendancy in recent times and, I will argue, can trace its roots back to earlier strands of Anglican social thought. For want of a more precise label, I will call this loose grouping the Catholic Socialists. They share a sense that the Christian faith does not need to be translated into middle axioms to contribute to political debate in a pluralist society, but rather *is* its own social, political and economic vision. They also share a commitment to radical critique of the status quo on this basis and to more mutualist, cooperativist, communitarian forms of socialism rather than to statist solutions. This tradition might include such diverse figures as Ken Leech, community theologian in East London, Tim Gorringe, professor at Exeter University, Michael Northcott, professor at Edinburgh, John Milbank, professor at Nottingham, Graham Ward, professor at Manchester and, arguably, Rowan Williams, who was Archbishop of Canterbury.

In differing ways, they have expressed a wariness towards liberalism and its alliance with free market capitalism, a strongly internationalist and environmentalist concern, along with a recognition that what is required is not simply state interventions on the basis of justice, but more fundamentally new forms of business and commercial practice to achieve transformation at the level of the economic base. This certainly sounds closer to the integralist thinking of *Caritas in Veritate*. This perspective has gained a new ascendancy through the influence of more post-liberal and communitarian thinkers, such as Stanley Hauerwas and Alasdair MacIntyre in recent years. Meanwhile their influence in turn can be connected with broader cultural shifts, such as the breakdown of a liberal consensus in the face of more extreme pluralism and the marginalization of religion through a more vigorous secularism, which has curiously led to a revival of theological self-confidence.

Furthermore, this integralist Anglican tradition can be seen as not just a recent maverick departure from the dominant 'conservative liberal' perspective, but in fact a return to elements of an earlier tradition of Anglican social thought. We can certainly trace direct precursors of the more communitarian, confidently Christian, politically radical analysis we have been describing in the Anglo-Catholic 'Christendom group' in the early twentieth century, and slightly earlier in the work of Henry Scott Holland and the *Lux Mundi* school, including R. C. Moberly and Charles Gore. This latter group stand slightly closer to the 'conservative liberals', and we might group with them the important writings of the Anglican economist R. H. Tawney, Michael Ramsey, Archbishop of Canterbury, and in fact certain aspects of Temple's own work (his more idealist and unapologetically Christian moments).

More broadly, we can see something which, at the least, is quite different from the 'distinction of planes' model in the thought of the grandfather of Christian socialism, F. D. Maurice (see Morris 2005, pp. 158–60). In particular, his ecclesiology, with its universal reach and refusal of clericalist distinctions of laity from clergy, his theology of communion, for which the Church *is* itself a social reality, and his theology of creation, with its sense of all creation as graced and his refusal of any notions of pure nature, seems remarkably close to the integralist position set forth in the mid-twentieth century by Henri de Lubac (which stands behind Ratzinger's theology and *Caritas in Veritate*) (Morris 2005, p. 128, n. 149; pp. 135, 149, 169, 173, 203). This should not come as such a surprise when we recall that both were in differing ways influenced by patristic, Platonic philosophies (in Maurice's case, with a Coleridgean flavour; while for de Lubac in a more Augustinian mode) rather than the Aristotelianism which had influenced neo-scholastic ways of thinking (Morris 2005, pp. 37–43, 46–9).

We can also suggest that Anglican ecclesiology and soteriology, from Maurice, back to Hooker and even in proto-form in someone like Tyndale preserved, in common with the Orthodox churches, an earlier Carolinian/Byzantine model of Church and society, and a more deification model of grace and nature, unaffected by the Hildebrandine, Tridentine, neo-scholastic, and Vatican I developments which had made the distinction of planes model seem so appropriate to Roman Catholicism (see Ramsey 2009, chs 11 and 13; Williams 2004, chs 1 and 3; Hooker 1907, chs 1, 2, 55, 56).

Such a lineage might make integralism seem a hopelessly old-fashioned Constantinian model unsuited to the challenge of the present day. However, we should not forget that Maurice and de Lubac were each already responding to the challenge of secularism and even the rise of atheism in ways which were not just about reasserting control, but in the confidence that nothing is beyond the limits of grace. Likewise we have seen how it is ultimately such an integralist position that in fact offers a *more* radical analysis and response to our contemporary situation. If this argument is correct, then it is the case that not only are there important similarities between the message of *Caritas in Veritate* and recent Anglican social thought, but also an Anglican perspective can help to rescue the encyclical from the stale conservative/liberal debate and reveal its radical theological heart. On the other hand, this reading of the encyclical can encourage Anglicans in moving on from the 'Niebuhr in ecclesiastical drag' model of social thinking, towards something that is at once more Christian and more radical.

Beyond this, we can make an even more bold or perhaps just mischievous claim: that some of the key ideas of *Caritas in Veritate* have received their most fulsome treatments and indeed may even have partially originated within Anglican thought. We can note, for example, that John Burnaby, Oliver O'Donovan, and John Milbank have been among the most important defendants of the Augustinian notion of charity as reciprocal gift exchange, and in the latter case has applied this to the economic sphere (Burnaby 2012; O'Donovan 1979; Milbank 2003; 2009). We can also recall that mutualism, cooperatives and association were much discussed by Maurice, the Anglican legal and economic historians J. N. Figgis, and R. H. Tawney, and the British Christian 'guild socialists' (Morris 2005, p. 143; Tawney 1920; see also Milbank 2009, ch. 4). Also that one of the key Roman Catholic exponents of distributivist ideas was the convert from the Church of England, G. K. Chesterton. Finally, that many of the basic ideas of the *ressourcement* movement which contributed to de Lubac's integralism and the position of *Caritas in Veritate*, such as the concern with historical development, or the return to the Fathers instead of neo-scholasticism, had some of their roots in another famous convert, John Henry Newman (de Lubac 1998, pp. 431–3). These converts may well have brought some of their intellectual 'patrimony' with them, so that both traditions are already more ecumenically interdependent than they might realize. It seems then as if Anglicans may have more sympathy for this encyclical and more of a contribution to make concerning its interpretation and reception than many would think.

References

John Atherton, 1992, *Christianity and the Market*, London: SPCK

Tina Beattie, 2009, 'Church's Idealisation of Sexuality May Be Root of Abuse', in *Irish Times*, 3 November

Benedict XVI, 2009, *Caritas in Veritate: Charity in Truth*, ET, Dublin: Veritas

John Burnaby, 2012, *Amor Dei: A Study of the Religion of St Augustine*, new edition, Norwich: Canterbury Press

Henri de Lubac, 1988, *Catholicism: Christ and the Common Destiny of Man*, ET, San Francisco, CA: Ignatius Press

1985, *Faith in the City: A Call for Action by Church and Nation: Report of the Archbishop of Canterbury's Commission on Urban Priority Areas*, London: Church House Publishing

Gustavo Gutiérrez, 2001, *A Theology of Liberation*, ET, London: SCM Press

John Habgood, 1988, *Confessions of a Conservative Liberal*, London: SPCK

Richard Harries, 1992, *Is there a Gospel for the Rich?*, London: Mowbray

Richard Hooker, 1907, *Ecclesiastical Polity Book Five: Volume Two*, London: J. M. Dent & Sons Ltd and New York: E. P. Dutton & Co. Inc.

David Jenkins, 2000, *Market Whys and Wherefores*, London: Cassell

John Milbank, 2003, *Being Reconciled: Ontology and Pardon*, London and New York: Routledge

John Milbank, 2009, *The Future of Love: Essays in Political Theology*, London: SCM Press

Jeremy Morris, 2005, *F. D. Maurice and the Crisis of Authority*, Oxford: Oxford University Press

Michael Novak, 2009, 'Pope Benedict XVI's *Caritas*', *First Things Online*, 17 August, www.firstthings.com/onthesquare/2009/08/pope-benedict-xvis-caritas-1

Oliver O'Donovan, 1979, *The Problem of Self-Love in St Augustine*, New Haven, CT: Yale University Press

Oliver O'Donovan, 1996, *The Desire of the Nations: Rediscovering the Roots of Political Theology*, Cambridge: Cambridge University Press

Adrian Pabst (ed.), 2011, *The Crisis of Global Capitalism: Pope Benedict XVI's Social Encyclical and the Future of Political Economy*, Eugene, OR: Cascade Books

Ronald Preston, 1993, *Religion and the Ambiguities of Capitalism*, London: Pilgrim Press

Michael Ramsey, 2009, *The Gospel and the Catholic Church*, Peabody, MA: Hendrickson Publishing

Peter Sedgwick, 1997, 'Theology and Society', in David Ford (ed.), *The Modern Theologians: An Introduction to Christian Theology in the Twentieth Century*, Oxford: Blackwell, pp. 286–310

Peter Sedgwick, 1999, *The Market Economy and Christian Ethics*, Cambridge: Cambridge University Press

R. H. Tawney, 1920, *The Acquisitive Society*, New York: Harcourt Brace

William Temple, 1956, *Christianity and Social Order*, Harmondsworth: Penguin

George Weigel, 2009, '*Caritas in Veritate* in Gold and Red: The Revenge of Justice and Peace (or So They May Think)', *National Review Online*, 7 July, www.nationalreview.com/article/227839/caritas-veritate-gold-and-red-george-weigel

Rowan Williams, 2004, *Anglican Identities*, London: Darton, Longman & Todd

Notes

1 For Anglicans sympathetic to the papal encyclical tradition, we could think of Oliver O'Donovan, Michael Banner and John Milbank.

2 See Tina Beattie's well-argued piece on the gender blind spots of the encyclical (2009).

3 The phrase 'distinction of planes' comes from Gustavo Gutiérrez. See Gutiérrez 2001, pp. 88–100, for his discussion of the development of this model by Maritain and others as a response to the collapse of Christendom, and his critique of this in favour of the more radical integralism of de Lubac and de Montcheuil. For an excellent summary of what is meant by 'integral humanism', see de Lubac 1998, pp. 353–6.

4 It is striking, for example, that Temple does not shy away from the Christian nature of his economic and social vision, and also has an account of the co-inherence of justice and love, and of guild models of association, which is not so far removed from *Caritas in Veritate* (see Temple 1956, pp. 93, 76–7, 106).

5 E.g., Habgood 1988; Jenkins 2000; Harries 1992; Sedgwick 1999. In fairness we should note that there are of course shades of difference in this tradition: so, for example, in the report *Faith in the City*, Selby and Jenkins all stand at the more radical end politically and economically and, as we have indicated, Temple retains more of an explicitly Christian integralist agenda than many of his heirs would claim.

6 From a response to a question at the conference 'A Particular Place' at Westcott House, Cambridge, 16–18 September 2009.

11

The Possibility of Christian Culture[1]
(2012)

In this paper I want to say a few words in defence of the notion of the possibility of a Christian culture or cultural Christianity. Such a notion requires defending today, not just because it sounds to some like an argument for joining the English Defence League, but because, more seriously, it has come under attack not so much from those outside the Church, as from a significant body of Christian theologians. While these criticisms begin from entirely legitimate concerns, it is my claim that they are implicated in certain novel departures from Christian tradition in modernity and ultimately depend upon an overly angelic anthropology that renders key traditional Christian practices incoherent. By looking at the notion of 'culture' in Samuel Taylor Coleridge and T. S. Eliot, I hope to show how Anglican Christians defended the traditional Christian belief in the possibility of baptizing culture against the rising individualistic political philosophy from the late eighteenth century onwards, offering what remains one of the most important criticisms of this philosophy to date. And by focusing on Christian culture and society, rather than Christian states, I want to argue that it is impossible for Christians to renounce the question of power altogether, even if they would prefer the Church to avoid *political* power in the narrower sense. This is because, after Michel Foucault, as it were, we can see that even the most local, small-scale Christian practices, such as communicating the gospel or caring for others or bringing up children, are forms of power. This has consequences for the continuing viability of a catholic ecclesiology and missiology today, in a more pluralist and individualist society (but we may have to leave that to the discussion to draw out).

First, what is the opposition to notions of a Christian culture? I am not primarily concerned here with non-Christian opposition to Christian culture, such as the National Secular Society's endless campaigns against public prayers and Christian symbols in public life, which is at least more comprehensible, although some of these arguments would be relevant to that debate as well. My concern today is with specifically *Christian* opposition to Christian culture, such as we have seen recently for example in Ekklesia's opposition to Church schools.[2] It is my impression that this Christian opposition to Christian culture derives from a strange mixture of two theological streams: evangelical Protestantism and liberalism, and their common mind can be seen when it is followed to its *terminus ad quem*, in a suspicion at least or outright rejection of infant baptism. So we can see the first stirrings of this opposition to the idea of Christian culture in the radical Protestant movements of the sixteenth and seventeenth centuries. Their position derived from an opposition to the worldly corruption of the medieval Church and what they saw as the dilution of the perfectionist ethical tradition of the Sermon on the Mount and the early Church, through its accommodation to worldly power. This was what later generations would come to call 'Constantinianism' and the Anabaptist solution was to separate from the world and found a new Church consisting of freely consenting rational adults, rather than those simply 'brought up' as Christians within a Christian culture.

While the majority of Protestant traditions, following Luther and Calvin, did not follow this path, this critique of cultural Christianity remained present within Protestant thinking, resurfacing at various points. Kierkegaard takes up the challenge again in the nineteenth century with his blistering attacks upon the reduction of European Christianity to bourgeois conformist respectability. In the twentieth century Karl Barth and Dietrich Bonhoeffer continued this critique with particular force in relation to the accommodation of German cultural Christianity with National Socialism, while John Howard Yoder and Stanley Hauerwas have given currency to a new generation of anti-Constantinians in their powerful attacks on the identification of Christianity with America. I have much sympathy with all of these critiques of the *corruptions* of Christian culture, but I do not think one need take the subsequent step of saying that there can be *no such thing* as a Christian culture. It is this latter move which seems to me to derive not from any particularly Christian insight but from the influence of liberal political philosophy. This philosophy, for quite understandable historical reasons concerning the opposition to forms of political tyranny and enslavement, placed a great stress upon the individual as completely free and rational, a blank slate forming his own destiny. Such a view of the human subject downplays the important ways in which *who* we are, including our very capacities for reason and freedom, are not simply inert, self-possessed givens, but are *developed* through *time* and through *relations* with others. And this – development through time and through relations with others – is what we call 'culture'.

Samuel Taylor Coleridge's *On the Constitution of the Church and State* was published in 1830 as a somewhat belated response to the Roman Catholic Emancipation Act (1829) and is his major work of political thought. It attempts to provide an account of the English Constitution that is at once historical and ideal, describing how things have developed and what their true purpose should be. In this we see his mature philosophical method, which has moved beyond the Hartleyan materialism of his youth while also rejecting the abstract ahistorical rationalism of René Descartes, in favour of a historicized Christian Platonism, in which ideas are manifest through the unfolding of history. This enables him to synthesize elements of the English Common Law tradition going back to Richard Hooker with the Romanticism and historical idealism of post-Kantian German philosophy. It also means he shares with Edmund Burke, Johann Gottfried von Herder and others much of the wider Romantic critique of the Enlightenment philosophy which had found expression in the French Revolution, of which Coleridge had originally been a supporter. Although this counter-Enlightenment tradition is sometimes described as conservative, it also has genuinely radical elements (and again perhaps we will have to wait for the discussion to draw these out!).

Coleridge begins his argument with the claim that the National Church is the third estate of the realm which holds together and grounds the forces of permanence (represented by the hereditary rights of property) and progress (represented by commerce and the professions). The role of the National Church is 'a continuing and progressive civilization' and for this purpose some of the nation's wealth ('the Nationality') is set aside from private ownership to sustain this task (Coleridge 1972, p. 33).[3] 'The proper *object* and end of the National Church', according to Coleridge, 'is civilization with freedom' (p. 43). Civilization is understood in the broadest sense, not just in relation to public life: 'civilization is itself but a mixed good, if not far more a corrupting influence,' he says, 'where this civilization is not grounded in *cultivation*, in the harmonious development of those qualities and faculties which characterize our *humanity*. We must be men in order to be citizens' (pp. 33–4). The National Church is concerned with the work of culture: the formation of individuals and communities as human. Its role is educational, and in this sense while there are moments that sound rather docile to our ears (as when he speaks of training up 'obedient, free, useful, organisable subjects, citizens, and patriots' (p. 43)), there are other moments when this role is conceived in explicitly progressive and radical terms as disseminating knowledge and encouraging development and social mobility. For example, it is the task of the National Church to secure for *all* subjects 'the hope, the chance, of bettering their own or their children's condition' (p. 58). Coleridge explicitly conceives this task in relation to the transmission of values through time, which again he expresses in such a way as to be progressive as well as conservative: the National Church is to 'preserve the stores, to guard the treasures, of past civilization, and thus to bind the present with the past; to perfect and add to the same, and thus to connect the present with the future; but especially to diffuse [them] through the whole community' (p. 34). It is worth remarking that this is in essence a manifesto for universal education as a national responsibility, precisely not just for purely instrumental utilitarian reasons, but for the cultivation of human beings in community. This 'NATIONAL EDUCATION,' is according to Coleridge, 'the *nisus formativus* of the body politic, the shaping and informing spirit, which *educing*, i.e. eliciting, the latent *man* in all the natives of the soil, *trains them up* to citizens of the country, free subjects of the realm' (p. 37). Not only this, but Coleridge also makes reference to the need for the 'nationality' to make provision for those who through no fault of their own are incapable of economically supporting themselves, anticipating in some ways later arguments for the welfare state.

Two things are worth noting here in relation to Christianity. Despite Coleridge's vocabulary, he explicitly refuses to identify the National Church with the clergy or even essentially the Christian Church. The 'National CLERISY' as he calls it, should consist of 'the learned of all denominations', not just parish clergy, but also university lecturers and school teachers, all involved in education, science, and the liberal arts (p. 36). Likewise he claims that there was a Levitical National Church in the Old Testament as there was a Druidical National Church in ancient Britain. The *Christian* Church is *not* the same as the *National* Church, which has more this-worldly ends (morality rather than salvation). While the National Church may hold temporal power, the *Christian* Church as such is supranational and purely spiritual in its power. If the Christian Church in England fulfils the role of a National

Church, then it is only as a 'collateral object' (p. 100). We can see here how Coleridge's idea of the National Clerisy *could* be developed by Matthew Arnold and others to provide an initially ecumenical and subsequently secularized account of the role of the state in providing culture, which continues to be influential in British public life today (think of the BBC, as well as something like Stefan Collini's defence of the humanities (2012)).

But we might also notice some alternative notes in Coleridge's argument here, which would not support this secularizing conclusion. For on the one hand, Coleridge does not want the national clerisy to be completely subsumed under the state's control, or identified with temporal power (which he sees as the problem with the Roman Catholic Church and Islam). The setting aside of land to provide an independent income and its government by convocation rather than parliament ensure this. Coleridge is not an Erastian. The dynamic tension between Church and state is a distinctively Christian achievement. And yet they are not to be separated either. For, as he puts it quoting Proverbs 29.18: 'Where no vision is, the people perisheth' (p. 46). Without the religious concern for *ultimate* ends, we will become a society dominated by instrumental utilitarian 'understanding' rather than reason and its ideas. This is what Coleridge sees in the Britain of his own day. It seems therefore that for Coleridge, religion cannot be dispensed with in favour of public morality; the National Church cannot hold to a purely civil religion. 'Religion, true or false, is and ever has been the centre of gravity in a realm, to which all other things must and will accommodate themselves' (p. 53). We might go further than this and suggest that the very idea of a National Church as a function which all cultures have, waiting to be fulfilled by some particular religion is an ahistorical abstraction, as Coleridge himself suggests with his comments on Islam and Roman Catholicism. Rather, the particular conception of the role of a 'national clerisy' that he has outlined has a peculiarly *Christian* history, which might not be detachable from this origin. Likewise Coleridge's insistence that the Christian Church is something public rather than individual suggests that its shaping of culture will not be *purely* collateral. 'The Christian Church', he says, 'is not a secret community … it is objective in its nature and purpose, not mystic or subjective, *i.e.* not like reason or the court of conscience, existing only in and for the individual' (p. 99). Culture, we might say after Foucault again, is a form of power, even if it is 'spiritual' rather than purely coercive.

It is this second, anti-Arnoldian interpretation of Coleridge which I think can be seen influencing T. S. Eliot's high Anglican defence of the notion of a Christian culture in *The Idea of a Christian Society* of 1939 (henceforth ICS) and *Notes towards the Definition of Culture* of 1948 (henceforth NDC). In the light of the succumbing of European civilization to the twin barbarisms of Soviet Communism and German National Socialism, Eliot considers what a Christian society should look like. He refuses simply to identify Christianity with liberal democracy, arguing that the Western democracies are Christian only negatively in that they have not yet positively become anything else. The more evidently post-Christian nature of the civilization Eliot inhabits in relation to Coleridge enables him to be much clearer about the specifically Christian nature of his claims. His central claim is that the 'Christian should be satisfied with nothing less than a Christian organisation of society – which is not the same thing as a society consisting exclusively of devout Christians' (ICS, Eliot 1976, p. 27).[4] He follows Jacques Maritain in arguing that the Christian society of the future will necessarily be a pluralist society (ICS, p. 34). He also refuses to identify a Christian society purely with the question of Church establishment and the state. Rather, 'The State is Christian only negatively; its Christianity is a reflection of the Christianity of the society which it governs' (ICS, p. 35). He distinguishes three elements to a Christian society: the Christian State, the Christian Community (by which he means something like the wider cultural ethos), and the Community of Christians (by which he seems to have in mind something like Coleridge's clerisy, but conceived in a more mystical, artistic, religious sense, as the spiritual elite who keeps the genuinely Christian element of a Christian society alive). There are some problems with how Eliot conceives the role of this latter group, although the suggestion of some sort of spiritual division of labour need not be so ridiculous. But it is the second group, the Christian community, which has most interest for the question of culture. For here Eliot is concerned not so much with conscious religious self-description or assent to particular articles of doctrine, as in 'the substratum of collective temperament, ways of behaviour and unconscious values ... What we are seeking is not a programme for a party, but a way of life for a people' (ICS, p. 14). This phrase occurs again in *Notes towards the Definition of Culture*: 'we can see a religion as the *whole way of life* of a people, from birth to the grave, from morning to night and even in sleep, and that way of life is also its culture' (NCD, p. 103). Here Eliot, the extreme cultural elitist, is trying to speak of popular culture. 'For the great majority of the people', he says, 'religion must be primarily a matter of behaviour and habit, must be integrated with its social life, with its business and its pleasures; and the specifically religious emotions must be a kind of extension and sanctification of the domestic and social emotions' (ICS, p. 24).

In the later essay he presses home this anthropological Bourdieuian point that culture includes the most prosaic practices of everyday life: 'Derby Day, Henley Regatta, Cowes, the twelfth of August, a cup final, the dog races, the pin table, the dart board, Wensleydale cheese, boiled cabbage cut into sections, beetroot in vinegar, nineteenth century Gothic churches and the music of Elgar' (NCD, pp. 103–4). If at times Eliot may seem to sound as if he believes that he and the spiritual elite stand above habitual, cultural Christianity, at other times he recognizes in a more Wittgensteinian direction that 'behaviour is also belief' and that this is just as true of elite cultures, so that 'even the most conscious and developed of us live also at the level on which belief and behaviour cannot be distinguished' (NCD, p. 104).

Eliot's stress on Christian culture leads to a typically Coleridgean emphasis on education as the dissemination of culture and the formation of ways of life: 'A Christian education', he says, 'would primarily train people to be able to think in Christian categories, though it could not compel belief and would not impose the necessity for insincere profession of belief' (ICS, p. 22).

Eliot is also able, with the benefit of hindsight, to draw out more clearly than Coleridge the implicit critique of liberalism in their notion of culture. If culture is neither purely natural, but rather historical, and yet also not simply artificial, but organic and oriented towards the ultimate ends ordained by God and made known through reason, then it cannot simply be wiped away in the manner of the Jacobins and replaced by positive law. To put it more strongly, there can be no acultural society or, as Eliot will argue, if culture and religion are ultimately inseparable, no purely secular culture either. 'The Liberal notion that religion was a matter of private belief and of conduct in private life … is becoming less and less tenable,' he says (ICS, p. 17). For Eliot, the Liberal attack on culture is more dangerous than it realizes: 'By destroying traditional social habits of the people, by dissolving their natural collective consciousness into individual constituents … Liberalism can prepare the way for that which is its negation' (ICS, p. 12). This may have its uses, but cannot be the final word. Liberalism, he says, 'is a necessary negative element ... a negative element made to serve the purpose of a positive is objectionable' (ICS, p. 13).

For Eliot, Arnold's mistake was to think of religion as a part of the more fundamental category of culture, whereas, Eliot claims, culture is 'essentially, the incarnation (so to speak) of the religion of a people' (NCD, p. 101). This means that no culture can appear or develop without a religious basis, just as there can be no religion without culture (NCD, pp. 101, 105).

I hope that this has given you a brief flavour of this Anglican tradition of reflection upon the relation of Christianity and culture. Time constraints mean that its implications and potential problems will have to be left for our discussion![5]

References

John Baillie, 1945, *What is Christian Civilization?*, Oxford: Oxford University Press

Samuel Taylor Coleridge, 1972 (1839, 3rd edn), *On the Constitution of the Church and State According to the Idea of Each*, London: J. M. Dent & Sons Ltd

Stefan Collini, 2012, *What are Universities For?*, London: Penguin

T. S. Eliot, 1976 (1939, 1948), *Christianity and Culture: The Idea of a Christian Society and Notes towards the Definition of Culture*, San Diego, CA, New York and London: Harcourt, Inc.

Notes

1 A seminar paper delivered at the Society for the Study of Theology annual conference, University of York, 26–28 March 2012.

2 (John perhaps has in mind the campaigns of the Accord Coalition set up in part with the help of the Ekklesia think-tank. Although not against schools having a Christian ethos, it campaigns for inclusivity in schools and an end to religious discrimination in school staffing and admissions policies. It proposes that all state maintained schools should provide Personal, Social, Health and Economic education and that assemblies and Religious Education should teach the full range of both religious and non-religious beliefs in society. Accord had been the subject of a fringe meeting of the General Synod of the Church of England on 8 February 2012. See www.ekklesia. co.uk and www.accordcoalition.org.uk)

3 Further references by page number in parentheses in the main body of the text will be to Coleridge 1972 until indicated otherwise.

4 Further references to Eliot 1976 will be by page number in parentheses in the main body of the text.

5 (There is one note on John's manuscript suggesting he would have liked to have explored the reaction of John Baillie to T. S. Eliot's ideas (Baillie 1945).)

12

After Temple? The Recent Renewal of Anglican Social Thought (2014)

What is 'Anglican social thought' and what is its contemporary situation? The continuing social effects of the global economic crisis of 2008–9 have led to a widespread questioning of the fundamental political and economic models by which we live.[1] The post-war statist Keynesian model of regulated welfare capitalism had been under attack in Europe and America from representatives of the neo-liberal Chicago school of economics and the 'Washington consensus' throughout the 1980s and 1990s for destroying personal responsibility and restricting enterprise and creativity. Now it seems as if that consensus in favour of unregulated global 'free' markets is itself under attack for the way it has disembedded capital from its social context. This separation has encouraged reckless and irresponsible profiteering that, ironically, destroys the social cultures and virtues upon which flourishing and stable economies and markets themselves depend.

One perhaps surprising element of this questioning of fundamental economic and political models in Britain as elsewhere was the way popular expressions of protest such as the Occupy movement looked to the Church, even if only symbolically, to represent the vision of human flourishing that seemed to be lacking in the political and economic models of Left and Right. The Church of England was somewhat caught on the hoof by this unexpected attention and has sought to respond by returning to its own resources for thinking about social and economic questions, or what we shall call Anglican social thought. The very notion of Anglican social thought is a contested one, both because of the contested identity of Anglicanism itself and also because, in contrast with the obvious comparison of Roman Catholic social teaching, there is no one authoritative body of magisterial texts to which appeal might be made.[2] Nevertheless, for much of the latter half of the twentieth century there was a broadly coherent 'school' of British Anglican social thinking that dominated most official output from the Church institutions and hierarchy and shaped much academic and popular writing in these areas in Britain. This is the 'William Temple tradition', which takes its name from the mid-twentieth century Archbishop of Canterbury credited with producing a blueprint for the post-war social reconstruction of Britain. Many senior figures within the Church continue to look back to the heyday of this tradition as a golden era when the Church either played a major role in shaping public policy or, as in its last great example of the 1985 report *Faith in the City*, at least shaped debate by providing the principal critique of government policy. But for a variety of reasons, both external and more substantial, this Temple tradition has faced something of a crisis and decline of influence in the last twenty years.

This can be linked with the emergence of a very different political and religious climate in Britain, more pluralist and less susceptible to the sort of consensus that seemed possible in the immediate aftermath of World War Two. It can also be linked to the rise of a different dominant theological climate, which could broadly be called post-liberal. I do not believe, however, that these challenges and the waning of the Temple tradition represent the end of Anglican social thought. On the contrary, there has been a blossoming in this period of new and vibrant expressions of Christian social and political thought from prominent British Anglicans in the academy and within the ecclesiastical hierarchy, which are now beginning to find new institutional and cultural expressions. While these new developments may initially seem less coherent and less self-consciously Anglican, I will argue that there are common theological and methodological themes that they share, partly in response to the changed circumstances of the Church of England, and that this merits their description as a new phase, or renewal, of Anglican social thought. In particular I will argue that they are all indebted in various ways to the philosophical critiques of Enlightenment liberalism and its account of reason and the secular. Following from this, they share an 'ecclesial turn', a renewed interest in the Church itself as embodying an alternative social vision to that of secular liberal economics or political thought, and a greater doctrinal confidence, in the sense of expecting the Christian tradition to have its own resources to engage with social and political problems rather than presuming the Church must always defer to secular social sciences and political ideologies on these questions. I will offer a summary of some of the key figures in this recent post-liberal renewal of Anglican social thought and a narrative of how this strand has developed over the last twenty years, showing how these ideas were absorbed into the mainstream of Anglican social thought across the spectrum of British theological opinions.

This theological renewal found public and 'magisterial' ecclesial expression in the ministry as Archbishop of Canterbury of Rowan Williams, who as such can be seen as a new 'Temple' for the current generation of Anglican social thought, both in the sense of bringing together many of the developments of the last twenty years and providing them with a national public audience, and also in the sense of becoming a symbolic reference point and example for subsequent Anglican social and political thinkers. Williams's work is important to the narrative of the development of this tradition because it indicates that this renewed theological and ecclesial confidence need not be, as some have seen it, a 'sectarian' turn, a spurning of the world and a retreat into a theological fortress mentality. Rather, this recent renewal of Anglican social thought can in fact (at least in many cases, if not all) embody an 'integral Christian humanism'. What this means will be explained more fully shortly, but the phrase is borrowed from mid-twentieth century Catholic theology, where it referred to the account of the 'integral' relationship between grace and nature, reason and revelation, in the works of Henri de Lubac and other figures of the *ressourcement*, who opposed the more dualistic two-tier accounts of the neo-scholastics. This origin is significant in that it indicates how this direction in Anglican social thought has been developed partly through ecumenical dialogue, rather than being something exclusively Anglican. However, it can also be argued that this integral Christian humanism has significant continuities with earlier Anglican social thinking, prior to (and perhaps not even excluding) Temple. I will refer to some of these late nineteenth and early twentieth century roots of Anglican social thought in order to see what might be decisive and of contemporary interest in the tradition viewed in this longer perspective. Finally I will make some brief comments about the various questions particularly highlighted by this renewal of the tradition of Anglican social thought and some of the challenges it faces.

The Temple Tradition

As Alan Suggate indicates (2014), Archbishop William Temple (1881–1944) was a towering figure in twentieth century Anglican social thought. What had begun as 'Christian socialism' (meaning Christian social concern rather than a fully fledged political ideology) with a small group of clergy and lay people around F. D. Maurice in the mid-nineteenth century had risen in the early twentieth century to influence every level of the Church's life, and this move was perfectly represented by Temple, who was the product of this tradition. Significantly, Temple was able to bridge the two dominant groups in early twentieth century Anglican social thought: the more establishment, ecumenically minded, statist and reformist, and generally non-partisan tradition of the Christian Social Union of B. F. Westcott and Charles Gore (whose proposals were often similar to the views of the Whigs or Fabians), and the more controversial, Anglo-Catholic, associationalist, Romantic and anti-industrialist radical tradition of the Church Socialist League, the Christendom Group and the Malvern Conference (which was closer to the distributivism of Roman Catholics such as Hilaire Belloc and G. K. Chesterton).[3] While bishop of the key industrial city of Manchester, Temple had been unusual among his fellow bishops in being a member of the Labour party (although he left before being made Archbishop of York) and also organizing the major ecumenical Conference on Christian Politics, Economics and Citizenship (COPEC) in 1924. It was, however, Temple's famous book, *Christianity and Social Order*, originally published in 1942 as a set of proposals for the reconstruction of Britain after the war and seen as a blueprint for the welfare state, that sealed his reputation for the post-war generation as achieving a level of Christian influence over public policy that was difficult to match before or since (Temple 1956). As Suggate reminds us, Temple's own views were a strange mixture of philosophical idealism with Gore's theological incarnationalism, Maritain's Catholic natural law with Niebuhr's Lutheran social pessimism, and pluralist mutualism with Fabian–Keynesian economic theories (Suggate 2014; 1987).

The 'Temple tradition' that took its name from him, however, and that dominated Anglican social thought during the post-war period but especially in the 1970s and 1980s, tended to draw particularly on the more 'liberal' elements of his thought: using the language of 'middle axioms' and empirical research to seek a rational consensus that could supposedly transcend the particularities of a specific religious perspective; and having a social pessimism (Niebuhr's 'realism') that looked to the state to resolve the agonistic individualism of human nature embodied in the market through legislative regulation and intervention. The William Temple Foundation, based in Manchester, has been one of the strongholds of this tradition, particularly through the work of Ronald Preston, professor at Manchester University, and John Atherton, at Manchester Cathedral (for example, Preston 1993; Atherton 1992). We could also, however, include the work of John Habgood, Archbishop of York; David Jenkins, Bishop of Durham; Peter Selby, Bishop of Worcester; Peter Sedgwick, Principal of St Michael's College, Cardiff; and Richard Harries, Bishop of Oxford, as well as many of the publications of the national Board for Social Responsibility in this category of 'conservative liberalism' (to borrow Habgood's phrase, which is taken up by Sedgwick).[4] All these authors are characterized by a basically liberal (Kantian–Weberian) analysis of modernity, with its increasing secularization and pluralism, while at the same time, in varying degrees, wanting to continue the historic role of the established Church in addressing the nation. As a result, all tend to offer comment on contemporary politics and economics that seeks to speak in the categories of 'natural reason', more or less independent of specifically Christian claims, and therefore supposedly acceptable to all, regardless of their beliefs; while at the same time they end up offering at most only very modest critiques of the status quo.

This methodology (the famous 'middle axioms') developed out of the work of the Christian Social Union in the earlier twentieth century and their concern to influence policy through the use of empirical research. This approach often presents itself as embodying a certain form of broad inclusive 'Anglican' national consensus, against what is seen as the pietism and absolutism of more extreme 'partisan', integralist alternatives such as Catholic liberation theology or evangelical communitarian thought. It is difficult to miss the episcopal, establishment nature of this strand of Anglican social thought, and it has often been expressed through responses to government reports (what has been termed the 'Royal Commission' methodology) and interventions in the House of Lords. As this methodology suggests, its focus was primarily national politics rather than global questions. Among the theological influences, one of the principal figures for this later tradition was, as already indicated, the American Lutheran Reinhold Niebuhr, whose distinction between 'moral man' and 'immoral society' seemed to enable a 'realistic' engagement with the limitations of worldly power (in a classically liberal way. See, for example, Niebuhr 1935 and 1960). In its day this Temple tradition provided the Church of England with a credible discourse of moderate social criticism and legislative reform to engage with national debates during the post-war era dominated by the regulated welfare capitalism of Wiliam Beveridge, John Maynard Keynes and the Bretton Woods agreement. When this consensus first came under attack in the 1980s it was able to absorb elements of more radical positions such as liberation theology in order to respond to the challenge (as in *Faith in the City*). This should remind us that although the liberal Temple tradition was dominant in this period it was not the only voice in Anglican social thought, as others such as Ken Leech, Tim Gorringe and Chris Rowland explored more liberationist approaches within both the Church and the academy while, as Jonathan Chaplin indicates (2014), Anglican evangelicals adopted their own approaches.[5] Increasingly, however, the capacity of the dominant Temple tradition to speak to the changing situation as well as its internal theological coherence began to come under question.

Critiques of Enlightenment Liberalism: MacIntyre and Hauerwas

Direct attacks on the Temple tradition have been few, but its waning has undoubtedly been due to the prominent theological and philosophical critiques of its underlying philosophy of liberalism. Within a wider postmodern turn to critiques of the Enlightenment in the 1980s and 1990s, the forceful anti-liberal positions of Roman Catholic philosopher Alasdair MacIntyre and the originally Methodist theologian Stanley Hauerwas have been particularly significant in theological circles. In *Three Rival Versions of Moral Enquiry* and *After Virtue*, MacIntyre takes from Marx and Nietzsche the critique of the claims of enlightened reason to offer one, neutral, universal truth upon which everyone is supposed to agree when they have transcended the allegedly arbitrary and conflicting claims of particular (usually religious) traditions and worldviews (MacIntyre 1981 and 1990). This Enlightenment rationalism is itself a particular tradition and worldview like any other, arising at a particular moment and embodying the interests of a particular group (the liberal European bourgeoisie). Its claims to universal self-evidence have often justified darkly imperialist projects masquerading as serving progress and freedom. MacIntyre famously claimed at the end of *After Virtue* that the future of ethics would instead be likely to be sustained through a new dark ages by small communities with disciplines and virtues such as St Benedict's religious houses (MacIntyre 1981, p. 263). Yet this need not lead to a closed irrationalist communitarianism, for MacIntyre refuses to retreat into sceptical, postmodern relativism. Instead he argues that the very possibility of critique presumes some shared commitment to truth, even if that truth is not a 'view from nowhere' that can be securely grasped and possessed. He speaks therefore of 'tradition-based reasoning' embedded in social and historical practices, but open to dialogue, interaction and development, and looks to Aristotle and Aquinas as examples of this.

Stanley Hauerwas developed this MacIntyrean approach, combining it with his reading of Wittgenstein to see ethics not principally as a set of universal rational principles but as embedded ways of life and material practices, or traditions. Such an approach tends to lead to a greater stress on the distinctiveness of the Christian tradition instead of looking for some universal consensus. Likewise it is therefore inclined to more radical critique of the status quo. Influenced by Karl Barth's attack upon theological liberalism and by John Howard Yoder's Mennonite rejection of 'Constantinianism', Hauerwas developed a critique of liberalism, especially in its contemporary American form, that is more specifically theological than MacIntyre and also more polemical. For Hauerwas, liberal accounts of freedom substitute an abstract procedural account of freedom as choice for more classical accounts of freedom as oriented towards real shared goods and ends. Hauerwas rejected the rationalist foundationalism of Kantian and utilitarian ethics as simply particular narratives of freedom and salvation, embedded in their own communities and histories rather than universally self-evident to all. In contrast he proposed that 'the Church is a Social Ethic' because it is a 'Community of Virtues' and because the 'gospel is a political gospel' (Hauerwas 1984, pp. 99, 102). Hauerwas was increasingly influenced by Roman Catholic thinking during his time at the University of Notre Dame, but thoroughly rejected the 'two-tier' account of ethics embodied in most natural law theories with, on the one hand a universal set of principles supposedly available to all people of goodwill on the basis of reason alone and, on the other, a more particular set of distinctively Christian virtues established on the basis of revelation. For Hauerwas, 'being Christian is not equivalent to being human' (Hauerwas 1984, p. 55). Lest this be misunderstood as an extreme Protestant rejection of any Christian humanism, Hauerwas goes on to explain that this is primarily for epistemological reasons:

> to be Christian is surely to fulfil the most profound human desires, but we do not know what such fulfilment means on the basis of those desires themselves ... While the way of life taught by Christ is meant to be an ethic for all people, it does not follow that we can know what such an ethic involves 'objectively' by looking at the human. (Hauerwas 1984, p. 58)

The initial reaction of many within the Temple tradition of Anglican social thought to this challenge was often to dismiss Hauerwas and his followers as 'sectarian' or guilty of 'irrational fideism'. This however was to misunderstand how Hauerwas's underlying theological matrix differs from both Barth and Yoder. Hauerwas rejects any simplistic two-tier division or opposition between reason and revelation in favour of a much more 'integralist' account of their relationship: 'I find the traditional distinction between natural knowledge of God and revelation to be misleading. All knowledge of God is at once natural and revelatory' (Hauerwas 1984, p. 66). Beneath the frequent polemics, Hauerwas takes a similarly 'integralist' approach to the question of the Church and the world, which is more complicated than simply rejecting the world: 'Church and world are thus relational concepts – neither is intelligible without the other ... As the church we have no right to determine the boundaries of God's kingdom' (Hauerwas 1984, p. 101). Perhaps the point to note here is that the difference between integralist and two-tier accounts of nature and grace, reason and revelation, does not map directly on to the difference between liberal accommodationalist and more oppositional stances on the relationship between the Church and the world. This is partly because of the distinction of the ontological and epistemological elements of the question, so that an ontological integralist might still find herself in a minority position of opposition to the wider culture in specific situations. We can see this in the different forms that Hauerwas's interventions have taken across his career and particularly on different sides of the Atlantic (see Hauerwas 2001, chs 12 and 13; Hauerwas 2004).

Between them MacIntyre and Hauerwas have changed the landscape of British Christian ethics and given birth to a post-liberal generation much more sceptical about the capacities of 'neutral secular reason' or of achieving a universal consensus. This new generation of theologians has learned to be particularly sceptical towards the principal ideology of contemporary Western consumer capitalism, namely the belief in freedom as abstract choice without any orientation to shared goods or ends. At the same time they tend to be more attentive to the social and historical embeddedness of particular theological, political and economic visions, and therefore much more interested in the life of the Church as embodying a set of practices that set forth a distinctive theological vision of the world. Such an emphasis on cultural formation draws attention to the gaps in classical liberal economic theories, whether of the Right or Left, which focus instead upon the 'rational' choices of the individual or the state, abstracted from the specificities of culture that actually shape these decisions in relation to particular ethical visions of the common good. This post-liberal approach also draws attention to the variety of relationships and institutions between the state and the individual from families, businesses, schools, charities, local communities, churches and so on – that embody and transmit these values (sometimes called 'civil society'). As we shall see later, all this means that the current generation of Anglican social thinkers have various philosophical reasons to be more sympathetic to more historical, cultural and ethical approaches to economics than to the classical models of the Austrian school or the neo-Keynesians.

The Development of this Critique within Catholic and Evangelical Anglican Thought: Milbank and O'Donovan

While this alternative approach to religion and social and political ethics initially developed outside Anglicanism, both MacIntyre and Hauerwas were soon to be influential within the Church of England and their positions were developed in important ways by the two most prominent British Anglican academic political theologians of the last twenty years, Oliver O'Donovan and John Milbank, who now have both influenced the generation after them.

John Milbank, coming from the Anglo-Catholic tradition and taught by Rowan Williams, with a background in intellectual history, argued in *Theology and Social Theory* that '"scientific" social theories are themselves theologies or anti-theologies in disguise' (Milbank 1990, p. 3). By investigating in MacIntyrean fashion the genealogy of secular social science, Milbank sought to unveil hidden theological positions that continue to operate and oppose to them a 'postmodern

Augustinianism', which followed Hauerwas in seeing the Church as an alternative social vision, with its own politics based on an ontology of peaceful difference rather than violence. Milbank situated this project within an older tradition of Anglican social thought: the Anglo-Catholic anti-Fabian 'Christendom' tradition of 'guild' or mutualist socialism of V. A. Demant, Conrad Noel, Thomas Hancock, J. N. Figgis, R. H. Tawney and Donald MacKinnon, stretching back to the rather more diverse figures of S. T. Coleridge, J. H. Newman, W. G. Ward and F. D. Maurice in the nineteenth century. Milbank rejected the agonistic individualistic ontology of self-ownership that lay behind modern liberalism, with its presumption that humans cannot agree about common goods and ends so must simply find defensive mechanisms of coexistence. Milbank is often accused of wanting to recreate a Romantic fantasy of medieval Christendom, but while he does look to medieval Christian culture for constructive resources, he has always argued that he is interested in constructing an alternative modernity rather than simply reactionary nostalgia. In a number of earlier articles, more recently collected in *The Future of Love*, Milbank made his debts to the Anglican 'sacramental socialist' traditions more clear. Here he brings together philosophical debates about the gift with a Maussian anthropological account of gift exchange to offer his own Trinitarian social theology of charity as the relational exchange of gifts. This sounds very close to the similarly Augustinian account of charity offered by Pope Benedict XVI in his encyclical *Caritas in Veritate* (see Chapter 10). Milbank also offered some examples in the same book of how this position might apply to concrete contemporary concerns, including the international 'War on Terror', the defence of public goods such as the National Health Service and the welfare state in Britain, more mutualist and socially responsible models of business and finance and the need for humanizing limits on the economy to protect the 'sanctity of life, land, and labour', such as a living wage and limits on usurious interest rates (Milbank 2009). Milbank and the ecumenical radical orthodoxy movement, which he inaugurated with two other Anglo-Catholics, Catherine Pickstock and Graham Ward, have continued to develop this 'integralist' Anglo-Catholic perspective on social questions, refusing the two-tier separation of reason and revelation, grace and nature, and insisting with Hauerwas that the Church is an alternative politics to liberal capitalism. Although their original focus was primarily academic and theoretical, some of this group have been involved in more pragmatic policy interventions in recent years on the

Left ('Blue Labour') and Right ('Red Toryism'), often making common cause with Roman Catholic social teaching and the post-liberal advocacy of civil society.[6]

Oliver O'Donovan, the leading British evangelical Anglican political theologian, began from a more traditional ethicist's approach, moving into political ethics with *The Desire of the Nations* and *The Ways of Judgement* (O'Donovan 1996; 2005). While O'Donovan is not uncritical of the historicism of MacIntyre or the anti-Constantinianism of Hauerwas, he shares with them an 'excitement' over the 'Great Tradition' of political theology (O'Donovan 1996, p. xi). For him too, theology must 'break out of the cordon sanitaire' of modernity that separates religion and politics, for 'theology is political simply by responding to the dynamics of its own proper themes' (O'Donovan 1996, p. 3). O'Donovan is often grouped with Milbank, Hauerwas and MacIntyre as a 'modernity critic'. In fact his account of liberal society and political thought is complex: identifying positive elements he sees as deriving from the Christian tradition (the concern for liberty, mercy, equality and free speech) before going on to describe how all of these elements can be distorted to take the form of 'Anti-Christ' (O'Donovan 1996, pp. 252–84). There is no doubt that, for O'Donovan, Christian political ethics should be authentically Christian and even evangelical, reflecting his sympathy for Barth, because all of the political order must submit to the authority of Christ.

In a significant Anglican departure from MacIntyre and especially the early Hauerwas, O'Donovan and Milbank both refuse to simply give up on Christendom. O'Donovan responds specifically to Hauerwas's charge of 'Constantinianism' by arguing that Christendom was simply what happens when the rulers of this world submit (with varying degrees of sincerity) to Christ, rather than a sinister alliance with corrupting power. Christians should not cling to power for its own sake and may need to know when they will be required to return to the catacombs rather than submit to alien demands, but actively to desire the persecution of the Church is to be perverse. O'Donovan stresses the way the secular was originally a *Christian* creation, stemming from the distinction of dual authority (priestly and royal) in the medieval period, and is more positive about this development than Milbank. This might seem slightly to qualify his 'integralism' in a more two-tier direction, by contrast with Milbank and Hauerwas. A similar qualification might be detected in O'Donovan's defence in *Resurrection and Moral Order* of natural law (O'Donovan 1994). For O'Donovan this is the basis of a moral realism embedded in the created order, against relativist histori-cism. He insists, however, that the existence of a universal moral order is an ontological rather than epistemological claim, so that this reality is not immediately available to everyone on the basis of reason alone but is only known through the vindication of the created order in the historical proclamation of the resurrection of Jesus Christ (O'Donovan 1996, p. 19). This is certainly not the same as more liberal Enlighten-ment accounts of nature as completely autonomous from the divine and independently knowable without the aid of revelation.

O'Donovan does not have so much to say about social and eco-nomic questions, but his evangelical account of natural moral order and his constitutionalist defence of the legitimacy of Christian use of political power and law have been very influential on the current gener-ation of Anglican social thinkers, particularly among evangelicals (see Chaplin 2014). There remain significant differences between Milbank and O'Donovan, as we have seen, but I have sought to argue that, by contrast with the Temple tradition, there are sufficient similarities in their accounts of reason, the secular, liberalism, Christendom and the political role of the Church to indicate why the recent post-liberal revival of Anglican social thought is not confined to one 'wing' of the Church of England but brings together elements from the evangelical and Anglo-Catholic traditions, as we will show in a moment.

A New 'Temple'? Rowan Williams

Rowan Williams was more of a contemporary of Milbank and O'Don-ovan than someone influenced by them, but it makes sense to consider him here after them. This is because, while his views on social and political thought were undoubtedly an influence upon Milbank and to a lesser degree O'Donovan, his significance in terms of identifying the contemporary renewal of Anglican social thought is more recent. During his time as Archbishop, Williams brought this renewed theological tradition out of the academy to bear on national and international social and political questions in ways that parallel his predecessor Temple. This engagement at once contributed to the wider dissemination of the recent post-liberal renewal of Anglican social thought within the Church and broader public discourse and inevitably led to its being adapted in significant ways (adopting a tone that is more self-consciously 'public' and inevitably is received as more 'magisterial').

Williams comes from the Anglo-Catholic socialist tradition and was involved with various successors to the Christendom movement in the 1970s and 1980s (for example, the Jubilee Group and the Christian Socialist Movement). Philosophically he was influenced particularly by Gillian Rose's Hegelian critique of Kantian–Weberian sociology, while theologically he was shaped by ecumenical engagements with Barth's critique of theological liberalism and by various integralist approaches to theology and politics (especially the Eastern Orthodox theologies of Sergei Bulgakov and Vladimir Lossky, and the Roman Catholic *nouvelle théologie* of Henri de Lubac and Hans Urs von Balthasar). (See Williams 2007, especially chs 4, 5 and 6.) Within Anglican thought, Williams tends to look back before Temple to the Anglo-Catholic sacramental incarnational tradition of Gore (despite sounding a Barthian warning about the dangers of this incarnationalism becoming an uncritical naturalism), more mutualist and environmentalist socialist traditions, and the legal pluralist tradition of political thought represented by J. N. Figgis at the Community of the Resurrection in Mirfield (see Williams 2000, chs 6, 14 and 15). He has also traced this 'radical integralist' political vision back to earlier English authors, including Tyndale and Hooker (see Williams 2004, chs 1 and 2).

In his more recent collection *Faith in the Public Square* (where he acknowledges his debts to Milbank and O'Donovan among others), Williams gathers together his lectures on political themes from his past ten years in office and summarizes some of their common themes: a philosophical critique of 'programmatic secularism'; an account of the state as a 'community of communities' 'rather than a monopolistic sovereign power', supporting a 'pluralist' and 'decentralized' pattern of social life; and a 'sacramental' approach to the material world against the 'mythology of control and guaranteed security', calling for a 'sober and realistic scaling down of our consumption and pollution' and rejecting the 'fantasy that unlimited material growth is possible' by asking what is growth *for* (Williams 2012, pp. 2–5). Williams has long been making the sacramental socialist argument, which has strong affinities to the British New Left of the 1960s and also the environmentalist movement, that the way the market commodifies basic human goods necessary to life has alienating effects upon everyone, and especially the poorest. He has insisted instead, against liberalism, that there are real basic human goods beyond simply choice (see, for example, Williams 2003). When it comes to the state, however, his earlier writings show a more optimistic account of the state's role in the delivery of social goods, combined with a strong sense of its providentially secular role distinct from the Church (as Anna Rowlands helpfully describes in her analysis of his earlier essay on Barth's political theology (2014)). In *Faith in the Public Square* this position has developed subtly. Without abandoning his account of the importance and quasi-secularity of the state, we can now also detect the development of a shift away from a more formalist account of the state towards one that pays greater attention to how its particular constitutional structures are historically dependent upon Christianity. This is combined with an account of the limits of the state in relation to the importance of civil society, which builds on Figgisite legal pluralism to defend the Church against the incursions of the state but also offers a subsidiarist account of why social flourishing should not be left to the state alone.

Within Williams's work we can see then a similar critique of Enlightenment rationalism and liberalism to that of MacIntyre, Hauerwas, Milbank and O'Donovan, combined with a similar return to the political resources of the classical Christian tradition (Williams cites Augustine and Aquinas as forerunners of the 'pluralism' he is describing). More fundamentally, Williams resists any two-tier natural law appeal to a consensus founded on neutral secular reason in social and political questions in favour of one that is integrally theological all the way down. However, this does not mean that he simply speaks in dogmatic terms or refuses to engage with non-Christian thinkers. Indeed, perhaps because of the intended audiences (international bankers, the Trades Union Congress and so on), some of these pieces are often less explicitly theological on the surface than the writings of Hauerwas, Milbank or O'Donovan. But this should remind us that theological integralism does not equate to a dogmatic or sectarian refusal to engage with the world. Rather, for the theologians of the French mid-twentieth century *ressourcement*, for whom the term integralist was first coined, this rejection of the two-tier approach and the return to theological sources was precisely for the sake of a more thorough engagement with the contemporary world.[7] If there is no 'pure nature' and no neutral 'secular' reason, no ontological separation of the sacred and the secular then, against Barth and perhaps the earlier Hauerwas, all reason and truth and nature is always already theological and thus cannot be simply excluded and ignored.

This point might enable one to defend the often celebrated 'inclusivity' and 'engagement with the world' of the Temple tradition as authentically Anglican without seeing this as somehow entailing a commitment to Enlightenment liberalism or a dilution of distinctively Christian content. Williams shows us that it is possible to have a theological integralism and open engagement with a pluralist society. As I have argued elsewhere, Anglicans, who have in part rediscovered 'integralism' through ecumenical dialogue in the twentieth century, may well have reason to find that it runs much deeper in our own theology, piety and polity. This would be because Anglicanism's identity since the Reformation has generally rejected the two-tier approach to grace and nature, reason and revelation in late scholastic Aristotelian thought, and its dialectical reconceiving by Luther, in favour of more patristic Platonic integralist models. Likewise Anglican polity has tended to preserve earlier Byzantine and Carolingian models of Church and state against the strict separation that began to open up in the Hildebrandine reforms of the eleventh century and was consolidated in the Counter-Reformation. Of course these Anglican philosophical and ecclesiological traits come with their own peculiar dangers (naturalism and Erastianism respectively).

This brief account of the social and political thought of Rowan Williams has sought to show how he embodies many of the elements of the recent renewal of Anglican social thought. In particular he brings together the political questions about the nature and role of the state with socio-economic questions about the role of ethics in relation to the global market. The ways he does this indicate how the recent renewal can draw upon an earlier, pre-Temple, more integralist, associationalist and sacramental tradition of Anglican social thought, including figures such as Maurice, Gore and Figgis, even as it faces the new challenges of a very different national and global situation.

The Next Generation of Anglican Social Thought

I have argued that Milbank and O'Donovan, despite their differences, represent a renewed perspective in Anglican social and political thought in the last twenty years, one more indebted to MacIntyre's and Hauerwas's critiques of liberalism than the Temple tradition. I have also suggested that Milbank and O'Donovan already modify MacIntyre's and Hauerwas's positions in ways that make them arguably more Anglican and show how such positions can be connected with earlier strands of Anglican social thought up to and including Temple. While I have grouped Williams with Milbank and O'Donovan as part

of this revival in Anglican social thought, he also shows what this tradition looks like when voiced from the same pulpit, as it were, as Temple.
By this move the revival breaks out of the academy, becoming more
'public' while also remaining thoroughly 'ecclesial'. It also marks the
completion of the move of this tradition from the somewhat scorned
periphery of Anglican social thought in the 1980s, into the very centre.
This move and the adaptations in style that go with it (becoming less
polemical and theoretical and more 'public' and practical) can be seen
in what I have termed the next generation of theologians within this
renewed tradition. I will now offer a very brief survey of these developments in the work of Graham Ward, Catherine Pickstock, Michael
Northcott, Nigel Biggar, Robert Song, Michael Banner, Jonathan
Chaplin, Malcolm Brown, Sam Wells and Luke Bretherton.

Graham Ward, the Anglo-Catholic Regius Professor of Divinity in
Oxford, was one of the founders of the radical orthodoxy movement
with John Milbank, but has developed his own earlier work on the 'postmodern city' and his reading of Hegel to shape an account of Christian
discipleship as fundamentally political, echoing the 'sacramental socialism' of Williams and Milbank in his exploration of the questions of
materiality and culture, and the contemporary situation of religion and
globalization (see Ward 2009). Catherine Pickstock, the other founder
of radical orthodoxy, based in Cambridge, has focused on liturgy as a
fundamental political and anthropological category in dialogue with
various American Marxists also critical of secular liberalism (Pickstock
2005, 2012). Michael Northcott, based in Edinburgh, has been one
of the principal Anglican theologians to engage with questions of climate change in relation to globalization and international development
(see especially Northcott 2007). Nigel Biggar, O'Donovan's successor
in Oxford, has developed the McDonald Centre for Theology, Ethics
and Public Life and has sought to use the work of Jürgen Habermas
to engage in public discourse while retaining a Barthian theological
integrity (see, for example, Biggar 2011). Robert Song in Durham uses
Jacques Maritain and the Canadian Anglican George Grant to argue
for a similar critical engagement with liberalism, while Michael Banner
in Cambridge might also be situated within this 'O'Donovan' Anglican
ethical tradition, and is currently drawing upon social anthropology to
provide a more sophisticated engagement with actual material practices than previous empirical approaches (Song 1997; Banner 1999).
Jonathan Chaplin also comes from the evangelical end of Anglicanism
and has used the political philosophy of the Dutch Calvinist Herman

Dooyeweerd to develop a theological critique of secular liberalism in dialogue with Milbank, Hauerwas and O'Donovan, with the same stress on pluralism and civil society that we have seen in Milbank and Williams (Chaplin 2011).

How has this renewal affected the Church beyond the academy? Malcolm Brown is Director of the Mission and Public Affairs Division of the Archbishops' Council and comes out of the Manchester William Temple tradition, but nevertheless sees Milbank and Hauerwas as 'a necessary and timely corrective' to the underlying liberalism of that tradition, but one that itself needs to be opened out into a public theology for a pluralist society (Brown 2010, p. 113). Sam Wells and Luke Bretherton illustrate the British Anglican development of the Hauerwasian tradition in exactly this sort of direction, away from an American anti-Constantinian Mennonite position towards something more like a pluralist Christian society 'from below'. Wells, formerly Dean of Duke University Chapel and now Vicar of St Martin-in-the-Fields in London, has applied Hauerwasian categories of narrative and character formation to think through the pluralist context of Anglican ministry in engaging with secular and other agents to establish projects such as community regeneration (see, for example, Wells 2006). Bretherton, an evangelical lay Anglican, until recently based at King's College London but now at Duke University, has used the 'broad-based model of community organizing' developed by the agnostic Chicago Jew Saul Alinsky, and made famous by Barack Obama and in Britain by London Citizens, to develop a similar account of how the Church might engage in the public sphere without abandoning its theological integrity. He warns against the Church's co-option by the state, which is 'more of a Trojan than gift horse', and insists against John Rawls that theological reasons can be articulated in the public realm (Bretherton 2010, p. 58). He looks to post-liberal theo-politics as a 'faithful witness' (after Hauerwas, John Paul II and the O'Donovans) engaging in ad hoc partnerships with those of other faiths and none, within a liberal constitutional–legal order that does not presume common beliefs. He provides studies of examples of this at the local, national and international levels, including the language of sanctuary in asylum and 'fair trade'.

This very brief survey has been confined to current British Anglican academic theologians and their growing influence upon the wider Church of England, especially through the offices of Archbishop of Canterbury and Director of Mission and Public Affairs. A more total account of Anglican social thought would need to include the role of the major charities connected with the Church of England in shaping the Church's discourse about social and political questions, particularly the international aid and development societies Christian Aid and Tearfund (both ecumenical) and the specifically Anglican charities, including the mission agencies (CMS, US), the Mother's Union and the more domestically focused Children's Society and the Church Urban Fund. Attention would also need to be paid to the debates and reports generated by the Church's central synodical bodies (see Brown 2014b), and the effect of a number of new theo-political think tanks, such as Ekklesia, ResPublica and Theos. These additional perspectives would make for a more complex story. This account of the renewal of Anglican social thought has concentrated on the development of particular theological ideas within the academy and their dispersal within the Church, but of course the influence is not all one way; these ideas were themselves shaped by events in the world. Similarly there are significant exceptions to the patterns that have been traced here, which might become more evident in a broader account that was less focused on theology and the academy: Anglican social and political thinkers who have either sought to continue to develop the more liberal Temple tradition (especially from the perspective of sociology of religion) or have taken various liberationist stances (including black, feminist and queer theologies).

Common Themes

My aim, in focusing on British Anglican social and political theologians of the last twenty to thirty years, has been to show that while they may not conceive of themselves as a 'new movement' with anything in common, let alone as distinctively 'Anglican', what we can observe across many of these writers is indeed a broadly coherent shift in Anglican social thinking, under the influence of MacIntyre, Hauerwas, Milbank and O'Donovan, and becoming 'mainstream' through the archiepiscopate of Williams, away from the post-war Temple tradition, towards something more theologically confident and ecclesial but, as is perhaps more obvious in the light of its second generation, no less Anglican and certainly not 'sectarian'. Although this renewal is far from monolithic, a number of common themes can now be observed. We have seen a critique of the 'neutral' secular liberalism of Kantians such as Rawls, which dominated post-war social and political thought in the West, and the presumption that there is a universal rational basis upon which a consensus can be built with all people of goodwill. We have seen a renewed appreciation of the importance of the cultural and historical formation of social, political, economic and ethical questions. This has enabled a 'post-liberal' turn to tradition-based modes of reasoning, leading to a renewed confidence in the Church's capacity to use the theological resources of its own tradition to think about social problems. There is therefore in many of the figures we have considered a broad rejection of the two-tier model of public theology with its rationalist natural law theories separate from more specifically Christian claims, in favour of a more integralist approach. This need not necessarily entail ruling out a more theological account of natural law though. Recent Anglican defences of natural law will tend to be more explicitly Christological and more historicist and therefore more open to the possibility of development. As a result of all this, Anglican social thought has become more explicitly doctrinal and ecclesial once again, without retreating from public debate in an increasingly religiously pluralist society. Against the classical liberal stress on ethics as an essentially secular, rational matter for the state or individuals, there has been a recovery of the sense of the Church as itself a social ethic, or a culture. This has been combined with a greater sympathy for pluralist views of society and increased attention to civil society and all the forms of association that fall between the state and the individual. There has thus been a renewed interest in both the global and the local, beyond the post-war preoccupation with the nation-state (although this temptation goes back much further for Anglicanism of course). This interest in questions of international justice and subsidiarist, mutualist and participatory distributions of power, reflects long-standing elements of Roman Catholic social teaching.

Ongoing questions and internal debates of course remain, as discussed in greater detail in some of the other contributions to the collection of essays on Anglican social thought edited by Malcolm Brown (2014a): between the majority of those mentioned here who continue to be interested in some sense in a Christian society and state, even if a pluralist one, and those who see the Church as essentially a gathered *ecclesia*, opposed to Christendom and the secular *polis* alike. There are also questions broadly corresponding to traditional divides between Roman Catholics and Protestants, or Thomists and Barthians, about the relative place of Scripture, tradition and natural law, and exactly how the relationship between the order of creation, the fall and the order of redemption should be understood. And yet the more striking element is in fact how these historic Reformation divides have been largely set aside and different traditions are quite ready to learn from each other's resources. Here the intra-Anglican common ground between evangelicals and catholics reflects the wider ecumenical convergences in social thinking by which British Anglicans have been affected. It would be important in this respect also to consider the work of the Anglican Communion and the World Council of Churches in shaping British Anglican social and political thought, especially on international questions such as globalized trade and finance, development, migration, international law and war. The renewal of Anglican social thought that has been described here may have some elements of a distinctively British Anglican flavour (perhaps especially the integralism and historicism, the sympathy for Christendom and the emphasis on the idea of a Christian state, and some elements of the particular approach to questions of gender and sexuality), but none of these are exclusively Anglican, and indeed it would be a misunderstanding of the Church of England's ecclesiology to look for such exclusively Anglican features. We might note here in passing that, while not a theologian in the same sense as his predecessor, the new Archbishop of Canterbury, Justin Welby, could also be connected with these developments: coming from a strand of evangelical Anglicanism that has not been lacking in social awareness, he has also learned considerably from Catholic social teaching. His views expressed in the Parliamentary Commission on Banking Standards indicate his recognition that the culture and governance systems of global finance must be reformed, while his comments on how the Church should support credit unions and other forms of social lending to help rescue people from payday lenders suggest that he thinks the Church can offer more by showing alternative ways of doing things than simply preaching at the state.

Contemporary and Future Challenges

From these common themes we can also see a certain basic agreement among the current generation of Anglican social and political thinkers, crossing theological and political divisions, concerning what are the most pressing contemporary issues and practical challenges of today. I will conclude by simply summarizing these questions that have kept coming up in the work of various authors.

Secularism and Pluralism

The methodological debates explored in this essay can be understood as different responses to a post-Christendom situation, in which the Church cannot presume that the political authorities or most of the population will share a Christian vision of society. Strongly secularist voices will contest the right of Christians to express their faith in the public sphere. And yet the novelty of this situation can be overstated. T. S. Eliot and Temple in the 1930s and 1940s already described a Britain only vestigially Christian, while still advocating a Christian society and state, precisely on the grounds that the alternative is something worse than neutrality. Meanwhile the diversification of the religious traditions represented in Britain through immigration seems largely to have strengthened the role of religion in public life, and recent politicians from across the political spectrum have paid lip service to Britain continuing to be a Christian society. In this context, despite the emotive talk in some quarters of the persecution of Christians by the state (particularly in relation to questions of sexuality), others have spoken of a post-secular turn to British political life, in common with much of Europe, enabling theological arguments and religious organizations to play significant roles in public debate and the provision of public services. It is interesting here that within debates about multiculturalism and immigration, Williams and others have re-imagined Anglican establishment in terms of hospitality beyond both liberal cosmopolitanism and ethnic or racial nationalism.[8] It is worth noting that this post-secular turn entails a move beyond the strategy of attempting to find a neutral rational consensus towards more self-confidently theological and ecclesial interventions which, as Bretherton particularly indicates, are no less afraid of ad hoc alliances with those of other faiths and none.

The Welfare State

Perhaps the most urgent domestic issue in Britain (although with parallels throughout Europe and the United States) is the social effects of the remodelling of the welfare state represented by the political agenda of cuts and austerity in the light of the global recession. If the welfare state was perhaps the greatest 'achievement' of the Temple tradition, its vulnerability to attack now suggests the need both to articulate a more confident account of its Christian ethical and theological foundations and to recognize and reform the weaknesses of its bureaucratic non-participatory structures, so as to be more genuinely empowering and socially and economically sustainable. The effects of current changes upon the most vulnerable in society have already been picked up by Anglican charities such as the Children's Society and the Church Urban Fund, and taken up by the bishops in national debate. While there has been much criticism of the exclusive focus on the state in the post-war settlement, most of the thinkers we have been considering recognize that the continuing protection of the most vulnerable will remain a task in which the state plays a key role, even if this will often be in collaboration with other groups and must avoid entrapping people in relationships of unnecessary dependence.

International Development and the Global Economy

One of the consequences of debates about globalization and the advocacy work of international aid charities such as Christian Aid and Tearfund is the realization that international inequalities of wealth are a moral, social and political question, rather than a purely economic one. Campaigns such as Jubilee 2000 and the Millennium Development Goals (including episcopal and synodical endorsements) represent this realization entering the mainstream of British church life. The global economic crisis of 2008 has, as mentioned earlier, led to a widespread renewed rejection by Christian thinkers of the economic rationalism of the free market 'Washington consensus'. As Roman Catholic social teaching has been arguing for many years, this neo-liberal view of economics is, in its impersonal exclusion of the personal *moral* dimension to society, curiously similar to its apparent opposite, the previous statist Weberian post-war consensus. Both are examples of what Catholic social teaching calls rationalist, materialist 'economism', with little room for the ethical. Anglican social thought, like Roman Catholic social teaching, is by contrast not finally a purely rational political or economic theory, so much as the insistence that both politics and economics are inescapably *ethical* questions, beyond the deliberations of reason alone. The renewed insistence on the moral nature of the economy has led to a number of significant concrete proposals that all reflect the belief that property and profit, finance and industry are not ends in themselves but must be ordered to the common good. These developments include a recovery of Christian critiques of usury to ask questions about limited liability, responsible debt and the international regulation of finance, and calls for the closing of tax loop-holes. The development of 'fair trade', 'social enterprise', and 'social finance' has questioned the model of 'morally neutral' free trade as the only route to development, while calls for greater economic and industrial democracy have led to the reconsideration of more mutualist models of corporate governance and participatory systems of worker ownership. The recovery of a Christian theology of labour has led to demands that labour conditions should not only be safe but also appropriate to the dignity and responsibility of the human person and remunerated with a living wage, so that the entire economy is ordered to vocation, employment and the distribution of goods, rather than simply the increase of capital and social inequalities at the national and international levels. Similarly, the questions of the 'outsourcing' of labour and of migration are usually considered only at the level of populist protectionist anxieties or of narrowly economic utility, rather than in terms of their complicated role in relation to global human solidarity and development. Finally there is also a renewed recognition that economic development is often bound up with and limited by other political questions, such as violent conflict or political corruption. In this light the position of many Anglican leaders and theologians on the Iraq war and other conflicts, weapons of mass destruction and the development of structures of international law should be seen as part of the renewal of the Anglican social tradition. In almost all these ques-tions, Anglicans are often catching up with the work that has already been done by Roman Catholic social teaching.

Gender and Sexuality

Although these questions have been particularly fraught internally for the Church of England and the Anglican Communion in relation to issues such as gay marriage and women clergy, there is an undeniable awareness in recent years that questions of gender are social and polit-ical, rather than narrowly moral, and that likewise social and political questions frequently also concern questions of gender. As the Mothers' Union has powerfully argued, it is women who are usually among the worst victims of international social and economic inequalities as well as acts of violence, while on the other hand the family, and especially women, play a crucial role in education, development and the trans-mission of social virtues. As reproductive health has become increasingly politicized in international development agendas, Anglicans have found themselves in an interesting position: openly in favour of contraception in ways that not all religious groups are able to be, while also supportive of the family and opposed to regarding abortion as just another 'reproductive right' in ways that differentiate the Anglican position from secular liberals. If this position can be held by those from a diversity of theological positions within Anglicanism, alongside a consistent global advocacy against the persecution and oppression of women and homosexuals, which has been repeatedly affirmed by various Lambeth conferences, then this could well be a crucial witness to both sides of the Western sexual culture wars that now affect the worldwide Church and the wider international community.

The Environment

However accurate the various predictions of environmental apocalypse may be, it is clear that the world will struggle to sustain a growing population with a lifestyle consuming at the rate of first-world nations now. For this reason ecological questions are also questions concerning international equity and economic development. In this light a number of the authors we have been considering have asked whether the current economic model of development and growth needs to be revised in favour of more sustainable economic models that restore a more harmonious relation between humans and our natural resources. This reflects the arguments already mentioned that there are human and social goods that cannot simply be subordinated to the limitless pursuit of profit and that require ultimate protection by national and international law.

These will be the questions facing the new generation of Anglican social and political thinkers in the years ahead. If the 'Royal Commission' approach of the Temple tradition is no longer so viable, we may well see a more diverse range of responses than before, including attempts to embody critiques and alternative practices, rather than simply writing reports about them. Nevertheless, as we have seen, rejuvenated by ecumenical influences and a rediscovery of some of its own earlier traditions, Anglican social thought ought to be in good health to engage with these challenges.

References

John Atherton, 1992, *Christianity and the Market*, London: SPCK

Michael Banner, 1999, *Christian Ethics and Contemporary Moral Problems*, Cambridge: Cambridge University Press

Hilaire Belloc, 1912, *The Servile State*, London: Foulis

Nigel Biggar, 2011, *Behaving in Public: How to do Christian Ethics*, Cambridge: Cambridge University Press

Phillip Blond, 2010, *Red Tory*, London: Faber & Faber

Luke Bretherton, 2010, *Christianity and Contemporary Politics*, Oxford: Wiley-Blackwell

Malcolm Brown, 2010, *Tensions in Christian Ethics*, London: SPCK

Malcolm Brown (ed.), 2014a, *Anglican Social Theology: Renewing the Vision Today*, London: Church House Publishing

Malcolm Brown, 2014b, 'The Case for Anglican Social Theology Today', in Malcolm Brown (ed.), *Anglican Social Theology: Renewing the Vision Today*, London: SPCK, pp. 1–27

Jonathan Chaplin, 2011, *Herman Dooyeweerd: Christian Philosopher of State and Civil Society*, Notre Dame, IN: University of Notre Dame Press

Jonathan Chaplin, 2014, 'Evangelical Contributions to the Future of Anglican Social Theology', in Malcolm Brown (ed.), *Anglican Social Theology: Renewing the Vision Today*, London: Church House Publishing, pp. 102–32

G. K. Chesterton, 1926, *The Outline of Sanity*, London: Methuen

1985, *Faith in the City: A Call for Action by Church and Nation: Report of the Archbishop of Canterbury's Commission on Urban Priority Areas*, London: Church House Publishing

Maurice Glasman, 1996, *Unnecessary Suffering*, London: Verso

Charles Gore, 1928, *Christ and Society*, London: George Allen & Unwin

Timothy Gorringe, 1994, *Capital and the Kingdom*, London: SPCK

John Habgood, 1988, *Confessions of a Conservative Liberal*, London: SPCK

Richard Harries, 1992, *Is there a Gospel for the Rich?*, London: Mowbray

Stanley Hauerwas, 1984, *The Peaceable Kingdom*, London: SCM Press

Stanley Hauerwas, 2001, *Wilderness Wanderings*, London: SCM Press

Stanley Hauerwas, 2004, *Performing the Faith: Bonhoeffer and the Practice of Nonviolence*, London: SPCK

David Jenkins, 2000, *Market Whys and Wherefores*, London: Cassell

Kenneth Leech, 1997, *The Sky is Red: Discerning the Signs of the Times*, London: Darton, Longman & Todd

Alasdair MacIntyre, 1981, *After Virtue*, London: Duckworth

Alasdair MacIntyre, 1990, *Three Rival Versions of Moral Enquiry*, Notre Dame, IN: University of Notre Dame Press

F. D. Maurice, 1842, *The Kingdom of Christ*, London: Rivington

John Milbank, 1990, *Theology and Social Theory: Beyond Secular Reason*, Oxford: Blackwell

John Milbank, 2009, *The Future of Love*, London: SCM Press

John Milbank and Adrian Pabst, 2014, 'The Anglican Polity and the Politics of the Common Good', *Crucible: The Christian Journal of Social Ethics*, January–March, pp. 7–15

Jeremy Morris, 2005, *F. D. Maurice and the Crisis of Authority*, Oxford: Oxford University Press

Reinhold Niebuhr, 1935, *An Interpretation of Christian Ethics*, New York: Seabury Press

Reinhold Niebuhr, 1960, *Moral Man and Immoral Society*, New York: Charles Scribner's Sons

Edward Norman, 1987, *The Victorian Socialists*, Cambridge: Cambridge University Press

Michael Northcott, 2007, *A Moral Climate: The Ethics of Global Warming*, London: Darton, Longman & Todd

Oliver O'Donovan, 1994, *Resurrection and Moral Order*, Leicester: Apollos

Oliver O'Donovan, 1996, *The Desire of the Nations: Rediscovering the Roots of Political Theology*, Cambridge: Cambridge University Press

Oliver O'Donovan, 2005, *The Ways of Judgement*, Cambridge, MA: Eerdmans

Adrian Pabst (ed.), 2011, *The Crisis of Global Capitalism: Pope Benedict XVI's Social Encyclical and the Future of Political Economy*, Eugene, OR: Cascade Books

Catherine Pickstock, 2005, 'The Poetics of the Eucharist', *Telos*, No. 131, Summer, pp. 83–91

Catherine Pickstock, 2012, 'Liturgy and Modernity', in William T. Cavanaugh, Jeffrey W. Bailey and Craig Hovey (eds), *An Reader in Contemporary Political Theology*, Grand Rapids, MI and Cambridge, UK: Eerdmans, pp. 139–55 (originally published in *Telos*, No. 113, Fall, 1998, pp. 19–40)

Ronald Preston, 1993, *Religion and the Ambiguities of Capitalism*, London: Pilgrim Press

Christopher Rowland and Mark Corner (eds), 1989, *Liberating Exegesis: The Challenge of Liberation Theology to Biblical Studies*, Louisville, KY: Westminster/John Knox Press

Anna Rowlands, 2014, 'Fraternal Traditions: Anglican Social Theology and Catholic Social Teaching in a British Context', in Malcolm Brown (ed.), *Anglican Social Theology: Renewing the Vision Today*, London: Church House Publishing, pp. 133–74

Peter Sedgwick, 1999, *The Market Economy and Christian Ethics*, Cambridge: Cambridge University Press

Robert Song, 1997, *Christianity and Liberal Society*, Oxford: Oxford University Press

Alan M. Suggate, 1987, *William Temple and Christian Social Ethics Today*, Edinburgh: T. & T. Clark

Alan M. Suggate, 2014, 'The Temple Tradition', in Malcolm Brown (ed.), *Anglican Social Theology: Renewing the Vision Today*, London: Church House Publishing, pp. 28–73

William Temple, 1956, *Christianity and Social Order*, Harmondsworth: Penguin

Graham Ward, 2009, *The Politics of Discipleship: Becoming Postmaterial Citizens*, London: SCM Press

Samuel Wells, 2006, *God's Companions: Reimagining Christian Ethics*, Oxford: Wiley-Blackwell

B. F. Westcott, 1887, *Social Aspects of Christianity*, London: MacMillan

B. F. Westcott, 1893, *The Incarnation and Common Life*, London: MacMillan

Alan Wilkinson, 1998, *Christian Socialism: Scott Holland to Tony Blair*, London: SCM Press

Rowan Williams, 2000, *On Christian Theology*, Oxford: Blackwell

Rowan Williams, 2003, *Lost Icons: Reflections on Cultural Bereavement*, London: Continuum

Rowan Williams, 2004, *Anglican Identities*, London: Darton, Longman & Todd

Rowan Williams, 2007, *Wrestling with Angels: Conversations in Modern Theology*, London: SCM Press

Rowan Williams, 2012, *Faith in the Public Square*, London: Bloomsbury

Notes

1 In addition to colleagues engaged in this project (the dialogues and subsequent collection of essays in Brown 2014a), I am particularly grateful for conversations with Matthew Bullimore and for his feedback on an earlier draft of this chapter.

2 Although, as I am often reminded by Roman Catholic friends, the magisterial tradition in Roman Catholicism is both internally more diverse and only part of the picture, despite what some would say. As I shall argue, a plurality of voices need not indicate the absence of any identifiable coherence.

3 For some of the background see Norman 1987; Wilkinson 1998; Morris 2005; Maurice 1842; Westcott 1887; 1893; Gore 1928; Belloc 1912; Chesterton 1926.

4 E.g., Habgood 1988; Jenkins 2000; Harries 1992; Sedgwick 1999. In fairness we should note that there are of course shades of difference in this tradition; so, for example, *Faith in the City*, Selby and Jenkins all stand at the more radical end politically and economically and, as we have indicated, Temple himself retains more of an explicitly Christian integralist agenda than many of his heirs would claim.

5 For the more liberationist approach, see, e.g., Leech 1997; Rowland and Corner 1989; Gorringe 1994. It is arguably the case that British Anglican liberationists have been more indebted to a 'New Left' ethical reading of Marx than the narrowly materialist, agonistic and deterministic Marx of Soviet orthodoxy, which has been criticized in some other forms of liberation theology. I would argue therefore that these Anglican liberationists, while in some ways they resemble the liberal Temple tradition, have much more in common with the more post-liberal approach that I will go on to describe, particularly in their more radical global, mutualist and environmentalist concerns.

6 See Blond 2010; Glasman 1996; Pabst 2011. For the ways in which these projects are particularly 'Anglican', see Milbank and Pabst 2014.

7 This can be seen in Williams's reading of Vatican II in his address to the Roman Synod of Bishops, 10 October 2012: http://rowanwilliams.archbishopofcanterbury.org/articles.php/2645/

8 See the Queen's extraordinary Jubilee speech at Lambeth Palace, 15 February 2012: www.royal.gov.uk/LatestNewsandDiary/Speechesandarticles/2012/TheQueens speechatLambethpalace15February2012.aspx

Acknowledgement of Sources

The editor and publisher are grateful to the following publishers for giving kind permission to reproduce the following essays:

'The Politics of Forgiveness: A Theological Exploration of *King Lear*', *Modern Theology*, Vol. 17, No. 3, July, copyright © 2001; and 'Creatio Ex Nihilo and the Divine Ideas in Aquinas: How Fair is Bulgakov's Critique?', *Modern Theology*, Vol. 29, No. 2, April, copyright © 2013. Reproduced with permission of Blackwell Publishing Ltd.

'Work, prayer and leisure in the Christian Tradition', *Crucible: The Christian Journal of Social Ethics*, Jan–Mar, copyright © 2011; and 'After Temple? The Recent Renewal of Anglican Social Thought', in Malcolm Brown (ed.), *Anglican Social Theology: Renewing the Vision Today*, London: Church House Publishing, copyright © 2014. Reproduced with permission of Hymns Ancient & Modern Ltd.

'Work and Labour', in Nicholas Adams, George Pattison and Graham Ward (eds), *Oxford Handbook of Theology and Modern European Thought*, Oxford: Oxford University Press, copyright © 2013. Reproduced with permission of Oxford University Press.

'Bulgakov's move from a Marxist to a Sophic Science', *Sobernost*, Vol. 24:2, copyright © 2002. Reproduced with permission of Sobernost, with thanks to Revd Prof. Andrew Louth.

'Proofs and Arguments', in Andrew Davison (ed.), *Imaginative Apologetics: Theology, Philosophy and the Catholic Tradition*, London: SCM Press, copyright © 2011, and Grand Rapids, MI: Baker Academic, copyright © 2012. Reproduced with permission of Hymns Ancient & Modern Ltd, and Baker Publishing Group.

'What is Radical Orthodoxy?', *with Matthew Bullimore* in *Telos*, No. 123, Spring, copyright © 2002. Reproduced with permission of Telos Press Publishing.

'Jacques Maritain: Pre-Conciliar conservative or Thomist liberal democrat?', *Theology*, Vol. CXIII, No. 871, Jan/Feb, copyright © 2010. Reproduced with permission of SAGE publishing.

'Integralism and Gift Exchange in the Anglican Social Tradition, or Avoiding Niebuhr in Ecclesiastical Drag', in Adrian Pabst (ed.), *The Crisis of Global Capitalism: Pope Benedict XVI's Social Encyclical and the Future of Political Economy*, Eugene, OR: Cascade Books, copyright © 2011. Reproduced with permission of Wipf and Stock Publishers, www.wipfandstock.com.